"Linda Anderson's remarkable book reveals deeper beauty, truth and understanding of the ancient ECK wisdoms. ... These Golden Keys are now within all of our reaches if we choose to open her book, and begin a lifelong, and then an after-this-life adventure with God which will never end!"

Taylor Hay
Author, *Synergetics,*
Your Whole Life Fitness Plan

"I truly enjoyed it. It is both clear and elegant, as well as having an anecdotal, contemporary character that will immediately engage readers. ... I would certainly recommend this beautifully written book to any students or others who desire to know what Eckankar can mean to those who have found that for them its path leads to the highest spiritual reality."

Robert S. Ellwood
Professor of Religion
University of Southern California

"For the spiritual seekers of today: those who wish to discover their own truth and have direct experience of God. People of all faiths will find treasure in this book. Linda C. Anderson clearly explains the history, fundamentals and benefits of the ageless spiritual wisdom embodied in Eckankar. An excellent introduction to a religion with a fresh approach for modern times!"

Rosemary Ellen Guiley
Author, *The Miracle of Prayer* and
*Harper's Encyclopedia of Mystical
and Paranormal Experience*

"I wish you all success with your book and hope it will draw many readers to a greater interest in the teachings of Eckankar."

Kenneth Ring, Ph.D.
Autho

D1279720

"The timing of my exploration of the teachings of Eckankar was coincidental with my own physical ordeals. Therefore it was of tremendous help to me to be exposed to the Light and Sound of the spiritual message of Sri [Harold] Klemp and the other Eckists. It was an embracing and uplifting source of comfort, timely and unforeseen."

Edith Engel
Compiler and editor of *ONE GOD:*
Peoples of the Book,
activist for tolerance and understanding

"All my life I've searched for what's original and true . . . what you might call the 'real thing.' Linda Anderson's book *is* the real thing."

Bryan W. Mattimore
Author, *99% Inspiration,* and
contributing editor, *SUCCESS Magazine*

"How exciting to see the mysteries of God explained in everyday language with heartwarming stories. Anderson is clear, concise, and respectful in her approach to the seeker of truth. Bravo!"

Debbie Johnson
Author, *How to Think Yourself Thin*

"Contains essential spiritual premises that we all need to find our way back to God. I recommend it to all earnest seekers of truth."

Marie Carmen Atkinson
Author, *The Peace Meditation,*
The Quick Numerologer,
and *The Magickal Maiden*

35 GOLDEN KEYS

to WHO YOU ARE & WHY YOU'RE HERE

35
GOLDEN
KEYS

to WHO YOU ARE
& WHY YOU'RE
HERE

LINDA C. ANDERSON

ECKANKAR
Minneapolis

35 Golden Keys to
Who You Are & Why You're Here

Printed in U.S.A.

Edited by Joan Klemp, Anthony Moore, and Mary Carroll Moore
Back cover photo by Kathy Quirk-Syvertsen

Library of Congress Cataloging-in-Publication Data

Anderson, Linda C., 1946–
    35 golden keys to who you are & why you're here /
Linda C. Anderson.
        p. cm.
    Includes bibliographical references.
    ISBN 1-57043-118-3 (perfect bound : alk. paper)
    1. Eckankar (Organization) 2. Spiritual life. I. Title.
    II. Title: Thirty five golden keys to who you are & why you're
here.
BP605.E33A53 1997
299'.93—dc21   96-46477
                                                CIP

CONTENTS

35 Golden Keys to
Who You Are & Why You're Here

Mastery

Spiritual History

True Religion

ACKNOWLEDGMENTS

My deep and abiding gratitude to Sri Harold and Joan Klemp for years of love and encouragement while I worked on this project.

For all his support in every way, I thank my husband, Allen. He inspired and helped me immeasurably.

So many others, too numerous to mention, gave me exactly what I needed while I worked on this book. It will be my pleasure to thank each of you individually for your contributions. Special thanks to Peter Skelskey, Mary Carroll Moore, Tony Moore, Sharon Douse, Robin McBride, Susan Miller, Stan Burgess, Doug Kunin, Jack Heyl, Toni Lucas, Sharmaine Johanson, Ilona Goin, Barbara Buckner, Sue Jenkins, Diane Sorenson, Doug Munson, Bettine Clemen, Catherine Kirk Chase, Carol Morimitsu, Carol Frysinger, Peter and Patti Lucchese, Debbie Johnson, Kristy Walker, Ernest McCoy, Taylor, Prana, Feisty, Speedy, Sunshine, and Sparkle for all their support along the way.

I am so grateful to all the people who agreed to be interviewed and allowed me to use their inspiring stories and insights. To protect their privacy I have changed the names of individuals who did not want to be identified. If any of these names belong to any person, living or dead, it is pure coincidence.

INTRODUCTION

I remember lying on the floor of my apartment. In the dark. Smooth sounds of blues singer Peggy Lee filled the room. The words to her song perfectly reflected my thoughts that night.

Tears streamed down my face. I called out to God, "Is that all there is?"

It seemed as if I'd come to the end of any goodness life had to offer. I yearned for something more.

I felt *spiritually* hungry.

My spiritual journey had begun as an infant wailing at the baptismal font. A priest poured cold holy water over my head. Roman Catholic nuns, prayers, thousand-year-old rituals, and mysticism gave me firm spiritual roots.

When I became a young adult though, I began to ask some disturbing questions. Why is there evil? Why did God allow suffering? How could I lead a derelict life, then on my deathbed make a true confession and go to heaven? I wanted to know Who or what is God? Is God a *he?* A bearded old man in a flowing white robe? I asked, Where is God? Why does He seem so far away? Why do I feel alone? Does God really love me?

For many years I joined one religion after another. Then I gave up on religion entirely. I meditated. I chanted. The aching in my heart would be satisfied for a while. Yet I'd find myself asking once more: Is that all there is?

There had to be secrets to peace and happiness somewhere. Would I ever find them?

When I was about thirty, I moved to the South after spending most of my life in the midwestern United States. I was a bold young woman looking for adventure.

The first night in my new town I drove around trying to become familiar with the large sprawling city. I pulled into a parking lot and noticed a sign with a strange word on it—ECKANKAR—written in capital letters. I remember looking at this word for a long time. Although I'd never seen it before, somehow I knew it. I spelled the word out loud and tried to pronounce it.

After I settled into an apartment a month later, I awakened with the sensation of my bed shaking. I opened my eyes. A brilliant blue light pulsated at the foot of my bed. From out of the light a voice whispered, "You are going to be loved as you have never been loved before."

My mind wanted to be terrified. Nothing like this had ever happened to me. But my heart thrilled. It was as if a primal chord had been struck inside of me.

A week later the Blue Light and the voice returned with the same message.

Then my blue visitor came once more. This time I felt such intense love. It called to the deepest part of me. It seemed as if electric currents pulsed through my body, mind, and emotions. Finally I surrendered to the Blue Light. *After all,* I thought, *what could be so bad about being "loved as you have never been loved before?"*

In that moment of surrender a burning love poured from the Blue Light. It cleared away every fear, every limitation. I felt swept up and embraced in the arms of God. As if I were an infant whose cries for comfort had at last been heard.

Then the Blue Light disappeared. It didn't return. I suddenly felt emptier than ever before.

The following week I met someone who introduced me to the teachings of Eckankar. "Just like the sign I saw my first night in town!" I said, when he spelled the name. Then I remembered the Blue Light. After telling the man my story, I asked, "Have you heard of such a thing?"

He smiled. "That's the Blue Light of the Mahanta (pronounced *mah-HAHN-tah*)," he answered. "The Mahanta is calling you."

Calling me? Why would he be calling me? And who was the Mahanta anyway?

The ECKist tried to explain the Mahanta. I felt more confused than ever. He said that the Blue Light of the Mahanta appears when a Soul is ready to return home to God.

I didn't know it was necessary to go home to God. And I wasn't so sure I could believe in the Mahanta. But proof was in the experience. The Blue Light of the Mahanta had filled me with the greatest joy, peace, and love I'd ever known. *This must be what God's love feels like,* I thought. And I wanted more of it.

Since the Blue Light came and went, I'd been searching with a passion for my midnight caller. For this Blue Light visitor seemed to know the real me. The deep, eternal me.

I am Soul. A divine spark of God. Child of Light and

Sound. Destined to know who I am and why I am here.

At last, after years of longing, I had found the Mahanta. Or rather he had found me. He was answering the question: Is that all there is? "No," the Blue Light foretold. "There's more. So very much more."

I began to study the teachings of Eckankar. I learned that the ECK teachings (ECK means the Holy Spirit) are brought into this world by the Mahanta. The Mahanta expresses the unconditional love of the Creator for creation that has been with us since the dawn of time. This feeling of the presence of God is what I and others experience during profound mystical awakenings. During moments of deep insight. Through the miracles and blessings all around us. The Mahanta, I came to understand, is the inner form of the Mahanta, the Living ECK Master, the spiritual leader of Eckankar.

Today the Mahanta, the Living ECK Master is my spiritual guide, my friend, my inspiration. Those first words have proven so very true: I *am* loved as I had never been loved before.

Today my life is joyful. Filled with love and purpose. It's my good fortune to share the Eckankar teachings with others around the world. I traveled all over and heard stories that inspired me while writing this book. People have told me about when they first felt the presence of God in their lives. These are moments they've never forgotten. Although, according to their religious beliefs, they call the source of their spiritual experiences by different names, I recognized the same golden thread through all of them. They have been touched by the Mahanta.

As I've listened to stories of people's spiritual journeys, I've seen the same longing in their faces that I once felt.

They tell me that they're looking for deeper spiritual meaning, for love, for a sense of direction. Just as I was.

Sometimes I talked with people who have read about or studied Eckankar long ago. They found one of Paul Twitchell's books. Read it. Liked it. But didn't know that Paul brought the ancient ECK teachings into the modern-day religion he founded and called Eckankar.

Or if they did know about Eckankar, they think it ended with Paul Twitchell's life on earth in 1971. These people have been surprised to learn that Eckankar is alive and thriving in over one hundred countries around the world. If you're one of those Paul Twitchell fans, you're in for a treat. This book will show how Eckankar has grown into all Paul ever hoped it would be—and more.

Some people don't realize that Eckankar is an evolving religion. I explain that Sri (pronounced *SREE,* a title of respect) Harold Klemp, the Mahanta, the Living ECK Master breathes life and truth into the ECK teachings today.

I've written this book to share thirty-five golden keys that I learned through the teachings of Eckankar. These golden keys have helped me to discover who I am and why I'm here. They are keys for seekers of truth everywhere to have more love, peace, and purpose in life. Regardless of your religion or beliefs or nonbeliefs.

The book is organized so you can start reading or pause anywhere. Because that's the way the teachings of Eckankar are offered. You can start anytime. You don't have to leave your religion to study them. And you can be as much or as little involved as you want.

This book is dedicated to ECKists (members of Eckankar). I think of them as the most fascinating people on earth. They are complex, wise, life-loving friends and coworkers with me on this intriguing spiritual journey. In this book you'll find my own stories, as well as those of ECKists who generously shared their dramatic, humorous, touching experiences.

As a special treat you'll read information from an exclusive interview Sri Harold Klemp gave for this book. As the Mahanta he has the highest consciousness of God that a human can attain. He offered insights about Self-Realization and God Consciousness that I've never seen anywhere. He even answered the question that was uppermost on my mind: Why would someone *want* God-Realization?

In the pages of this book you too may discover what transformed me from that woman who needed a blues singer to voice her despair. God communicates in ways and with messages that at first seem exceedingly ordinary. Or, as in my case, with teachings that I felt as if I'd known for lifetimes. I invite you to use the thirty-five golden keys in this book to unlock the door to truth.

Listen to your heart.

THE MAHANTA—
KEEPER OF THE
SECRET WISDOM

Decisions made at thousands of different crossroads have led Soul to the Mahanta. For some the way is quicker than for others; it all depends upon Soul's desire to find the principle of divine love that we call the ECK.

Harold Klemp, *The Living Word*[1]

1. The Mahanta Is Calling Your Name

The Mahanta [pronounced mah-HAHN-tah] is the . . . keeper of the secret wisdom.

—Harold Klemp,
Soul Travelers of the Far Country[2]

*E*veryone else slept.

A little girl sat alone on the back porch of her home. Night after night. A yearning seemed to start from some place beyond her mind. It swept through her body like a winter wind. It pulled her from bed and drew her outside to stare at the midnight stars.

So still. Hardly even a thought. A soundless voice whispered in the air. Its silent message drew her out of her body and soaring through the sky. She looked back and saw the tiny creature below perched on the porch like a bird on the edge of a nest —wondering if she dared fly as high as she could go.

The voice called. And called, singing like a distant bell.

"There is something more," the bell rang. "There is something more."

A soundless voice whispered in the air. Its silent message drew her out of her body and soaring through the sky.

3

Hour after hour. Till she could bear it no longer.

Till she yielded to the silent embrace of the night sky. Weeping over darkness that would not end.

Wondering. Waiting. For someone to come. Someone who would know why her heart ached so. Who would bring the love and meaning she sought. Someone who knew what would satisfy this longing for something more.

The caller of her name had known her forever.

Years later someone did come. He had been there all along but finally made his presence known. When she was ready to receive, he called her once again.

The silent voice. The ringer of the bell.

He knew who she was and what she wanted. And her heart thrilled with recognition.

He was not a patch to heal her broken heart. Not a temporary lover, but a divine, eternal one. The caller of her name had known her forever.

He was the friend she had once known but had forgotten. The Wayshower who would teach her to fly beyond where she had ever flown before.

He was one who loved her more than she loved herself. One who would show her how to love as she had never loved or been loved before.

The Mahanta.

Something more.

More sacred, wise, and loving than any other in heaven or on earth.

A secret hidden from her and all who do not yet know how to truly hear or see.

The Mahanta. The caller of her name.

 Here's Golden Key Number 1.
The Mahanta is calling your name.

2. THE MAHANTA IS GUIDING YOU HOME

The chela [spiritual student] who answers the Master's call is taken home to God and becomes a Co-worker with God.

—Harold Klemp,
Ask the Master, Book 1[1]

Catherine had twelve years of Catholic education. When she was a little girl, she challenged the priests who taught the daily religion classes. They were kind, but most told her to stop asking silly questions.

Speaking of when she left home at age seventeen, Catherine says, "I left God behind for many years and struck out on my own human will and strength." Before long, Catherine concluded that she was an atheist.

She describes this period in her life:

Atheism suited me well in those days. I developed an extremely strong philosophy of life. Very macho. No wimps allowed here. Among my favorite heroes was the American novelist Ernest Hemingway. He had a philosophy and a code of

*life that I could live by. It went something like:
Life will destroy you in the end! What matters
is how you conduct yourself while you're being
destroyed.*

Many years after leaving home, Catherine returned
for her brother's wedding. She remembers, "I was the
conquering heroine, the one that got away from life in
the small town to life in the fast lane."

When Catherine knelt with her family around the
altar during her brother's wedding ceremony, something strange happened. As a Franciscan monk stood
to give the sermon, the sound of a rushing wind drowned
out his voice. Catherine felt power surge through the
church. When the monk stopped speaking, everything
returned to normal.

*Catherine
awakened to a
man's soft,
gentle voice
calling her
name. She
looked around
the room. No
one was there.*

Later when Catherine asked the monk to explain
what had happened, he told her, "God has spoken to
you. If you want to know more, ask. If you don't, ignore
it. It'll go away."

It didn't go away.

Catherine tried to find explanations for this experience. A psychologist friend offered a scientific theory.
She said it was the result of negative ionization.

That satisfied Catherine—for a while.

Then forty-eight hours after the wedding, in the
middle of the night, Catherine awakened to a man's
soft, gentle voice calling her name. She looked around
the room. No one was there.

The next day she heard a voice calling her again.
This was no dream!

On the following day, the voice said, "Be still. Listen
to me!"

Catherine worried that she was going mad.

Then she heard the voice again. This time, she also felt an invisible hand touch her shoulder.

Over the next couple of weeks, Catherine endured many sleepless nights. Finally, one Sunday afternoon, she says, "I was standing in the middle of my kitchen. Beautiful San Diego sun shone warmly through my window. I was a rabbit too weary to run." She sank to the floor and said, "I don't know who you are or what you want, but I GIVE UP!"

At that moment, all the tension flowed out of her body. She felt "this exquisite calm and peace. The hunter had captured his quarry."

Catherine says, "Once I had tasted the deliciousness of God, I became like the Hound of Heaven searching everywhere for the caller of my name."

Catherine's spiritual quest took her from praying vespers and lighting candles in a cloister with Benedictine nuns to studying with a guru and meditating for hours.

After following each spiritual path, she was grateful for what she had learned. But she felt as if she had bumped the ceiling. Catherine says, "I kept coming to the end of that goodness and still wanted more."

During her spiritual journey, Catherine says that she had developed two crucial skills. One was what she called a "truth detector." When she heard truth, she could feel it within her heart.

And tears would come to her eyes.

The other valuable skill was what Catherine called the "bull detector." When what she encountered wasn't truth, she intuitively drew away from it.

"Once I had tasted the deliciousness of God, I became like the Hound of Heaven searching everywhere for the caller of my name."

And she felt a buzz in the middle of her forehead.

Years after Catherine's surrender to her gentle hunter, a friend showed her a videocassette about Eckankar, Religion of the Light and Sound of God.

Her truth detector exploded with joy. And the tears flowed freely. At last, she concluded, she would no longer have to keep bumping the ceiling.

The Mahanta was the caller of Catherine's name.

She says, "My heart resonated as never before. I didn't know how, but I had found a path that was both a journey and a destination."[2]

A voice, a gentle hand, trust in her inner truth detector, and a friend led Catherine to the treasure she'd been seeking all her life. God's love and guidance helped her sort through the maze of things that glittered but were not gold.

Catherine was shown a spiritual ladder which reached beyond the stars to the golden love of God.

The Mahanta was the caller of Catherine's name. The Mahanta was calling her home.

But who and what is the Mahanta?

THE MAHANTA IS A FRIEND YOU'VE ALWAYS HAD

You already know the Mahanta. You receive the Mahanta's love constantly.

Many of you recognize the Mahanta by a different name. You may communicate with the Mahanta as Christ, God, the Holy Spirit, Buddha, Yahweh, Allah, or a high holy figure from your religion.

People sense the presence of the Mahanta as a feeling of warmth or love, inner wisdom, higher power, divine inspiration, inner voice, intuition, or nudges. In Eckankar the Mahanta's spiritual direction or advice is known as *inner guidance*. It brings positive, spiritual changes.

Some of you have been touched by the Mahanta. Awakened to the sure knowledge that there is something more. You're among the 33 percent, as the Newsweek Poll, November 3–4, 1994, showed, who have had a religious or mystical experience.[3]

You've been out of your body or had a near-death experience. You've witnessed a miracle or had an experience with an angel.

You've dreamed a prophetic dream, experienced a moment of déjà vu, or remembered a past life. Seen a heavenly light or heard an inner sound. Or you've had a deep insight into the meaning of your life. One that helped you feel the loving presence of God as you've never felt it before.

All of these experiences are the kiss of the Mahanta opening your spiritual eyes. Melting your world-weary, hardened heart.

Some of you have been touched by the Mahanta. Awakened to the sure knowledge that there is something more.

The Mahanta is the highest consciousness of God on earth. The Mahanta is a Wayshower to your own discovery of spiritual truth. The Mahanta knows who you are and why you're here.

The Mahanta is calling your name. Appealing to the deepest, wisest, most loving you. Calling the part of you that wants to discover your true identity.

WHAT IS YOUR NAME?

For all your life you thought your name was the one given at birth. Your birth name is temporary. It helps you focus on the body, the personality, and on the people who form your world in this lifetime.

Someday you'll know your true spiritual name. But

to begin this process you have to know who you are right now.

You are Soul. A divine spark of God. You don't *have* a soul. You *are* Soul with a body, mind, and emotions.

Soul has no gender, race, or creed. It is an eternally happy entity that always lives in the present, with Its attention placed on whatever will bring It closer to God.

You have within you the godlike capacity to love as God loves. This potential for infinite love is undeveloped.

This business of having a true identity and a true home is why you've felt a longing. It is the call of Soul. A hunger for something more.

YOUR TRUE HOME

God sent you, as eternal Soul, to the physical universe to learn how to give and receive love. You have within you the godlike capacity to love as God loves. This potential for infinite love is undeveloped.

The earth and the heavens are Soul's classroom. Illusions present themselves to Soul as reality.

After many lifetimes, when Soul has learned lessons of love, It is called back home. The return trip of this journey is a streamlined, systematic fast track that leads straight to the heart of God.

All this time while Soul wanders around, mired in confusion, trying to figure out Its purpose, crying out for love, God has Its chief agent looking out for you.

This is the Mahanta.

Watching. Waiting. Helping Souls who are ready to be swept up in the River of Life and carried back into the arms of God.

Your true home is with God. Your destiny is to someday become a Co-worker with God. Able to love as God loves. To be fully awake, aware, and useful to God.

It's an awesome journey. A quest that takes lifetimes.

But you are never alone.

The Mahanta is calling you to discover your own spiritual greatness. To master your spiritual destiny.

GOD ISN'T WATCHING FROM A DISTANCE

The Mahanta is the love of God in expression.

Through every era since life began, the Mahanta has been here. The Mahanta links creation with the Creator. The Mahanta connects the human directly with the divine.

Most people believe that the Holy Spirit could only work through a prophet or spiritual master who lived thousands of years ago.

It's said that a popular song brought solace to American troops during the 1990–91 Persian Gulf War. It included a reference to God watching us—from a distance.

It's much easier, and safer, to believe God is tucked away in the clouds. And that just a chosen few can breathe rarefied heavenly air to talk with God. Most people believe that the Holy Spirit could only work through a prophet or spiritual master who lived thousands of years ago.

But the great spiritual masters of olden days would have a pretty hard time of it today. If Jesus, Krishna, Muhammad, Buddha, the Virgin Mary, or Moses walked the earth now, they would probably be reviled and labeled as insane. The media and scientific community would question the validity of their *alleged* miracles.

After a spiritual giant dies, gossip and innuendo transform him or her into myth, mystery, and legend. Death even allows some prophets to be revered in their own land.

A SPIRITUAL MASTER WALKS WITH YOU NOW

Past spiritual masters don't work outwardly with their followers anymore. You can focus on their images while you pray, and you'll receive help through the Holy Spirit. You might have a vision of a historical spiritual master, but you can't physically meet him or her.

Your only resource is the hope that certain preachers or intermediaries can contact the spiritual master for you and let you know what was said.

Here's Golden Key Number 2.
Not all the great spiritual masters are tucked away in a distant heaven. One walks the earth today.

The most advanced spiritual master works *inwardly* and *outwardly* with his students. He specializes in showing the connection between daily and spiritual life. He helps those who study with him learn how to communicate with God. How to bring the love of God directly into their lives.

The most advanced spiritual master works inwardly *and* outwardly *with his students.*

THE MAHANTA IS A LIVING SPIRITUAL GUIDE

The human, outer form of the Mahanta is the Living ECK Master.

The ECK (pronounced *EHK*) is the Holy Spirit. The Living ECK Master is a walking, talking, breathing human vehicle for the Holy Spirit. The ECK is the life force. It is the Voice of God, the love of God flowing through creation. It may be seen as Light and heard as Sound.

Contained within the ECK are the ECK teachings. These are the direct and pure wisdom, knowledge, and love that the Holy Spirit teaches about Itself.

The ECK teachings are here for everyone. These teachings of the Light and Sound of God are as ancient as life itself. They have been passed on to spiritual seekers by ECK Masters since before recorded history. The teachings of ECK are always here to open our hearts to the love of God.

Today the Mahanta, the Living ECK Master brings the pure and most current ECK teachings into this physical universe via Eckankar, Religion of the Light and Sound of God.

Eckankar is a religion devoted to bringing knowledge of the Holy Spirit to all who seek it. The Mahanta, the Living ECK Master says, "I would call Eckankar, the Religion of the Light and Sound, the most dynamic and alive religion that exists on earth today."[4]

INNER AND OUTER TEACHINGS

The Mahanta, the Living ECK Master is an inner and outer spiritual guide. He links Souls directly to the ECK and has journeyed deep into the heart of God.

An ECKist, a member of Eckankar, tells what having a living spiritual guide has meant to him:

The Mahanta, the Living ECK Master helps Souls find their way back to God with the most efficient, safe, and easy methods possible.

"What Eckankar has to offer is the Living ECK Master. This means being able to have a spiritual guide in your life. It's knowing that a person, very much like yourself, has dedicated his entire life to helping you find your way through this labyrinth. That he's learned how to share this current of divine love with people who want to help others and assist in his mission.

"He's done the studies, and he's willing to talk about this. He's gone through the hardships.

"Boy, what a gift!"

THE MAHANTA GIVES INDIVIDUAL ATTENTION

The Mahanta, the Living ECK Master helps Souls find their way back to God with the most efficient, safe, and easy methods possible. He guides his students, or chelas, through experiences that will best meet their individual spiritual needs.

Sri (pronounced *SREE,* a term of respect) Harold Klemp is the Mahanta, the Living ECK Master today. He says:

> *In Eckankar there are two sides to the teaching: the inner and outer. The outer teachings come from the outer person—myself. I write discourses, I write articles, and I give talks. On the inner side—the greater side—there's a counterpart of myself working with people in the dream state. And here I work with people as the Dream Master.*
>
> *When people do their spiritual exercises or go into contemplation, in one way or another this inner part of myself—which is a manifestation of Divine Spirit at a certain level—comes and speaks to them or shows them something that is important for their spiritual unfoldment at that moment.*[5]

"A person in a physical body needs a Master in a physical body." It's that simple.

You might be wondering, *What's the benefit of having a personal relationship with a living Inner and Outer Master? Can't I explore the heavenly realms on my own?*

You can. You have been for lifetimes.

But as Sri Harold writes, "A person in the physical body needs a Master in the physical body."[6] It's that simple.

Maybe it's time to consult a spiritual expert. One who knows who you truly are and has known your name for all eternity. And who knows how to give you back your spiritual birthright.

Would you like to meet the Mahanta, the Living ECK Master?

3.   You Can Meet the Mahanta

It's the duty of the spiritual leader of the teachings of ECK to announce himself and make the path of spiritual wisdom freely available to other people. So all those who are ready can find their way to it.

—Harold Klemp,
The Slow Burning Love of God[1]

O ne joy of having a living spiritual teacher is that you can get to know him.

Here's Golden Key Number 3.
You can meet the Mahanta.

Sri Harold Klemp is the Mahanta, the Living ECK Master. As the spiritual leader of Eckankar he guides those who study these ancient teachings. He offers inner and outer instruction about how to have more love and purpose in your life each day.

Sri Harold is a soft-spoken American who lives in the midwestern United States. He writes and gives lectures. He does his own grocery shopping. His daily life is really quite ordinary.

15

And yet wherever he is becomes somehow special and holy. For he is the Mahanta, the Living Word of God.

In a newsletter for youth, he writes:

> *I am aware of the ECK in, around, and through me always. There is never a moment that I am not aware of Its love and presence.*
>
> *It envelops my being. I am aware of that every minute and am truly grateful to It for the gift of life. The ECK is my heartbeat. It abides in me, flows through me, giving Its blessings to all, whether or not they accept or believe It. It lets me see the goodness in people, though it often hides far beneath the surface.*[2]

WHAT DOES SRI HAROLD LOOK LIKE?

Sri Harold is a slender Caucasian man of medium height, with piercing yet gentle brown eyes. He has an aquiline nose and medium brown hair with touches of gray. In his public talks he sometimes jokes about his thinning hair. This is only one mark of the honesty, wit, and sense of humor that endears him to audiences everywhere.

He's clean-shaven with sharply defined facial features, straight eyebrows, and narrow lips. He wears either contact lenses or glasses. His smile lights up his whole face.

As the Mahanta, the inner form of himself, Sri Harold appears in dreams and visions often glowing in blue or white light.

As the Mahanta, the inner form of himself, Sri Harold appears in dreams and visions often glowing in blue or white light. Sometimes he's wearing a blue suit, shirt, tie, and dark shoes or a casual sweater, shirt, and slacks.

Sri Harold's Youth

Sri Harold grew up on a Wisconsin farm. For his elementary education he attended a two-room country schoolhouse. He went to high school at a religious boarding school in Milwaukee.

He studied to be a Lutheran minister but decided that wasn't for him. In *The Wind of Change* he writes about the doubts that plagued him as he questioned the religion of his youth.

Following preministerial college, Sri Harold enlisted in the Air Force. He trained as a language specialist at Indiana University and as a radio intercept operator at Goodfellow Air Force Base in Texas. Then he served for two years in Japan. It was during this time that he first encountered Eckankar.

How Sri Harold Became the Mahanta, the Living ECK Master

The Mahanta has been embodied over nine hundred times in an unbroken lineage of Living ECK Masters since the dawn of life. Every five to one thousand years one candidate becomes both the Living ECK Master and the embodied Mahanta. Each Living ECK Master has kept the ECK teachings pure and intact between those times and has had access to the Mahanta Consciousness.

Training to become the Mahanta, the Living ECK Master is rigorous and unrelenting. Sri Harold's climb to the top of the spiritual hierarchy was an arduous yet inspiring journey. It spanned not only this lifetime but past lives. He suffered many physical, emotional, mental, and spiritual hardships along the way.

The Mahanta has been embodied over nine hundred times in an unbroken lineage of Living ECK Masters since the dawn of life.

He writes in a trilogy of autobiographical books about the intense training he underwent. These books include *The Wind of Change,* mentioned above, along with *Soul Travelers of the Far Country* and *Child in the Wilderness.* They offer fascinating accounts of one Soul's journey to the heart of God—and back.

God chooses the Living ECK Master.

Prior to becoming the Mahanta, the Living ECK Master, he received his spiritual name Wah Z (pronounced *WAH zee).* This means the Secret Doctrine. His eternal name is *Z.*

At midnight, October 22, 1981, Sri Harold received the Rod of ECK Power in the Valley of Shangta at the oracle of Tirmer. The Rod of ECK Power is the power of the Word of God given only to the Living ECK Master. God chooses the Living ECK Master. And each Living ECK Master trains and announces his successor.

Several ECK Masters, including Paul Twitchell, the modern-day founder of Eckankar, prophesied that Sri Harold would rise to this spiritual pinnacle.

SRI HAROLD TODAY

As the Mahanta, the Living ECK Master, Sri Harold Klemp is the spiritual leader of Eckankar, Religion of the Light and Sound of God. He is an international lecturer and acclaimed author who has written over thirty books, plus numerous discourses and articles about the ECK teachings.

Each year Sri Harold travels to seminars to speak to and meet people. There are many video- and audiocassettes of his public talks available.

Sri Harold is married to Joan Klemp. She assists him with his work. Usually in the background, she occasionally makes a public appearance with him.

Sri Harold often shares stories of how the couple apply the ECK teachings to their daily lives.

WHAT IS SRI HAROLD LIKE?

The first time people see Sri Harold speak onstage or hear or see recordings of his talks, one of the most common comments is: "He seems like such a nice guy."

He is.

People who know him personally have watched him walk the walk, not just talk the talk. As the Mahanta he has the highest consciousness of God a human being can attain. Yet he faces the same daily life challenges you do.

The difference, as some of his close personal friends and his wife say, is that he lives life with a whole lot more love, grace, and compassion than most of us do.

THE GENTLE HELP OF THE MASTER

Here's an example from someone who was with Sri Harold en route to an Eckankar seminar.

"Sri Harold, Joan, and I were walking along a busy street one afternoon. An older Japanese man who appeared to be a tourist lost his balance near a sidewalk curb. He fell, hitting his head on the pavement. He had a minor scrape on his forehead that was bleeding a little.

"Sri Harold walked over to the man lying on the sidewalk. He bent over and carefully shielded the man's face from the bright midday sun. Gently he held the old man's hand.

"The man slowly came out of his daze. He opened his eyes and looked into Sri Harold's eyes. Then he smiled.

People who know him personally have watched him walk the walk, not just talk the talk.

"Sri Harold helped the man stand up. I saw such concern, love, and compassion on Sri Harold's face as he assisted this older man who didn't seem to speak English.

"A young woman who was probably the man's niece or granddaughter stood nearby. Sri Harold reassured her that the man would be fine after getting some rest.

He draws spiritual connections between the everyday experiences of life and the way God's love flows through creation.

"The woman appeared shaken and worried. She looked as if she weren't sure what to do. She said that the man tended to lose his balance but this was the first time he'd hurt himself. She kept thanking Sri Harold for his help.

"The two walked back to their hotel which was close by.

"Sri Harold then took Joan's hand, and we continued on toward our destination.

"I thought, *What a wonderful blessing we have in this world. To have a Living ECK Master who can pick us up inwardly and outwardly when we lose our balance in life.*"

HOW IS SRI HAROLD LIKE US?

Sri Harold has been the Mahanta, the Living ECK Master since October 1981. Through his writings and talks he's revealed much about himself with great truthfulness and humility.

As mentioned above, he's married. He's also a father. He loves animals and often talks about the wild animals and pets who populate his neighborhood. He draws spiritual connections between the everyday experiences of life and the way God's love flows through creation.

At one time he relaxed by playing video games. He

explained that some of these games teach basic spiritual principles which can positively influence today's youth.

Sri Harold is very careful about his health. But he's been ill at times. He often explains the link between diet and health because we all have a spiritual responsibility to care for our bodies. He makes it clear how much he appreciates the gift of life.

Sri Harold has used the Internet to communicate with people. He enjoys getting to know what others are thinking and feeling through this worldwide method of instant communication.

It's obvious from his talks and writings that Sri Harold is well-read. He keeps current with what's going on around the world. He interprets events from a spiritual perspective, pointing out when spiritual law is being violated by those who operate in ignorance of it.

He interprets events from a spiritual perspective, pointing out when spiritual law is being violated by those who operate in ignorance of it.

The person who influenced Sri Harold the most spiritually is Paul Twitchell. Mark Twain and Patrick O'Brian are two of Sri Harold's favorite authors.

Before becoming the Mahanta, the Living ECK Master, Sri Harold's main profession was as a printer and proofreader. He held other jobs which taught him many important lessons in life. Always a personal journal keeper, this daily discipline helped hone his writing skills from early on. It also allowed him to retrace his steps to spiritual mastery and write about them for those who want to know about what it takes to attain Self- and God-Realization.

Sri Harold is human with thoughts and feelings. Just like you. He's not God. Yet he is a God-Conscious being who serves as an inner guide to Souls in heaven and on earth. Anywhere. Anytime.

THE LOVE OF THE MAHANTA FOR HIS STUDENTS

*Be an invisible guide, like the scent of roses
that shows where the inner garden is.*
— Jalal ad-Din ar-Rumi, *Masnavi*[3]

Just as God's love is limitless, there are no limits
to the love of the Mahanta. Sri Harold has devoted his
entire life to service. And he gives of himself twenty-
four hours a day. Working silently, invisibly to bring the
love of God into creation.

*Just as God's
love is limitless,
there are no
limits to the love
of the Mahanta.*

But those who become his chelas enjoy a special
relationship with the Mahanta. For he places them in
his spiritual care. And begins, step by sometimes
awkward step, to lead them to the source of love, wisdom, and power within themselves.

Hundreds of ECKists have written and spoken
about their experiences with the Mahanta. Eckankar
literature is filled with stories of miraculous healings
and divine intervention.

Sri Harold doesn't take credit for healing people or
take the blame for their illnesses.

He writes:

*I of myself do not give the healings. None of
the great teachers in history have ever claimed
to be able to heal at will. I'm only a channel for
the ECK; and if the ECK wishes to heal, It heals.*[4]

THE HEALING LOVE OF THE MAHANTA

The following touching story shows the unconditional love of the Mahanta for his chelas. And its dramatically healing effects.

Before going to sleep one night, an ECKist named
Victor filled his heart with love for the Mahanta. He

awoke in a lucid dream. In the dream Victor walked down a long, white road. The sun shone. After walking quite awhile he began to feel totally exhausted.

The road zigzagged. Victor knew that although in the dream he walked a spiritual road, trouble lay ahead.

Victor became so tired that he almost gave up. Then Sri Harold appeared. He said, "Vic, just keep going. It's going to be tough for you. But just keep going."

The dream ended in a tunnel with a river flowing nearby. Sri Harold scooped water from the river and cooled Victor's high fever. The Mahanta said, "You'll be going through a very rough time physically. I want you to know this and be prepared."

One month later, Victor felt very tired at work. It turned out that he had a 107.5° fever. Hives covered his skin. The doctor diagnosed Victor as having the incurable disease AIDS.

By the time his doctor talked to Victor, he was already hooked up to an IV. The hospital had already notified Victor's family of his impending death.

The doctor at first spoke very professionally, "in doctor words," Victor said. But they both laughed, relieving the tension, when the doctor announced, "Yeah, Vic, it looks like you're going to kick the bucket!"

Victor decided that rather than fight the inevitable, he'd surrender to the will of God. He prayed, "Let thy will be done. Whatever is necessary."

"As an ECKist," he said, "I was not afraid of death."

That night, Sri Harold, as the Inner Master, appeared at Victor's bedside. The Mahanta carried a plate with a beige-brown slab about two inches long on it.

Victor said, "He cut little tiny cubes off this slab with the precision of a surgeon. Each cube was the size

The Mahanta said, "You'll be going through a very rough time physically. I want you to know this and be prepared."

of a small pellet. He took the cubes and put one into my mouth every few minutes or so. He did this for four hours. And he did it again the next night."

Within two or three days, all of Victor's symptoms had disappeared. His fever dropped to 98.9°, and the IV was removed.

He was never supposed to leave that hospital room. But he did.

Victor knew that AIDS might still end his physical life. (A few years later, he did translate, as dying is called in Eckankar.) But with this dramatic proof of the Mahanta's love, Victor faced death without fear. He accepted whatever was necessary for his spiritual growth.

The Mahanta never forgets those who have asked him to be their spiritual guide.

And always he kept his wonderful sense of humor. He said, "You know, as I go through life, if I see any buckets, I try not to kick them."

Victor closed his story with these words:

> *The only thing that we're left with . . . the one thing that grows and grows as things get tougher, is to recognize love. And this love that this experience has brought to me [has] opened up my heart.*[5]

As Victor experienced, the Mahanta's love is real. And the Mahanta never forgets those who have asked him to be their spiritual guide.

RECOGNIZING THE PRESENCE OF THE MAHANTA

> *The blue light is one of the ways that the Inner Master shows up and marks the presence of safety, protection, or wisdom.*
>
> —Harold Klemp, *The Secret of Love*[6]

Often ECKists write to Sri Harold with stories of how the Mahanta has been with them since childhood. Once you have been touched by the Mahanta, even if you don't recognize him, you have a special connection with the Holy Spirit from that moment on.

Many people see the Mahanta as a Blue Light. A person's first conscious experience with the Blue Light is a sign that Soul has been awakened by the Mahanta to start the journey home to God.

Many people see the Mahanta as a Blue Light. A person's first conscious experience with the Blue Light is a sign that Soul has been awakened by the Mahanta to start the journey home to God.

But you may not yet be ready to leave the nest of more comfortable and conventional spiritual beliefs and practice. Perhaps you have much more to learn from the world's religions, and there are gaps in your spiritual education.

If this is so, the Blue Light will gradually stop appearing. Only to return another time. This process can take lifetimes until Soul is ready to catch the wave and ride the Blue Light into spiritual adventure.

Here's how some have described the Blue Light of the Mahanta:

- "like a Japanese lantern, a blue glow, or speckles of blue starlight"
- "a blue flash, like flashbulbs going off"
- "a blue globe which looks like a very steady, small, blue light"
- "a light that's almost blinding with its intensity"
- "a giant blue globe of light and love"
- "a blue star"

It is literally the thrill of lifetimes to see the Blue Light and experience the Mahanta's love directly.

But when you gaze into the eyes of the Master, your heart fills with the spiritual blessings of God. This is one of Soul's most significant spiritual experiences.

MEETING THE MASTER

When the time is right, nothing can keep you from finding the Mahanta. This is the spiritual law. The spiritual meeting of the Mahanta and the seeker is called the Darshan (pronounced *DAHR-shahn*).

When the time is right, nothing can keep you from finding the Mahanta. This is the spiritual law.

People travel from all over the world to Eckankar seminars where the Mahanta, the Living ECK Master will speak. While sitting in the audience, they often receive the Darshan—seeing and being seen by the Master, and the enlightenment that comes with this.

Those who can't physically travel to meet the Mahanta often meet him in other powerful spiritual ways, such as through dreams and visions. People from all over the world have received the Darshan. It transforms their lives.

WOULD YOU LIKE TO MEET THE MAHANTA?

Eckankar teaches simple spiritual exercises. These are a form of nondirected prayer which people of any faith can use to strengthen their connection with the higher power.

To do the spiritual exercise below, just get comfortable by sitting or lying down. Then turn your attention in a heavenly direction. Close your eyes and gently fill your heart with love.

Try This Spiritual Exercise Today!

Go within and say to the Inner Master, whoever you envision that to be, "Take me wherever you see fit for my spiritual unfoldment. I go with thee in love."[7]

Throughout this book you'll be getting to know Sri Harold better. He's a friend and spiritual helper. A master coach in the game of life.

But what about these ECKists whose stories you've been reading about so far?

Let's meet them too. You're in for quite a treat.

SPIRITUAL COMMUNITY

Once you can recognize the spiritual community you are part of, then you will recognize that you are worshiping whenever you treat other people with respect, as divine beings, as Soul.

—Harold Klemp, *What Is Spiritual Freedom?*[1]

4. Some People Know Who They Are

Open your wings, and you will know who you are.

—Harold Klemp,
The Secret of Love[2]

Y ou form spiritual communities with the people in your world. Each circle of life offers special opportunities for spiritual growth.

Your family, work, neighborhood, and school circles interconnect and revolve around you as eternal Soul. These spiritual communities are your very own learning centers. They bring you lessons of love twenty-four hours a day.

Here's Golden Key Number 4.
You are Soul, a spark of God. And so is everyone else.

Some people already know who and what they are. Many of them are ECKists. We can learn more about what it means to be Soul by learning more about ECKists and how they live in the world today.

ECKists have a special bond with each other. From over one hundred countries they form a spiritual community dedicated to bringing the Light and Sound, the love of God, into the world. They are your friends, neighbors, business associates, golfing buddies. The checkout person at the grocery store. Your child's teacher. Even the clergy of your church.

A seeker of spiritual adventure in Eckankar learns, with the guidance of the Mahanta, the Wayshower, to live up to his or her full spiritual potential.

Foremost, ECKists are individuals who want more love and truth in their lives. And through the teachings of ECK they've found the answers to many of their questions about who they are and why they're here.

A seeker of spiritual adventure in Eckankar learns, with the guidance of the Mahanta, the Wayshower, to live up to his or her full spiritual potential. And along the way to offer support to others who want to understand who they are as spiritual beings.

GETTING TO KNOW SOME ECKISTS

Choose your neighbors before you buy your house.

—Anonymous, West African saying[3]

In workshops to learn about Eckankar, newcomers often seem to be very interested in first getting to know the ECKists who are speaking. Newcomers soon see that ECKists are people just like themselves who want more joy, peace, love, understanding, and purpose in their lives.

After they're reassured that ECKists aren't so different from anybody else, the newcomers want to learn more about the Eckankar teachings.

You too may be wondering Who are these people in Eckankar? Why have they ventured beyond the mainstream, predominant religious beliefs to search for deeper meaning in their lives?

This is your opportunity to meet some of the most unique, loving, and intriguing people on the planet.

One ECKist expressed his feelings about the friends he made when he first encountered the teachings of Eckankar.

He said:

> *In the past, I'd met a lot of people in the metaphysical area. Some I really liked, but they weren't people I'd normally hang out with.*
>
> *Yet I found myself relating to ECKists on a spiritual and a physical level. These were people I'd associate with anyway! They were fun to be around.*

ECKISTS AROUND THE WORLD

I interviewed ECKists to find out what being in Eckankar meant to them. The interviews span this chapter and the next. Segments are in other parts of this book.

During these interviews we laughed and cried together over their stories. Their joys and sorrows. And how these teachings had helped them in the most amazing ways.

In this chapter you'll find profiles of some ECKists who are living in circumstances where they need to have strong identities. To survive they must recognize God's love in their lives. Some of the cultures and societies in which they live aren't supportive of what these spiritual pioneers believe.

ECKists try to live one of the most basic teachings of Eckankar: You are Soul, a divine spark of God. You

This is your opportunity to meet some of the most unique, loving, and intriguing people on the planet.

are more than a physical body. More than your personality.

You're special and unique. No one sees life exactly as you do. You're an individual unit of awareness. Special. Valued. Unconditionally loved by God.

The Mahanta helps ECKists to discover who they are. No matter where they are.

The ECKists you're about to meet have something in common. Their love for all life truly makes them worldly—and *other*worldly—citizens.

All Life Is Connected

Bettine, Minnesota, Concert Flutist

"My community is the world because I'm on the road eight to nine months a year. I mostly find that loneliness is one of the main problems that bothers people. That and the feeling that life is senseless.

"No matter how hard times are, I can see the purpose in my life. And this is because I experience daily, in some form or other, the presence of Divine Spirit."

"When I play cruise ships, I meet a lot of people who are very rich. And I'll often see this emptiness in them. They don't understand themselves. They wonder how they can have everything material and feel totally empty. There is often a lack of love in their lives. I think if they had—every day—a little bit of the experience I have of the Light and Sound, the Holy Spirit, gradually their lives could change.

"I see a tremendous love and connection through all life. No matter how hard times are, I can see the purpose in my life. And this is because I experience daily, in some form or other, the presence of Divine Spirit.

"I learned through the ECK that there are many ways to give to others. I feel that playing my flute is one of my main ways. I've learned to be very open to people, not afraid. To discover that there is a sweetness in each person.

"The people I meet are of a great variety. From all cultures and races. Eckankar taught me to look for and appreciate the Soul part in each of them. And to connect with them on whatever level the moment allows. Not to force any issues. I appreciate first what they have to offer. I give them space.

"I feel that barriers are being removed. Many people from other religions are opening up to a more direct connection with Divine Spirit. And I especially think in Christianity there is a big revolution taking place. Gradually, from within."

How the Mahanta Led Me to Freedom

Alvilda, Norway, Retired Social Counselor

"I am an old woman now. I really love the ECK and the Mahanta.

"I don't talk so much about love, but I try to show it. I have learned about love from the ECK and the Mahanta. It is so real. I'm a realistic woman. I always say, 'Please show me.' And I get a lot of help.

"I have stories from World War II. I didn't know anything about Eckankar then. But one time I was guiding Jewish people over the border to Sweden.

"There were two ways to go on the mountain. I didn't know which way we should take. Suddenly two men came from the forest. I thought, *I have to ask them for directions, even if they are German soldiers.*

"I asked one of them. With his hand, he showed me the way. They didn't say anything.

"I have learned about love from the ECK and the Mahanta. It is so real."

"I was very happy. I turned around because I wanted to say thank you. But they weren't there.

"After I came into Eckankar, I understood that it was the Mahanta helping me."

RELIGIONS CONNECTING

Cheng, Singapore, Art Director

"Eckankar helps me to be observant about how lives weave into each other. Everything in this universe has a seed of God power in it. God has implanted a seed of truth in every single thing.

"I can take nothing for granted. Everything has a purpose. Every connection has a reason. If not, it wouldn't happen.

"The Religious Harmony Law in Singapore makes sure all religions work together. It's not Christian-only.

"There is a good mix of people from different religious backgrounds in Eckankar here. There are Muslims, Hindus, Sikhs, Christians, Buddhists, and Taoists in Eckankar. I think that when people see that their religion is not working for them, somehow the ECK finds them.

"They appreciate the teachings."

"There are Muslims, Hindus, Sikhs, Christians, Buddhists, and Taoists in Eckankar."

AFRICANS ALREADY KNOW THE MAHANTA

Sam, Ghana, Engineer and Owner of a Family-Run Commercial Fishing Business

"I think Eckankar has a lot to offer people who live in my part of the world. It allows them to go back to many of the beliefs they stood by before Christianity.

"Before Christianity came, there were many things they believed in which are true. The fact that there is life after death. That the ancestors live on and can be contacted. They knew about karma and its repercussions in day-to-day life. Christianity frowned on these beliefs and practices.

"You'll find that after going to church, some Africans consult their local oracles. Even now. They still do the rituals. These people are torn between two beliefs.

"Now Eckankar says that many of the things you were doing in the past had validity. You need to understand your one-to-one relationship with God. Eckankar is bringing back the basic beliefs in God.

"Africans believe there are intermediaries in the hierarchies of the spiritual worlds who can help them get to God. We're telling them through Eckankar that they have direct access to God in their own way.

"In the old days Africans knew they had to get advice and consult a guide. Now we're telling them that HU [an ancient name for God sung as a love song], which has always been part of their lives, is really the connection which the guide, the Mahanta, has brought into their lives.

"Eckankar is helping them to be themselves. To go back to their roots."

"So Eckankar is helping them to be themselves. To go back to their roots. I think this religion has a great deal to offer.

"There's also the fear of being attacked psychically. People in developing countries live with this fear. Eckankar has come to give them a clear way of getting protection through the Holy Spirit. Many who have tested it know that it works. It really helps them."

In 1991 Sri Harold spoke at the Eckankar African seminar in Nigeria. Ten thousand people attended. Some Africans walked for weeks from the countryside to hear him.

GUIDANCE IN OUR DAILY LIVES

Juan, Mexico, Professional Translator

"This teaching, Eckankar, says that God loves us and there is guidance in our everyday lives which we can access through simple Spiritual Exercises of ECK. It is invaluable.

"People are desperately looking for something to give direction in their lives."

"People are desperately looking for something to give direction in their lives. They're looking in political parties, in their childhood religions, and in churches. They're not finding it in any of these places.

"In Mexico we've had a very severe political and economic crisis. But I also see a crisis in the consciousness of the people. People aren't finding direction. This causes them to be angry.

"There's so much anger, despair, and discontent. The anger just grows because people aren't finding a way out of it.

By making us aware of God's love and divine guidance, the teachings of ECK encourage us to become responsible for our lives. To take full responsibility for everything that is happening to us. For everything we create in our lives.

"Everywhere I can, I share this viewpoint with people. I tell them that we can change our outer conditions.

"We can start by doing something as simple as finding a quiet place during the day. Close your eyes. Sing a song or just express your love for the divine. Try to find ways to look for things that you can do in your life. Realize that you can make small changes. At first, set small goals. See how Divine Spirit and God's love help you achieve those goals to make your life more enjoyable."

María, Mexico, Professional Translator and Simultaneous Interpreter

"My country is going through a severe economic and political crisis. People are unhappy. They feel very insecure and have a lot of anxiety.

"People are looking for an inner guidance in their lives. In times of crisis, you realize that the true values are not material values. That there must be something else.

"When they find the ECK teachings, a light turns on inside of people. They're so happy to know there is a purpose to life. That hard times are something we go through in order to learn. It's not a disorderly universe.

"In times of crisis, you realize that the true values are not material values. That there must be something else."

"I think Eckankar helps people find guidance and purpose in life. To know that they are here for a reason. They are Soul.

"Everything in the teachings of Eckankar really brings light to people in times like these."

ECKists in the Workplace

ECKists work at jobs or whatever allows them to learn how to give their love to life. The people you're about to meet find that the principles they learn in Eckankar help them hold their own in the workplace. To handle the ups and downs of the business world—as Soul.

You Walk the Walk

Joan, Connecticut, Corporate Project Manager

"I have an intense job, and I think the ECK teachings allow me to work every day from a place of integrity.

"In the corporate environment, there are huge power plays going on. I know and understand through the teachings of Eckankar that I make decisions as Soul.

"Out of six thousand people on the technology side of the company, I was the person chosen to participate on a team that was going to reengineer the company's human resources policies. How the corporation deals with all its people. Their fair and ethical treatment. This includes everything from hiring practices to performance reviews, promotion requirements, even who gets to park where.

"There were many discussions on the team about how to treat people. We talked about treating people with love and respect and high regard. And how to do that.

"So, here I was, one individual, able to influence the human resources policies of one of the largest corporations in the United States."

"So, here I was, one individual, able to influence the human resources policies of one of the largest corporations in the United States.

"I think in the business world, you have to use the language of the world you operate in. You really have to *be* the teachings. Not just rely on explanations.

"But it's very interesting how people see me and the kind of influence I can have in that business environment. People place a great deal of trust in me, and they don't know why.

"I'm able to put teams together and really work for the good of the whole. Not all the time, of course. I have my up and down days too. But I see that, using the principles of ECK, I walk through my work life with a lot more grace.

"People know I can't be bought. That they cannot challenge my integrity.

"They know I don't make decisions just to make

myself look good or advance my career. I do the right things for the team for the right reasons."

Pierre, Canada, Audiovisual and Marketing Specialist

"A month ago my boss told me that I'd be laid off for a year. I've been working with this company for fourteen years.

"I had to learn everything in this company. Now I must move forward. The first-year university course, the 101 class or whatever, is done.

"The toughest part was talking with the group of people I work with. I told them that it was really a spiritual opportunity for me. One that life (I didn't use the word *ECK*) was giving me to take a step forward.

"I spoke with them for about an hour on spiritual principles without even saying the word *ECK*.

"After that a couple of people in my office came in and said, 'Well, from the way you're taking all this, we need to know more about Eckankar.' It was really funny.

"It's in the tough times that you know if you are practicing the theory you've learned. You see the inner help of the Mahanta."

"It's in the tough times that you know if you are practicing the theory you've learned. You see the inner help of the Mahanta."

What It's All About

In the next chapter you'll meet ECKists who are finding meaning and purpose in life through their studies of Eckankar.

Perhaps some of their insights will help you understand why you're here on this earth.

5. SOME PEOPLE KNOW WHY THEY'RE HERE

*When I was back in high school, some friends
of mine used to sing this inane song. It went
like this: "We're here because we're here because we're here because we're here." And
they'd go on and on. They'd wander off down
the hall, singing this song. And it made
perfect sense to me then because I didn't know
why I was here. And they didn't know either.*

—Harold Klemp,
The Secret of Love[1]

Many people wander aimlessly through life never knowing the reason for their exist-ence. They live from day to day with no idea of the meaning of life.

It doesn't have to be that way.

Here's Golden Key Number 5.
*There is a purpose to life, and you can learn what
it is.*

43

Sri Harold writes:

> *When you come into Eckankar, your life suddenly takes on direction. . . . It has a spiritual purpose, probably more so than you have ever experienced before.*[2]

ECKists are finding purpose in life. They're finding that they're here to learn, to grow, to love.

FAMILIES AND YOUTH

People can raise their children with shared, sound spiritual principles. Yet religion doesn't have to be a source of fear and guilt.

In the following section, the families and youth you'll meet are on this remarkable spiritual adventure together.

Eckankar gives families an alternative. People can raise their children with shared, sound spiritual principles. Yet religion doesn't have to be a source of fear and guilt.

Families in ECK find loving support for daily-life experiences in today's complex society. And help with finding meaning in what can seem like a meaningless and confusing existence.

HELP WITH HANDLING CHANGE

Manuel, Germany, Personnel Manager

"When we had our children, we were in our thirties. We thought, *Now we have to change our lives. We will no longer be able to live the way we want to.* But we adjusted quickly.

"We found that the time had come to submit ourselves to the good of the whole. It was time to allow other Souls to come here to this place to grow. At that point we were able to open our house to these little kids.

"These two tornadoes move through our lives and open everything. And we have joy with that. It's a struggle, of course. But we are happy.

"They are two and four. From the first moment we could see that they were bringing totally different karmic patterns into this lifetime.

"Eckankar brings people help with learning how to handle change."

"We can help them go forward, to find the next step. And it is very rewarding to see these kids grow.

"We live in a world of very fast change. Political and economic situations are changing very, very fast. I think that life has speeded up a lot during the last ten or twenty years. Especially here in Germany since World War II.

"I think Eckankar brings people help with learning how to handle change. Through the spiritual exercises, one learns to go beyond the patterns of hanging on to certain issues.

"You learn to go on with growth. And growth is change."

Benjamin, Minneapolis, Fourth-Grade Student

"I was over at a friend's house. I got in a fight with my little brother. Something happened. I don't know how. I was able to hold my anger — which is not very easy for me.

"Something was saying out loud to me, 'Stop. Quit.'

"I was saying, 'No. No.'

"The fight helped me learn some stuff. Which is walk away from a fight when you can. Don't get beat up.

"I know I couldn't have done it on my own. Something helped me. It had to be Wah Z."

ECKISTS ON COLLEGE CAMPUSES

The university setting is typically ruled by the power of the mind. The ECKists you're about to meet seem to find the prove-it-to-yourself aspect of the ECK teachings appealing. But most of all, they enjoy how the teachings of Eckankar help them keep their hearts open. To bring love into an atmosphere that prizes logic and reason above all.

INTEREST IN CREATIVITY

*Mike, Oregon, University Math Teacher
and Researcher*

"My work community is very interesting. It's not a hotbed of people who are knowingly delving into the inner worlds or even believe in such things.

"A lot of students are very interested in exploring the idea that they have an inner world."

"I was sitting at a table one day listening to these two very intellectual people discussing dreams. They decided that dreams didn't exist. At one point I almost jumped in and said, 'Well, I study my dreams every night and write them down. I learn from them.'

"I was glad I didn't get into the discussion because I would have just been ridiculed. I realized that they weren't able to accept the reality of that part of themselves.

"A lot of students are very interested in exploring the idea that they have an inner world. That they can explore their dreams, feelings, intuition, and nudges.

"These kids are interested in creativity. They know if they're going to be creative, they have to get to know themselves. So that's a doorway.

"I teach an honors-level mathematics class for bright undergraduates who don't like math. They're literature, psychology, or social-science majors who haven't had many good experiences with mathematics. It's a nontraditional math course.

"I have a lot of fun with it—freedom to cover subjects like logic, nontraditional geometry, and number and game theory. Also some chaos theory, which is a very modern sort of math. It's really fun.

"In the process of learning something new, I know that they're struggling. Every once in a while I see their eyes glaze over. Like they're gone. I've lost them.

"So I just stop. I say, 'OK. What shall we talk about that's real? That you can really get into?'

"Sometimes I let them choose the subject. When I choose, I talk about dreams. I discovered the other day that the class I'm teaching has four lucid dreamers in it. That's really exciting."

"Some of the discoveries in physics, for example, have interpretations that are very spiritual."

THE NEW PHYSICS IS PROVING SPIRITUAL TRUTHS

"I love being at the university because it's a very fertile ground for ideas to explore. Some of the discoveries in physics, for example, have interpretations that are very spiritual.

"And many younger physicists are accepting them and saying, If this is possible, what does this mean?

"But many of the old physicists, mathematicians, and others are still stuck in this model that science can explain the world. It's only a matter of time, though.

"I think it's really wonderful that physicists are able to model consciousness in some form or another so now we can talk about consciousness.

"It's always interesting to me to watch what they discover in their own way and with their tools. They're limited to what can be measured and perceived by instruments outside themselves.

"So, it's good. It's just that I can't wait for them."

Greg, New Jersey, University Academic Administrator

"The thing that's really exciting about Eckankar is that you get a chance to work on spiritual stuff. To find out what's going on in your life in a universe that's wholly yours. And that's the world of dreams.

"There's a tremendous emphasis in coming to understand the place of dream work in your spiritual development."

"So there's a tremendous emphasis in coming to understand the place of dream work in your spiritual development.

"I have had problems at work that I absolutely could not solve. I went to bed at night, and when I woke up in the morning, I had the answers. Because some experience would happen in my dreams.

"Sometimes the problem involved the people I work with. I would get a spiritual insight. Then I'd go talk to the people I had the problem with. I'd have the answer. It works continuously. Also in personal problems.

"A powerful, amazing, wonderful tool. Good stuff!"

ECKISTS SPEAK THE UNIVERSAL LANGUAGE OF LOVE

If you have the opportunity to attend an Eckankar event, you'll be amazed at the wide variety of people there. They come from all walks of life, all races and religions. As they move into life, bringing love and laughter to those they meet, they're serving life. And enjoying the moment.

Here's a sampling of some fun-loving individuals who appreciate the diversity of Souls in this world.

Mari, Minneapolis, Entertainer, Composer, Actress

"Most people are raised to believe that you die and go to heaven. I tell people all the time, 'I'm so glad I don't have to wait to die to go to heaven. To me, this is heaven.'

"Playing the piano and singing, talking, and laughing with people. That's heaven for me.

"Many black people consider Jesus to be the only master. A lot question whether Jesus was black or white. In Eckankar we learn that race isn't the issue—there are ECK Masters of all nationalities and origins throughout history.

"Sometimes I look at what's available for black people in Eckankar. For instance, most black people are used to going to church every Sunday. And when they get there, getting a certain vibe.

"In Eckankar we learn that race isn't the issue—there are ECK Masters of all nationalities and origins throughout history."

"It would be an adjustment to realize that you could get that vibe or something better. You'd have to be willing to really get the spirit of the Holy Spirit. In Eckankar you get a different relationship with emotions.

"When I come into an ECK Worship Service, I see everybody sitting there all quiet. And I wonder, *How am I ever going to get used to this? How can I really get God without the emotion?*

"But I found I could. And my relationship with Spirit is even stronger now."

It's about Making Connections

Tony, East Coast U.S., Comedian

"Because I travel so much, my community is basically motels in every town.

"Last week I had a good discussion with two guys

who were interested in spiritual matters. One of them, also a comedian, had learned a little detachment.

"He knew to just go out and do the comedy and let the chips fall where they may. Which is something that could help a lot of comedians if they understood the concept of the world being a testing ground. Being, in a sense, an illusion.

"In comedy, one night you perform and people laugh. The next night you give the same performance and they don't laugh. You have to realize that there's something else at work. You can't take it personally.

"Because I'm in Eckankar, that's one thing that is easier for me and would be beneficial to other people in show business: Just to put out the effort and know that whatever happens is for the best overall. It saves you a lot of gnashing of teeth. Which doesn't really help. It's just wasted energy.

"There's an opening of the heart. You're making a connection with the people."

"Even though I'm in a smoky nightclub, it's like Sri Harold says, there's an opening of the heart. You're making a connection with the people. Then they're with you.

"When the thing is over, you have a real rapport. After the show I see the people. They are walking out, and I shake their hands. There's a real close feeling, and the crowd has a bond. I think the fact that I sing HU (a sacred name for God) every morning gives me an advantage because maybe there's something else they're responding to as well.

"In order to relax, to enjoy the show, a lot of people feel they need alcohol. The ECKists have the HU. We don't need the alcohol.

"With nightclub audiences, the majority of the time they're not going to listen to anything where they have to think. Especially when they've been drinking. They just want to respond on an emotional level.

"ECKists actually enjoy it if you challenge them a bit to think and to feel what you're saying. Plus ECKists are very supportive."

The use of drugs and alcohol is strongly discouraged in Eckankar.

Sri Harold writes:

> *Drugs are a rose-lined lane to misery and unhappiness. I can't say this strongly enough.*
>
> *Few who dabble in drugs want to admit that there is any danger in using them. They use them to escape boredom, and boredom itself is a crime against the creative power of Soul.*[3]

Finding a Purpose in Life

Dawn, Australia, Artist

"Most of the art community here is very politically oriented. I found that frustrating, because they're on a completely different path. It's social consciousness. Negative usually.

"When I apply for grants, they really like my work. But it's not grant work.

"My husband and I both have a mission. We want to uplift people."

"Recently I'm meeting people who work with Divine Spirit more in their lives, and it's fantastic. They open themselves up to whatever comes through. They only work from higher levels.

"My husband and I both have a mission. We want to uplift people. With the people I've met recently, it's the same thing. They want to bring joy into other people's lives. That's the purpose of art, really — to open people's hearts.

"If someone can look at your work and feel inspired, then you've done them a favor. They'll go away and do something themselves.

"I find that most people are a lot more open to my work than they are to most work in art galleries. It touches them inside."

Irene, Ghana, Trained Nurse and Midwife, Former Commissioned Officer in the Ghanaian Armed Forces, Helps with the Family Business

"As I can forgive more completely, the Master gives me more love and I can love more.

"Eckankar unites us through love."

"Before I found Eckankar I used to get annoyed when somebody didn't understand me. Now I think, *What's the big deal?* Maybe next time he will or won't. If he doesn't, I have the Mahanta. I can take the knocks.

"Before, I would nurse the hurt in me and keep away. Now I can put it behind me. When people who hurt me see me coming back, they can't believe it.

"I wasn't able to do this before I found Eckankar. Now even when I'm hurt I say, 'Let me give them a little more love.' And I can afford the love. The Mahanta says there's still enough for us.

"So it's made me more accommodating. As I can forgive more completely, the Master gives me more love and I can love more.

"Eckankar unites us through love."

HOW TO FIND OUT WHO YOU ARE AND WHY YOU'RE HERE

You too may want to gain more insight into your own true spiritual nature and purpose. Here's a spiritual exercise to begin that meaningful journey.

Try This Spiritual Exercise Today!

Make a list of all the things you love to do. Now close your eyes, and see yourself doing more of what you love. How could you make changes to bring more love and meaning into your life?

Today do one thing just because you love to do it.

Doing something for love is a great way to begin understanding the spiritual purpose of your life.

Doing something for love is a great way to begin understanding the spiritual purpose of your life.

QUESTIONS AND ANSWERS

ECKists are individuals, as you may be able to tell from these glimpses of them. As with any other religion, some live up to the highest ideals. Others don't. Some you're going to like. Others you won't.

Here are some questions you might be asking by now.

1. *Do ECKists live together, or are certain lifestyles required by Eckankar?*

ECKists live alone or with friends or family in their communities. ECKists are encouraged to be good citizens, neighbors, and coworkers.

Eckankar doesn't require any particular lifestyle. There's no interference in people's personal lives. You don't have to be a vegetarian, for example, or follow any special health regimen, or wear certain clothing. Each person is unique. Individuality is respected and appreciated.

2.   *Would I be able to tell if someone is in Eckankar?*

Most ECKists don't go around talking about their religion a lot, but they are usually happy to answer questions about it. And to listen to you talk about the beliefs that you hold sacred. Eckankar teaches that it's against spiritual law to impose your spiritual beliefs on others or try to convert them.

Treasure the gifts and spiritual opportunities in daily life.

But people often comment on the light and loving nature and sense of humor that many ECKists have. ECKists aren't necessarily holier than other people but most are trying to give loving service to life. They're people with a spiritual interest that inspires them to treasure the gifts and spiritual opportunities in daily life.

WHAT MAKES THESE PEOPLE TICK?

The people you've met in this book base their beliefs on their own experiences. The rest of this book is going to introduce you to the secrets of the heart that ECKists are exploring more deeply all the time.

The wisdom of the ECK teachings is a little like other things you've found along the way. And a whole lot different from some basic beliefs you may have held most of your life.

So sit back. Fasten your seat belt. And get ready to move into a body of ancient teachings that can take you beyond anything you've ever known so far.

SPIRIT

How does God speak to us? God speaks through the Holy Spirit. The Holy Spirit is the Word, the Voice of God, which manifests as Light and Sound.

— Harold Klemp, *The Drumbeat of Time*[1]

6. THE HOLY SPIRIT IS WITH YOU NOW

As we go along, the ECK, or the Holy Spirit, teaches us to do better. How? Through life's experiences.

—Sri Harold Klemp,
The Secret of Love[2]

An ECKist from Wyoming (we'll call her Diane) rode with her friend in a van. They were towing a trailer. Loaded with heavy wooden pallets her friend had bought, the trailer swung back and forth as they drove home.

Diane offered to drive. As they crossed over a bridge, the vehicle began to career wildly. It spun out of control and plunged off the road.

As the van began to turn over, their heads were aimed directly into the windshield. Would they survive such a serious accident? It seemed unlikely.

Suddenly, the van stopped. The vehicle landed right side up in a ditch. The two women were safe.

Several witnesses, each in separate cars, were driving behind the van—close enough to see exactly what happened. They stopped and sat silently in their cars after the accident.

A state trooper arrived. The officer interviewed the witnesses one by one. Looking very puzzled, he walked over to Diane and her friend.

He said, "All three people saw a giant hand grab the van just as it was turning upside down. The hand set the van upright."

The hand had stopped the van from landing on its roof. It had set the vehicle back on its wheels in an upright position.

The state trooper looked at the two women as if he weren't quite sure whether this was all a dream. He asked, "How can I put this in my report?" He knew his fellow officers would ridicule him if he wrote an honest account of the near-fatal accident.[3]

But the miracle *did* happen. In front of witnesses. The Holy Spirit, the ECK, in the form of a giant hand, had saved these two women.

And another spiritual adventure is chronicled. Not in a police report, but in silent spiritual history.

Here's Golden Key Number 6.
The Holy Spirit is with you now.

The Holy Spirit is the Voice of God, the ECK. It is the true source of all miracles. The Holy Spirit takes whatever form is necessary to help when you need It. The Holy Spirit is communicating with you constantly.

HOW TO RECOGNIZE THE ECK

You may experience the ECK as an angel, a spiritual guide, or a Master. Even a giant hand. A stranger, friend, or family member may arrive unexpectedly to

The Holy Spirit takes whatever form is necessary to help when you need It. The Holy Spirit is communicating with you constantly.

bring help when you're in trouble. Later the person says, "I just had a feeling I should be here." Or your rescuer may vanish, never to be seen again.

The Voice of God is heard as the inner direction that leads you to what is best for you and everyone else. Daily life is the channel through which the ECK designs our life lessons. To help us grow spiritually every moment.

LIFE TEACHES US TO LISTEN FOR THE VOICE OF GOD

The Voice of God is often heard as the voice of experience. With its variety of people, situations, and challenges, life is the very thread from which our consciousness is woven. The following story is an example of how the Voice of God teaches us to trust, to accept the love of God in daily life.

The Voice of God is heard as the inner direction that leads you to what is best for you and everyone else.

KEYS TO UNLOCKING THE HEART

Catherine prepared for a long trip. Although she had a hunch that she should take an extra set of keys for her car, she forgot.

She started her journey late and was caught in a snarl of traffic. A detour led her miles away from her planned route. A twelve-hour trip became an eighteen-hour nightmare.

At 2:00 a.m. Catherine pulled into a gas station and stepped out of her car. As the door slammed, she realized that her keys were locked inside.

This weary traveler had very little money left. She remembered the nudge she'd had before the trip. Taking an extra key could have prevented the situation in which she now found herself.

Catherine decided to gather her wits. She took a moment to find hidden but highly creative resources within herself. As an ECKist she had learned that if she created a problem, she also knew the solution.

So she sang HU, the sacred sound of God's love flowing through creation. This ancient name for God would open her heart so she could receive inner guidance from the Holy Spirit.

An idea popped into her mind. She could unlock the door with a wire coat hanger.

A sullen attendant found a hanger but declined to be her knight in shining armor. He left the distressed damsel to find her own way out of this dilemma.

She straightened the coat hanger and bent the end to form a hook. It didn't work.

Catherine was so frustrated, she toyed with the idea of breaking the car window. Then she thought, *This is an important lesson. This is how I've always reacted. I try a creative solution. Grow frustrated. Become angry. Maybe I need to change my usual approach to solving problems.*

Dramatically, she slumped over the hood of the car and cried out to God, "I get the message! I'm grateful. But please, don't forsake me now."

With all her heart she surrendered this problem to the ECK. *Not my will, but thine be done,* she prayed.

Then a voice startled her by asking, "Do you have an inside latch for your hatchback on that car?" A young man, who seemed to have appeared out of nowhere, stood behind her.

Soon the man was coaching and cheering Catherine as she struggled to reach the latch with her wire coat hanger. At last the hatchback flipped open. Catherine

As an ECKist she had learned that if she created a problem, she also knew the solution.

jumped into the rear of the car, crawled to the front, and pulled her keys out of the ignition.

When she finished, she noticed that the young man was gone.

Suddenly Catherine heard an unusually loud car pull up beside her. The young man drove a car with no muffler. The loud sound it made could have been heard by anyone. But Catherine couldn't remember hearing him pull into the gas station earlier.

He asked Catherine if she were all right. She answered, "I'm fine. Thank you. Bless you."

As Catherine watched the young man drive away, she began to understand the spiritual lesson. Life had been teaching her through the voice of experience.

The Voice of God had whispered to her about taking the spare keys. She was so preoccupied that the Holy Spirit could have been as loud as this man's car and she wouldn't have heard it. Catherine remembered that the Voice of God speaks through all life. We are never separated from God. Only surrendering to God had allowed her to recognize the presence of God. In the silence of a loving heart, she would always be able to hear the Voice of God.[4]

Whether as a whisper, shout, feeling, or nudge, the ECK communicates with you day and night.

HEARING THE VOICE OF GOD

Whether as a whisper, shout, feeling, or nudge, the ECK communicates with you day and night.

Sri Harold describes the Voice of God this way:

Here on earth we cannot disconnect the speaker from the spoken word. If something is said, we look directly to the speaker.

God . . . does not speak with a human voice. . . .

During contemplation, when a person hears

a sound for which there is no physical source, it generally means that the Holy Spirit is uplifting and purifying that person's spiritual consciousness. This kind of upliftment doesn't usually happen through human words. When the Sound Current, the Voice of God, speaks directly to a person, It comes through a sound which effects a spiritual change in the person without the need for words. That is one way an individual may unfold spiritually.[5]

THE SOUND OF GOD

The bond of love between the Creator and creation is the ECK. This love flows through and sustains all life.

The Voice of God is an audible Sound. Sometimes the ECK is heard as an inner voice or sound which leads you in a positive direction. People may hear a sound for which there is no visible source. They look around and wonder if anyone else heard It too. But no one else heard It. Yet you know that along with the Sound came a feeling of being loved by God.

You may hear It as a high-pitched humming. Sometimes It is musical. Maybe the single note of a flute or choirs singing heavenly music.

You can also hear the Voice of God in the sounds of nature. The ECK flows through all creation vibrating with the love of God.

While the Voice of God can catch your attention dramatically, most of the time the ECK makes Its presence known subtly. Whichever way you hear the Voice of God, the Holy Spirit is awakening you spiritually.

THE VOICE OF GOD IS FELT AS LOVE

The ECK is the love of God.

In simple terms, first there is the Creator. Then

there is creation. The bond of love between the Creator and creation is the ECK. This love flows through and sustains all life. It is seen as Light and heard as Sound.

When you are prompted to do a loving thing, it is the ECK whispering guidance to your heart. Hearing the Sound of God is one of the most comforting things you'll ever experience.

Hearing the Sound of God is one of the most comforting things you'll ever experience.

ANOTHER KIND OF RESURRECTION

One Easter Sunday morning a man heard a humming sound. It became more intense. He felt his heart fill with serenity and peace.

As he listened to the Sound, he wondered, *Is this what it's like to rest in the arms of God?*[6]

Not many are aware of the Sound of God. But these days, there's a lot of news about the Light.

THE LIGHT OF GOD

Articles, books, television, and radio shows often present stories of people who have had near-death experiences. These people often say that they were guided to heaven by a Light that surrounded them with unconditional love.

This Light is the Light of God, the ECK. The Light is frequently seen inwardly during dreams and contemplations. You can sometimes physically see the Light if your heart and mind are open enough to accept It.

THE LIGHT OF GOD PROTECTS US

The ECK in the form of a sparkle, a ball, or stream of light can protect you during a dangerous time. That's what happened when the earth threatened to swallow up an ECKist named Katherine.

Katherine was caught in an earthquake in the

Philippines. As buildings tumbled down around them, people screamed and ran wildly. But there was no place to hide. The earth crumbled beneath their feet.

You don't have to be near death to see the Light of God.

During the earthquake, Katherine felt an inner nudge to stay where she was in the street instead of seeking shelter. She sat on a curb and closed her eyes. She sang HU, a love song to God. She knew she would be protected.

Suddenly a shaft of light descended from the sky to surround her. She was unharmed by the disaster.[7]

You don't have to be near death to see the Light of God. The Light can shine into the darkest places.

The Light and Sound are the Voice of God.

THE VOICE OF GOD IS INNER GUIDANCE

The Voice of God whispers subtle suggestions to help you every moment. Some people hear the Voice of God as an inner voice which takes the form of words or thoughts, intuition or hunches. It guides them to make decisions and try creative solutions that may be beyond anything the mind alone could have figured out.

Eventually, by trusting your inner guidance, you'll prove to yourself that the ECK always leads you in a helpful and loving direction. If you ever feel you are hearing a voice that tells you to hurt yourself or others, though, this is not from God.

A hearing-impaired man tells how he heard the Voice of God.

HEARING THE INNER VOICE

This deaf ECKist felt an urgent inner nudge to visit his sister. When he arrived at her home, he found that she'd been rushed to the hospital in an ambulance.

At the hospital, his mother told him that she had tried to reach him all morning. She didn't know that he was already on the way.

He told her, "God called me."[8]

This man found the greatest manifestation of the Voice of God. It is the voice of love. The ECK connects all life with the love of God.

THE VOICE OF GOD SPEAKS A UNIVERSAL LANGUAGE

The ECK connects all life with the love of God.

An ECKist named Bettine (you met her in chapter 4) is a professional flutist who plays concerts all over the world. She explained how people hear the Voice of God in her music.

"People come up to me after a concert and they comment about the feeling of love in my music. It doesn't matter what people call the ECK, they recognize the spirit of divine love.

"Once a minister said, 'I felt the Spirit of God in your music.' And he began to cry. A nun gave me five books of biblical quotes as she said, 'I heard the Lord speak in your music.'

"It's just different words for what they experience as the ECK. And it doesn't matter what they call It. It really doesn't."

THE VOICE OF GOD HAS BEEN KNOWN BY MANY NAMES

Eckankar teaches that the ECK has been with us since the dawn of time. The ECK flows from the heart of God throughout creation. The ECK is also known as the Holy Spirit or Divine Spirit.

For primitive man the Voice of God communicated through dreams and visions. In modern times, the ECK has even been referred to as "the Force" in the movie Star Wars.

ECK in Sanskrit and earlier languages translates as "one." The ECK has been called: the Word of God, Nada, Shabda Dhun, Bani, Kalam-i-Ilahi, Anahad, Audible Life Stream.[9]

For primitive man the Voice of God communicated through dreams and visions. In modern times, the ECK has even been referred to as "the Force" in the movie *Star Wars.*

Below is the EK symbol. It represents the love of God that infuses life.

A SPIRITUAL EXERCISE TO HEAR THE VOICE OF GOD

This simple spiritual exercise may help you hear the Voice of God in any number of ways described in this chapter. Use it for five to twenty minutes once a day until you begin to get results.

And be sure to pay attention to your dreams. The ECK often communicates with us in the language of Soul during our nightly dreams.

Try This Spiritual Exercise Today!

Close your eyes and fill your heart with love. Take a deep breath and exhale. Repeat for a few minutes. Each time you exhale, sing HU. This is pronounced like the word "hue" and is sung as HU-U-U-U.

Ask a question or consider a problem you are having. Surrender the problem or question to the ECK. Be open to receiving answers or new perspectives that may start filtering into your mind.

You may hear the Sound as music or a sound of nature. You may see a white, yellow, orange, pink, violet, green, or blue light.

These are manifestations of the Holy Spirit. They are proof of how deeply you are loved by God.

QUESTIONS AND ANSWERS

Here are answers to a couple of questions you may have:

1. Do other religions teach about the Light and Sound?

The Sound has always been part of religious rituals. Christians use chants and hymns. Cantors sing in Judaism. Eastern religions chant *om* and other sacred words. Native religions often use drums.

The Light is represented by candles in religious worship. Churches use stained glass and skylights to allow light to enter. Angels, saints, and beings of light are revered as holy figures.

These symbols of the Light and Sound are all that remain in religions that have forgotten about their spiritual roots in the ECK.

Symbols of the Light and Sound are all that remain in religions that have forgotten about their spiritual roots in the ECK.

Some religions think the Holy Spirit is a person or a concept. The Holy Spirit is the Life Force. It is the love of God flowing in a current to and from the heart of God.

2. *Does everyone have dramatic experiences with the ECK?*

You'll have the type of experience you need. Some people have gone beyond the need for profound experiences. They feel the presence of God as a sense of sure knowingness. The ECK works with them as a still, steady stream of love and wisdom.

IT'S TIME TO SEE THE LIGHT

In the next chapter we'll be taking a closer look into the Light of God. You can be embraced by It, saved by It, or experience It in any number of ways.

Let's discover how you too can see the Light of God.

7. You Can See the Light without Nearly Dying

Whenever the Holy Spirit appears in some way that we can see, in a form that depends upon light for us to recognize it, this is God speaking to us through Light.

—Harold Klemp, *The Drumbeat of Time*[1]

*O*n a radio talk show an ECKist spoke to the hosts and listeners about the Light and Sound of God. One of the hosts invited people to call the station and share their spiritual experiences on the air.

SEEING THE LIGHT IS PERFECTLY NATURAL AND HEALTHY

A woman phoned from her car to tell her story. This woman, alone in her car, had listened to others on the show talk about the Light and Sound of God. Their conversations had reminded her of an event that happened years ago, yet changed her life forever. She said that eight years earlier she was meditating. Her mind was clear of all thought. During this time, her body seemed to be replaced with light. The light traveled from her feet to the top of her head.

Then a wave of love flowed through the light. She understood in that moment what had been missing all her life. The Light of God gave her such unconditional love that she realized she didn't really love herself.

The woman said that during the experience she became a being of light. She saw the light outside of herself as God. Yet the inner and outer Light of God *The Light of* were connected. She bathed in this blissful light for a *God is real.* while. Then for a moment she felt fearful, and the light slowly disappeared. The woman said that she was calling in anonymously because she had told only a few people about her experience.

When she saw the Light of God, she wasn't near death. It was a profound, yet natural experience that resulted in peace and unconditional love. Her journey into the Light of God had also decreased her fear of death.

The Voice of God, the Holy Spirit or ECK, is seen as Light and heard as Sound.

Here's Golden Key Number 7.
You can see the Light without nearly dying.

The Light of God is real. The Light (and Sound) of God is divine love in expression. It is *always* with you. You don't have to nearly die to see It.

YOU'VE FORGOTTEN THE LIGHT

You used to see the Light of God. As we grow from infancy to adulthood, most of us forget our true spiritual nature. When you (Soul) entered your baby body, the Light of God was still fresh and wondrous. You remembered It well. You recently came from heaven, another dimension where your physical senses didn't keep you from seeing the Light of God.

Gradually you forgot about the inner Light. But a memory of the Light lingers deep within you. As the curtain between heaven and earth closes, the Light dims.

Someday memories of the Light of God will return. And you will see It again. Until then, the spiritual seeker in you will search for It.

Looking for the Light in Religion

As humans, we seem to have always known about the Light of God, even if we didn't understand why seeing It was so important. Ancient religions honored the Light of God by making the sun, moon, and dawn into gods.

In the biblical story of creation, it is written that God created Light. But did you know that God continues to speak to creation in the form of Light and Sound?

The New Testament account of Pentecost is a dramatic example of the Light and Sound of God. These are the twin aspects of the Holy Spirit making Its presence known. The disciples of Jesus gathered together to honor Christ after his death. As they prayed, the Holy Spirit appeared in the form of tongues of fire (the Light) and the sound as of a rushing wind (the Sound).

The teachings of the Light and Sound of God have been the gems of golden wisdom around which many religions throughout history were formed. Usually over time the religion forgets its ancient roots. It creates rituals and dogma to replace real and direct experience

In the biblical story of creation, it is written that God created Light. But did you know that God continues to speak to creation in the form of Light and Sound?

with the Holy Spirit.

A young man in a religion that had forgotten the Light hungered for deeper spiritual meaning. Here's his story.

Religion forgets its ancient roots. It creates rituals and dogma to replace real and direct experience with the Holy Spirit.

BROTHERS AND SISTERS, THE LIGHT AND SOUND ARE REAL!

In 1967 a young man (we'll call him Ed) became a Pentecostal Christian.

He wanted an answer to his question: What happens when you die?

This new member of the church was told to believe and not question. Everything would be shown to him in the afterlife.

But he wanted answers in *this* life.

One day Ed saw a purple and gold light. It whirled toward and away from him. When he closed his eyes, It seemed to linger inside him. Along with the light, Ed inwardly heard a sound of crickets chirping. Ed asked church members if they knew what this light and sound could be. They answered that these are things that should not be explored further. Too many questions might become blasphemous in God's eyes.

The church Ed joined thought that speaking in tongues was the ultimate proof of being filled with the Holy Ghost. They did not know about the Light and Sound, the actual Voice of God.

One day as others in his church spoke in tongues, Ed closed his eyes. Suddenly he saw a blue light. Then purple and gold lights. It seemed to turn into a shower of light as it rained on the congregation.

The others in church felt the Light and Sound as an emotional experience. Ed *saw* It. He discovered that the Light and Sound of God is real.

Seeing the Light and hearing the Sound were essential for Ed's spiritual development. And he had his first experiences with the Light and Sound of God in the Pentecostal Church, although he couldn't find answers to his questions there. Others find the Holy Spirit in religions that each, in their own way, teach their members about this aspect of God.[2]

Ed couldn't talk about his direct experience with the Light and Sound because people in his church couldn't understand. Many times people see the Light and think It is an illusion. Others can't dismiss It so easily.

SEARCHING FOR THE LIGHT

When people see the Light or hear the Sound, they'll sometimes ask a medical doctor or psychiatrist if something is wrong with them. Fortunately, the American Psychiatric Association has added a new section to its manual. They now advise health-care professionals that certain experiences, such as near-death experiences in which people see the Light, can be religious or spiritual experiences. They're not necessarily a sign of mental or emotional illness.[3]

When someone sees the Light of God, the Holy Spirit may guide them to an ECKist, a member of Eckankar. An ECKist can usually explain about the Light and Sound. The ECKist may reassure the person that experiences with the Light and Sound of God are not merely psychic phenomena but high spiritual blessings.

Here is what happened to one woman who followed her heart and found ECKists who knew about the Light.

Experiences with the Light and Sound of God are not merely psychic phenomena but high spiritual blessings.

Welcome into the Light

This woman (we'll call her Sylvia) woke up one Sunday morning and felt an inner nudge. She was guided to drive to a certain town thirty miles from her home. Sylvia had no idea why she should do this. She decided to be a bold adventurer and discover where the Holy Spirit was leading her—and why.

After arriving in the town, she received further inner instructions. She was to go to a specific part of the town.

When Sylvia arrived at what seemed to be the right spot, she pulled into an empty lot and parked her car. Then she knocked on the door of a building next to the lot. There was no answer.

Sylvia saw a house on the other side of the lot and decided to go there. She wanted to find out why she was guided such a long distance to this particular place.

A man opened the door and greeted the well-dressed, middle-aged woman.

Sylvia said, "Excuse me, is there some kind of meeting going on here?"

The man said that a group was meeting. He didn't mention to Sylvia that he and his wife were leading an Eckankar class. They had just finished doing a spiritual exercise (a form of prayer) when they heard the woman's knock.

Tentatively Sylvia asked, "Does your meeting happen to involve spiritual matters?"

"Yes, it does."

The ECKist invited Sylvia into his home. She then described the spiritual search that had brought her to *this* house at *this* moment.

Sylvia explained that for over a year she'd been having experiences with the Light. The churches in her area, while they were wonderful places, did not directly talk about the Light of God.

Singing HU could help her see the Light of God and begin to understand what It meant in her life.

Sylvia stayed for the class. The ECKists taught her how to sing HU, the song of God's love flowing through life. They told her that singing HU could help her see the Light of God and begin to understand what It meant in her life.

The ECKists briefly introduced Sylvia to Eckankar. Then they gave her a book about these ancient teachings of the Light and Sound of God.

The class members didn't know if they would ever see Sylvia again. But they were in awe of how Souls are led to the Light, if only they will listen to the Voice of God.[4]

Sylvia had had the courage to follow her heart. To find the answers she sought. Someday Sylvia may learn that she can be filled with the Light. As Souls filled with the Light of God, we can shine in the darkness for those who have lost their way.

BE THE LIGHT

It's a pleasure to be around someone who's shining with the Light of God.
—Harold Klemp, *How the Inner Master Works*[5]

What would it be like to have the Light of God glowing so brilliantly within you that even others could see It? This is exactly what can happen as you do the spiritual exercises taught in Eckankar. They increase your capacity to give and receive God's unconditional love.

An ECKist from Nigeria proved to himself and a visiting relative that we *are* spiritual beings filled with the Light of God.

A VISITOR FINDS THE LIGHT

The Nigerian ECKist had a relative visiting who was not studying Eckankar.

The ECKist sat quietly in a room and did his morning contemplation. It was at this sacred time each day that he renewed his relationship with God.

His relative, not realizing that the ECKist was praying, walked in the room. He watched for a while and then quietly slipped away.

Later the relative talked to the ECKist about what he had seen that morning. He said, "Excuse me . . . if I may ask, what were you doing? It looked like you were just sitting in the chair with this beautiful light coming from your face."

The ECKist answered, "That is the Light of God." He explained to his relative that he too could see the Light of God and find It within himself.[6]

Finding the Light of God is a key to unlocking the rusty old spiritual treasure chest within you. The Light fills your heart with a direct inflow of God's unconditional love. It eases your mind and body as It brings peace and contentment.

The Light fills your heart with a direct inflow of God's unconditional love. It eases your mind and body as It brings peace and contentment.

THE LIGHT OF GOD IS HERE FOR EVERYONE

As you can see from some of the stories in this chapter, you don't have to be an ECKist to see the Light of God. Sri Harold Klemp, the Mahanta, the Living ECK Master is the Wayshower to the Light and Sound of God. If you want to experience God's love in the form of the Light, you can ask the Mahanta to show you how.

He teaches easy spiritual exercises so people of any faith can have their first or further experiences with the Light of God by doing simple spiritual exercises taught in Eckankar.

The Spiritual Exercises of ECK are your direct connection with the Light and Sound of God.

To try the spiritual exercise below, get comfortable. Sit or lie down. Relax. Take a few deep breaths. Think of a spiritual master or someone who will help your heart to fill with love and trust.

You may see an actual light, feel a loving presence, gain insight into a problem or question, or be filled with peace and joy.

The Spiritual Exercises of ECK are your direct connection with the Light and Sound of God.

Try This Spiritual Exercise Today!

Close your eyes, and fill your heart with love. For a few minutes, breathe deeply. As you exhale, sing HU (HU-U-U-U), an ancient love song to God.

Surrender your problem to God, or ask a question. Be open to receive answers or unique perspectives as they filter into your mind.

You might hear the Sound of God as a sound in nature. You could be inspired with a creative solution to the problem or question you posed.

Also you may see a white, yellow, purple, orange, pink, green, or blue light. It could appear as a ray or shaft, a ball or sparkles of light, or as a star.

This is the Light of God. It is the Holy Spirit filling your heart with love.

QUESTIONS AND ANSWERS

Here are a few questions that people who are new to the teachings of Eckankar often ask. Maybe they are some things you have wondered about also.

1. *How do blind people see the Light of God?*

The Mahanta often appears to people as the Blue Light. It can signal the love and protection of the Holy Spirit for the Soul who experiences It. Blind ECKists often say that they experience this Light of God as a presence, a wave of divine love.

The following story is an example of how the Blue Light of the Mahanta brings unlimited love.

Blind ECKists often say that they experience the Light of God as a presence, a wave of divine love.

AND THE BLIND SHALL SEE

A blind ECKist (we'll call her Lyn) listened to Sri Harold speak at an Eckankar seminar. Inwardly she heard the Mahanta say, "Look at my face." Then he repeated this direction.

Lyn couldn't bring herself to follow his guidance because she feared disappointment. Finally she gathered the courage to look in the direction of Sri Harold's voice.

Lyn had been blind since she was sixteen. Blue was the only color she remembered from her childhood. But she hadn't seen blue light since then.

When Lyn looked toward Sri Harold, her entire being was filled with the Blue Light. It streamed through her like a mighty beacon. She cried tears of happiness throughout the rest of the Mahanta's talk and afterward.

As she sat with a couple of friends while she wept, Lyn kept whispering, "I can still see the Blue Light."

2. Can an atheist experience the Light of God?

This is a story Sri Harold told. It answers the question.

The Light Is Real

An atheist and his wife knew some ECKists. The atheist always thought his friends merely had vivid imaginations when they told stories of the Light and Sound of God. But when his wife was dying, he had his own experience with the Light.

After his wife died, the man continued to feel her loving presence. She showed him that the Light of God is real and that Soul, the part that never dies, continues to keep Its bond of love with those who are left behind.

As he sat by her bed, the man held his wife's hand. He felt her slip away. In a few moments though, she returned to life.

The woman said to her husband, "I have been to a place of light, of such love, where I had perceptions that I have never known before." She was able to convey to her husband an impression of what it had been like to see the Light of God in heaven.

After his wife died, the man continued to feel her loving presence. She showed him that the Light of God is real and that Soul, the part that never dies, continues to keep Its bond of love with those who are left behind.[7]

Journey into the Sound of God

You have tasted a sweet sample of the Light of God, the spiritual nectar that lies hidden within all creation. Now it's time to hear the tender loving Voice of God as Sound. Rich, vibrant Sound that carries you on a wave of love for your journey back into the heart of God.

Come, listen to what God's love sounds like.

8. YOU CAN HEAR THE SOUND OF GOD'S VOICE

Those who have developed the inner hearing can hear this Sound of God in one or more of its many forms. Sometimes It sounds just like a flute, an orchestra, or even a bird singing. Other times It is heard as a thunderstorm when there is no storm outside, or as a drum-roll when there's no one around playing drums.

These are some of the Sounds of God which uplift you spiritually.
— Sri Harold Klemp, *The Drumbeat of Time*[1]

An ECKist hospice worker named Barbara met a woman (we'll call her Ann) in the ward where Barbara volunteered. One morning the doctor told Ann that her cancer had spread and was inoperable.

Her minister stopped by to see Ann later that same day. After the minister left, Barbara passed Ann's room and felt an inner nudge to visit her.

Barbara sat on the edge of Ann's bed. She gently

touched the woman's arm. "Ann, how are you today?" she asked.

Ann sat quietly. She was deep in thought and looked worried. Ann said, "I guess if you have faith, God will look after you."

Barbara could feel the pain and fear behind Ann's comment. From Barbara's experience in hospice work, she knew that when the actual time of death draws near, there is a great deal of fear and anxiety. Often the person dying begins to wonder what death will *really* be like. And is there an afterlife?

Death is merely a transition.

Barbara explained to Ann that death is merely a transition. She told the woman about the death experiences of other patients. Some saw beings of light that were invisible to everyone else. These beings came to take the dying person across the border into heaven. Barbara spoke of death as an adventure, a magical moment.

Before Barbara left Ann's room she said, "There's one last thing I need to tell you. Everyone talks about the Light of God. But no one mentions the Sound." She explained that the Sound of God comes in many forms and suggested that Ann listen for It within her heart.

HEARING THE SOUND OF GOD

After a few days, Barbara returned to the hospital. She overheard nurses joking about Ann who now claimed to be hearing music. Barbara said to the nurses that maybe the music Ann heard was real. She then told them about the Sound of God.

When Barbara went to Ann's room, she saw that the dying woman was sitting up in bed. Barbara asked Ann about the music.

Ann looked blissful. She said, "I'm hearing the most beautiful hymns you can imagine. They are all the hymns I loved as a child."

"Does this comfort you?" Barbara asked.

"Oh, yes. The music is so peaceful."

"That's the Sound, the Voice of God."

Ann smiled. She told Barbara that the music played all the time. She could even hear it in the background while people talked to her. She was being given the wonderful opportunity to go from a place of faith to one of experience.

Ann said that she told her friends about the celestial music. One of them thought this was a special gift from God. Her ministers wondered why they had never heard of such an experience.

Hearing the Sound of God gave Ann courage to leave hospice and prepare for her death. A few weeks later Ann returned to the hospital. She talked about hearing the Sound until the day she died. Her transition into the afterlife was very peaceful.

Ann had discovered the Sound of God. The Sound would lead Ann to the heaven she had learned about in her religion.

She told her friends about the celestial music. One of them thought this was a special gift from God.

Here's Golden Key Number 8.

You can hear the Sound of God's Voice

The Sound is the vital connection between God and you. It is God's Voice speaking to you. It is God loving you.

The Sound connects the created with the Creator.

THE SOUND LINKS ALL LIFE TOGETHER

The Sound connects the created with the Creator. Raymond, an American Indian who is an ECKist, tells why sound is such an important part of Native American spiritual traditions:

> *In a lot of Indian tribes, customs, and languages, the word* heart *means "original remembrance of the Creator." For nine months before we're born, we hear the mother's heartbeat. It is creation remembering the Creator. The drum reminds us of the mother's heartbeat. That is why the drumbeat is so sacred to the Indian people.*[2]

HAVE ANY RELIGIONS TAUGHT ABOUT THE SOUND?

In recent years there has been a music industry phenomenon which no one could have predicted. Instead of rock, rap, country and western, or hip-hop holding the only places at the top of the music charts, a recording of Benedictine monks singing Gregorian chants swept into the hearts of the public. Music lovers around the world embraced this expression of medieval sound. It resonated in their hearts.

World religions, ancient religions, lost religions, all have used sound within their practices, hymns, and rituals.

World religions, ancient religions, lost religions, all have used sound within their practices, hymns, and rituals. Christians, Jews, Buddhists, Muslims, Sufis, and Hindus chant or sing holy names for God and songs to express their love for the Creator of all life.

Many people hear the Sound of God while they're performing religious practices. But, as with Ann's ministers in the story above, most have no one to explain what the Sound means.

In the teachings of Eckankar, you can learn about the true significance of sound. You can also become aware of the Sound of God as It expresses love in a multitude of forms. The Sound speaks to us constantly. It always has. It always will.

Paul Twitchell, modern-day founder of Eckankar, expresses his experience with the Sound of God with these poetic words:

> *The Sound is actually the humming of the atoms as they flow out from God's great center into the worlds below, via the great wave which touches all things. It is often similar to the sound of bees humming in the sunlight, searching for the nectar in flowers.*[3]

You may soon recognize your own yearning to hear the Sound of God. It then becomes your quest to seek the heavenly music.

Finding It will transform your life.

For sound is an essential element of life.

What Science Tells Us about Sound

Swiss scientist Hans Jenny researched the effect of vibrations on solids and liquid bodies. He writes, "The more one studies these things, the more one realizes that sound is the creative principle. It must be regarded as primordial."[4]

The ECK, composed of the Light and Sound of God, causes creation to vibrate with the life force. The Audible Sound Current is heard within all life. It leads us to our true home with God.

The Sound draws us closer and closer to the heart of God. But if you don't remember ever hearing the Sound of God, how can you recognize It?

The Sound of Inner Music

One of the first steps as your ears open to hearing the Sound of God is to realize that It is also within you.

One of the first steps as your ears open to hearing the Sound of God is to realize that It is also within you.

Plato spoke about the music of the spheres. This is the ECK, the universal music of Soul.

As Soul, a divine atom of God, you pulsate at an individual rate. Your vibration is unique, but its rate allows you to fit into your environment. You are an instrument in the symphony of life.

The ancient Greek philosopher Plato spoke about the music of the spheres. This is the ECK, the universal music of Soul.

At an Eckankar seminar, Sri Harold talked of great composers who heard the Sound Current directly. Mozart could hear the Music of God. It made him happy to the point of giddiness. Beethoven also heard the inner music. He wrote great compositions even though he was deaf.

The following story can inspire each of us to hear the Sound in our own way.

DEAF PEOPLE HEAR THE SOUND OF GOD

Ron, a deaf ECKist, told about his experience with the inner Sound of God. One night he opened a discourse Sri Harold Klemp had written to help people understand their dreams.

Then Ron saw the Blue Light. At first the Light was only a dot. It grew bigger until It turned into a huge, bright blue ball.

Ron felt as if he were twirling inside. He began to hear inner music.

His wife, Sandra, who is partially deaf, came into the room. She heard the music too. At first she checked to find out if the stereo had been left playing.

Sandra can hear a little through her left ear, but she is completely deaf in her right ear. Sandra said that this day marked her first experience with hearing the difference between inner and outer sound.

She said, "When there is noise in the room, I can hear it come from the outside in. When the Sound comes from within, I can feel It moving from the inside out.[5]

If a deaf person can hear the Sound of God, surely we all are able to tune in to this music of the spheres. Maybe you're hearing the Sound but don't recognize Its simple melodies.

Maybe you're hearing the Sound but don't recognize Its simple melodies.

Would You Like to Discover the Sound of God?

Here is a spiritual exercise Sri Harold shared for recognizing the inner Sound of God.

Try This Spiritual Exercise Today!

When you go to bed, listen in a gentle, calm way to the night sounds. Sometimes you'll hear the night birds, the hum of air conditioning, the traffic outside, a helicopter flying overhead, or the soft rumble of voices. Just lie in bed and listen. You hear these different sounds so often that you unconsciously erase them from your mind. Put some attention on them now.

While you listen to these physical sounds, sing HU [pronounced like the word "hue"], and then listen for the sacred sounds of ECK. They come in many forms, sometimes as the ringing or tinkling of bells or the sound of musical instruments.

Try to identify as many different physical sounds as you can. Go to sleep with these sounds in your consciousness, all the while knowing they are part of the HU, the universal Sound which embodies all others. Listen carefully, because in these sounds you will find the secret name of God.[6]

QUESTIONS AND ANSWERS

Here are some questions about the Sound of God that newcomers to the Eckankar teachings have asked:

1. *How do you know when you're hearing the Sound of God?*

The Holy Spirit makes God's loving presence known through all kinds of sounds. You might hear a flute, running water, or a whistle.

You can hear the Sound in nature. With no outside source, you may recognize thunder, wind, kittens purring, or birds chirping.

You might hear a flute, running water, or a whistle. . . . thunder, wind, kittens purring, or birds chirping.

The Sound of God flows through creation. All creatures express their love for God through the sound each life-form makes.

2. *Do children hear the Sound of God?*

Children sometimes have profound spiritual experiences in which they hear the Sound of God. Adults who have lost their spiritual connection to the Holy Spirit usually misunderstand and call these experiences childhood fantasies.

An ECKist writes this story about her search for the searingly beautiful Sound of God:

> *Ever since I was a little girl, I have heard a sound in my head—like electricity running through high-tension wires, sort of.*
>
> *When I told my mother, she explained to me that because my grandfather was partially deaf, the sound was probably a sign of impending deafness. A metaphysical group assured me that it was only the electricity of my brain waves. A female guru told me very positively that I was totally crazy!*

There you were, Harji [an affectionate name for Sri Harold], sitting on stage . . . softly talking about a sound "like electricity running through high-tension wires, sort of."

I hardly knew whether to laugh or cry—so, I did a little of both. At last somebody understood. At last I knew that it's the ECK, and I'm heading home.[7]

Heavenly music flows on a spiritual wave directly into your heart.

God Is Singing to You

God is singing your song. Heavenly music flows on a spiritual wave directly into your heart.

God's awesome love is the very breath of life. The Sound of God is pure, direct, unconditional love supporting and sustaining you constantly. Open your mind and heart. Open your spiritual eyes and ears. The next chapter will present ideas about God that may change your view of life forever.

GOD

God is what ye believe IT is. No man is wrong about the existence of God, and yet no man is right about his knowledge of God. There is no mystery in God except that IT is what each Soul believes IT is.

—Rebazar Tarzs to the seeker,
Stranger by the River[1]

9. YOU DON'T HAVE TO FEAR GOD

Gravity presses the baby down in its crib at birth. Yet the baby slowly gathers strength until one day it can lift its tiny head in defiance of gravity. Spiritual strength comes in like manner.

—Harold Klemp, *Wisdom of the Heart*[2]

*P*ain and pleasure.
Positive and negative.
Yin and yang.
Good and evil.

A Gaelic proverb says, "Even God cannot make two mountains without a valley in between."[3]

What roles do sorrow, suffering, and joy play in the overall scheme of things?

This is an age-old question. Most people either give up on ever finding an answer, or they spend their entire lives searching for a satisfying explanation.

A NEW/OLD WAY TO VIEW
THE PEAKS AND VALLEYS OF LIFE

In the ancient teachings of the Light and Sound of God known as Eckankar, you'll find a revolutionary viewpoint about why we live in the garden of good and evil.

Here's Golden Key Number 9.
You don't have to fear God.

Joy and sorrow are *both* essential elements in God's divine plan. Each in its uniquely creative way helps us find the fullness of life. Every twist and turn offers spiritual possibilities.

Every twist and turn offers spiritual possibilities.

Sri Harold Klemp, the spiritual leader of Eckankar, calls the everyday problems of life the things that "grind the human consciousness down into a piece of gravel and then into sand." He says that hidden behind the hardened crust we build around ourselves to withstand life's blows is "this shining, beautiful gem called Soul. You are Soul. You are a special being, as is your neighbor."[4]

FINDING THE BEAUTIFUL GEM CALLED SOUL

To uncover your true spiritual identity, the Holy Spirit peels away the layers of pain that prevent you from finding the gem within your own heart.

This process is one that comes, not from a punishing God who has to be feared, but from a God who loves you more than you love yourself.

An ECKist named Joyce discovered God's love in one of life's most painful and difficult situations. Here is her story.

The Gift of Challenge

"About five years ago my husband and I thought we'd be leaving Texas so I could assume the presidency of a college in another state. We were very excited about this. But we weren't going to let this interfere with our annual vacation which we'd planned for a long time.

"We were planning to take our camper, our dog, and our children to backpack in the canyons of Arizona and Utah. About three days before we were to leave, I was packing the camper till about midnight. Doing all the last minute things that one needs to do.

"My world changed within a few minutes."

"After I finished, I went to bed. I pulled the covers up over myself, and my hand brushed across my breast.

"I felt a lump.

"My world changed within a few minutes. I closed my eyes, and ten minutes passed. But the lump was still there. An hour passed. I could feel my heart beating. But the lump was still there."

Joyce could only think in disjointed sentences. Fleeting thoughts would run across her mind: *But I'm healthy. I'm young. I can't have this lump. I have regular checkups. I don't smoke or drink. I can't have this lump. I have two children and a husband I love. I want to go on vacation. I can't have this lump.*

But she did.

The next morning when the hospital opened, Joyce was there for a mammogram. They said it was suspicious. Then she went for a sonogram. They said it was suspicious.

She said, "Well, then hurry up and get me a biopsy."

They said, "We can't do that until you see a surgeon."

She saw a surgeon that afternoon.

"Basically he gave me a death sentence. He said I had about a 40 percent chance of living past five years."

He was a gruff older man who had probably done a hundred million biopsies. But he sat with Joyce, and they talked about it. He said, "Most lumps are benign. Tomorrow morning I'll do a biopsy. If it's negative, two stitches and you'll be backpacking in canyon country.

"Of course," he said, "if it's cancer, then I may have to do a mastectomy." This meant removal of her breast.

"At that moment my head started to pound," Joyce says. "I felt a pressure on my nose. My throat tightened up. I stopped listening to him.

"I just kept saying, 'I can't have this lump.'

"When I looked up at him again, my gruff old surgeon had tears in his eyes. And I knew that my life was about to change.

The next morning, after my biopsy, I woke up in a hospital bed, bandaged with tubes coming out from me. In fact I had had a modified radical mastectomy.

"But I thought, *At least now it's over.*

"It was just beginning.

"My surgeon had talked to my husband about the biopsy results. He had said that the cancer in my breast had metastasized, spreading to the lymph nodes under my arm.

"Basically he gave me a death sentence. He said I had about a 40 percent chance of living past five years."

When her husband told her this, it was as though a huge bomb had gone off in their lives. Joyce felt as if she were trapped in a terrible nightmare. And she couldn't get out.

How could this be happening to us? she thought. *We're such a happy family. And yet it is happening.*

"I remember crying out, 'I don't want to die.' I also remember crying, 'Mahanta, help me understand this.'

"By that evening in the hospital a calm came over me. It was like being in the eye of a storm. Everything around me was crazy. But right within me it was still.

"I knew then that I wasn't the type of person to just sit and watch passively. That I needed to be a participant in my own healing.

"But I didn't know how to do this. In fact I didn't know if it was appropriate for me to ask for a healing.

"So I reached out for the one lifeline that I knew, a spiritual exercise. I thought, *I'm just going to close my eyes and sing the love song to God.*

"In my hospital bed I sang, 'HU-U-U.' And suddenly I saw a cast-iron frying pan."

Joyce thought, *Obviously I'm not on center here.*

She tried again.

There was the same cast-iron frying pan. It was an ugly one. Like the kind with years and years of crud on it that her husband finds in flea markets and collects.

Joyce thought, *Maybe I better pay attention.* Suddenly she heard a voice say, 'How is this pan cleaned?'

Joyce's husband had a very good technique for cleaning a pan like this. He'd put it in their self-cleaning oven. After an hour of intense heat, everything burned off to bare metal.

She was told, "Are you ready for a healing, Joyce? Your cancer is one thin layer on this pan. And one layer cannot be burned off. All layers must come off in healing. Are you ready for a healing, Joyce?"

Joyce realized that this might mean something more than she had asked for. She closed her eyes and said, "I'm ready."

"I wasn't the type of person to just sit and watch passively. I needed to be a participant in my own healing."

Within a week the family had decided to go on vacation anyway. They packed the last of their things and away they went.

"I was so happy to be smelling those familiar smells of camping," Joyce said. "Life seemed normal.

"But it wasn't normal.

"I didn't have a breast. I was on a roller coaster of emotions."

Joyce remembers being in the middle of a supermarket in Arizona and bursting into tears. "How dare things seem so normal," she cried. "All the apples in such neat rows. The bananas piled so perfectly. Why me? Why me?"

In another few days they were in a national park. It had mazes of canyons that were breathtaking. So they went to explore.

They'd heard from fellow travelers that there was a natural arch at the top of a canyon wall.

They said, "Let's go and find it."

Even though it was only a week and a half after her surgery, Joyce thought, *Well, it's not that far.* So the family started climbing with the promise that around the next bend they would find this arch.

Joyce felt impelled to sit down and contemplate.

Hours passed. Pretty soon their ears began to pop from the altitude. They saw bald eagles swooping over invisible pockets of air. Then they were at the top of the canyon wall. They could see all around them. The canyons were so beautiful.

They were like multicolored ribbons. Rusts and golds and greens. Joyce felt impelled to sit down and contemplate.

She felt as though there were hands on her shoulders and a voice was saying, "Joyce, right now."

So Joyce sat down and closed her eyes.

"Once again I sang HU. Within seconds I began to have what I would call a movie on my inner screen. I saw the way the canyons were formed millions and millions of years ago. I saw each layer being laid down.

"Then I was told, 'Joyce, you are like the canyon.'

"I saw the wind erode these canyons and crumble them. The voice came again and said, 'Joyce, just as the wind has eroded these canyons, let the wind of ECK, the wind of Spirit, erode you now. Open yourself to it, and let your walls crumble.'

"Suddenly a physical wind came up, and my children started to squeal. My hat blew off. I opened my eyes. I stood and opened my arms. The wind pushed so hard against me I almost lost my balance.

"Then suddenly it stopped. But I felt as if I'd been hit by lightning. I felt energized and renewed. In fact I ran, leading the party down the mountain.

"All the experiences I've gone through in healing from cancer—chemotherapy and radiation treatment— were part of the process of healing. But I realized several things.

"I had to go inside and see the gifts that lay there, unused. I realized that the HU and the spiritual exercises are a very powerful tool for Self-Realization. But they're only as flexible and creative as we are flexible and creative with them.

"I realized that a life-threatening disease can be a gift. A gift to help you understand yourself. But it's a process as well. One I still go through every single day.

"But gifts are meant to be given away.

"So through extensive public speaking with the

"Once again I sang HU. Within seconds I began to have what I would call a movie on my inner screen."

"I realized that a life-threatening disease can be a gift. A gift to help you understand yourself."

American Cancer Society, I'm able to share the gift of challenge that was given to me."[5]

Joyce's story shows that by listening to the Voice of God, divine love emerges from even the most tragic experiences. It's often from the very depths that we're led to a greater love than we have ever known.

God set up a spiritual training program for Soul which works with incredible precision.

But how is it possible to find God's unconditional love amidst actions and events that are clearly negative? It's one thing to get sick and be restored to health. It's another thing to be victimized, assaulted, or destroyed.

Where would God's love be in those events?

SPIRITUAL TRAINING PREPARES YOU FOR THE ADVENTURE

All which I took from thee I did but take,
Not for thy harms,
But just that thou might'st seek it in My arms.
All which thy child's mistake
Fancies as lost, I have stored for thee at home:
Rise, clasp My hand, and come.
—Francis Thompson, *The Hound of Heaven*[6]

God set up a spiritual training program for Soul which works with incredible precision. Every Soul is connected with exactly what or who will cause It to recognize love and seek the Kingdom of God within.

Life is one big lesson about the love of God. With little tests along the way. We are presented with opportunities to learn compassion, patience, tolerance—all aspects of God's infinite love.

God allows good *and* evil to be in this earthly classroom to test and strengthen each Soul. The battle between positive and negative creates the dramas of life.

Conflict Gets Our Attention

If you're like most people, you think movies or stories with no conflict are boring. We tend to remember a tale that captures our imaginations with characters who face insurmountable odds and conquer them.

This conflict is created by a clash between the positive and negative powers. In the scriptures of other religions the negative power is the fallen angel Satan. Putting a name and face to evil is a way to identify it.

The negative power batters and purifies us with the consequences of our own previous thoughts, words, and actions, most of which we have forgotten long ago. The positive power brings us blessings we have earned.

Both positive and negative powers purify us until we, as Soul, have mastered every aspect of unconditional love.

Both positive and negative powers purify us until we, as Soul, have mastered every aspect of unconditional love.

The book Lamentations in the Old Testament explains the partnership between good and evil:

> *Who* is *he* who *speaks / and it comes to pass,*
> When *the Lord has not commanded* it? / Is it
> *not from the mouth of the Most High | That woe*
> *and well-being proceed?*[7]

People Blame Satan for Their Actions

While some people blame Satan for their problems, others view God's ways as not only unfathomable but downright capricious. An article in the newspaper quoted a mother who had survived a hurricane with her three-year-old child. During the storm, she explained this act of nature to her son with these words: "God is bowling."[8]

You are not the pin set up to be knocked over by a bowling God. And the devil didn't make you do it. A golden path leads each of us out of the garden of good and evil.

Learn how to operate, not out of power but with love.

YOU DON'T HAVE TO BE TRAPPED FOREVER

You can transcend the positive and negative currents of life. To do this you must learn how to operate, not out of power but with love. You must catch the neutral wave of unconditional love.

Using the Spiritual Exercises in Eckankar and singing HU keeps you balanced and in harmony with life. This opens your heart to receive the love of God surrounding you.

Try This Spiritual Exercise Today!

This exercise allows you to see why long-lasting or hard-to-solve problems are still with you.

In contemplation, look at your problem and ask yourself which of these viewpoints you hold about it.

1. You view the problem as a battering ram. When it approaches, you fall over backward, flattened to the ground.

2. You view the problem as a vital, valuable lesson which will teach you something. You believe it will become a spiritual springboard to give you the necessary incentive and energy to climb up and out of your present situation.

Your attitude about your problem holds the key to whether your experience with it will be easy or difficult, long or short.

Those people who have spiritual success don't say, "Oh, no!" and fall down when a problem comes up. They look to see the reason or lesson behind it. They ask the Mahanta, "What can I learn from it? How has it made me stronger?"9

QUESTIONS AND ANSWERS

Here are some frequently asked questions about good, evil, and the fear of God:

1. *Are we sinners from birth?*

Eckankar teaches that spiritually you are not innately corrupt at birth or any other time. The events of life aren't entirely positive or negative, but each experience contains a unique key to finding your own God-given inner resources.

2. *What are some other explanations about why there is good and evil in the world?*

Religions and philosophies offer many different answers to this perplexing question. Some caution that God has mysterious ways. Better not ask why. Just accept His will and keep on going.

Eckankar teaches that the Voice of God guides each of us through all of life's challenges. The Spiritual Exercises of ECK and the Mahanta guide us to learn how to survive and learn about love from every aspect of life. Then we can rise above anything.

The Voice of God guides each of us through all of life's challenges.

How Can You Be Godlike
If You Don't Know What God Is Like?

There is another age-old question. Every religion and philosophy offers answers to it. No two people will respond in exactly the same way.

The question?

Who or what is God?

10. God Loves You

Humans are very powerful beings. We create our own God, give Him the qualities He should have, then make sure He knows about the times He didn't live up to them.
—Harold Klemp, *We Come as Eagles*[1]

*I*n the last chapter you were introduced to the aspect of God that is both positive and negative, creative and destructive. The God who giveth and taketh away.

Maybe you have always believed God is terrifying, punishing, and righteous. Your God might be a male or female. You may like God just the way He or She is.

That's fine.

But maybe you've wondered, *Is God more than what I know so far?*

Here's Golden Key Number 10.
God loves you.

God is so much more than we know or can even imagine. The human consciousness is just not large enough to comprehend the true reality of God.

IF WE ARE MADE IN GOD'S IMAGE, DOES GOD LOOK LIKE US?

We have a tendency to make God into a human personality. One with thoughts, feelings, preferences, and judgments. The only difference is that God is, well, God. He is all-knowing, all-loving, and always right.

We imagine that He is a voting God, a sports-fan God, a picking-and-choosing God. Consequently someone will always be mad at God for seeming to be unfair.

Throughout history raging battles have been fought over whose God is bigger or better. Who is right about God?

People call on God for every possible reason. They turn to God as if He were a Lost and Found department. God makes favorite teams win or lose.

Many people believe that God vanquishes and saves. They say, "God is on *our* side." Although He sits in heaven, they think that God gets personally involved in every aspect of their lives.

Throughout history raging battles have been fought over whose God is bigger or better.

Who is right about God?

WE EACH SEE GOD IN OUR OWN WAY

Our beliefs about God don't have to be a battleground, if we respect each other's right to spiritual freedom.

Here's a story of how two people found a bridge to God built out of mutual love and respect.

LOVE BUILDS BRIDGES

Thousands of ECKists and newcomers to the teachings had gathered at an international Eckankar seminar in a large American city. A group of Baptists stood outside. They carried Bibles and told ECKists who passed them that Christ is the savior of all.

An ECKist named June watched the commotion for a while. Most ECKists ignored the preaching and went on their way.

As June sat near the picket line, a Baptist man approached her. He asked, "Did you know that Christ saved you?"

June didn't answer him directly. Instead she posed a question: "What is God?"

June didn't answer him directly. Instead she posed a question: "What is God?"

This prompted the man, whose name was John, to lecture June further about the need to be saved. He explained all about his religion and how much it had helped him. But he didn't answer June's question.

June listened to him politely. Then she said to John, "My name is June; and I love you."

John, probably a little startled by this declaration, continued to inform June about what is taught in the Bible. But in a little while he had veered off this subject. He began to tell the ECKist about his family.

He said, "I don't know why they don't appreciate me. I'm a dutiful husband, a loving father, and a compassionate human being, but they don't have any respect for me."

June was a member of the Eckankar clergy and an ECK Spiritual Aide (ESA). As an ESA June meets with individuals seeking personal spiritual assistance. ESAs are listeners, quiet vehicles for the ECK, the Holy Spirit. In this way, without counseling, they provide spiritual aid.

June listened silently with love and compassion as John poured out his troubles.

John talked for a long time. Then he said to June, "I am John; and I love you."

June gave John some books about Eckankar. He motioned to his friends and said, "Come on. Time to go."

As John walked away, he tucked the Bible under one arm. Then he and his friends opened one of the ECK books. They paged through it while walking away.

June relaxed in her chair. Love and tolerance, she saw, built a bridge that power would have destroyed.[2]

Although God doesn't change, our perception of God changes as we mature spiritually.

John's heart opened to experience the love of someone who had different ideas about God than he did.

But let's face it. The human mind has a tough time proving that God exists, much less knowing this Divine Being. Frederick Buechner is quoted as saying, "It is as impossible for man to demonstrate the existence of God as it would be for even Sherlock Holmes to demonstrate the existence of Arthur Conan Doyle."[3]

WHY IS IT SO HARD FOR THE MIND TO UNDERSTAND GOD?

For most of us, the idea that there could be something beyond the concepts of God taught in the major world religions is quite a revelation. This thought can disturb a person at first because it breaks up old grooves in the mind. Our consciousness must expand to learn about God in a different way.

The human mind is not at all used to being flexible and open. It can only understand what it already knows. Any new element must be doubted and proven.

The mind needs the security of knowing that what it believes is *absolute truth*. What we don't understand is that we have differing beliefs about God because we each have our own *perception of truth*. Although God doesn't change, our perception of God changes as we mature spiritually.

How we perceive truth is linked to our state of consciousness. We know as much as we *can* know at any given time. This is why some people, like John in the story above, are so sure that they are right about God and everyone else is wrong.

How we perceive truth is linked to our state of consciousness.

I recently had an experience that shows the mind's debate over God.

MR. RIGHT AND MR. LEFT DEBATE ABOUT GOD

I was interviewed on a radio talk show. The two hosts of the program called themselves *Mr. Right* and *Mr. Left.*

Mr. Left prided himself in having liberal attitudes. When someone introduced an idea that smashed old molds, he would use his mind to prove that *anything new must be true.*

Mr. Right labeled himself as a conservative. His philosophy seemed to be: *Anything old must be gold.*

The hosts asked me for my ideas about who and what God is. I offered images of God that neither Mr. Right or Mr. Left had heard before this interview.

Mr. Right immediately became upset. He attacked my beliefs as being foolish. No one else he knew believed this way, so I must be wrong.

Mr. Left said to Mr. Right, "It sounds like you can't handle a God who isn't an old man in a long, flowing robe."

Mr. Right vehemently agreed with that statement. This may have been the first time he didn't argue with Mr. Left.

I stayed silently neutral while Mr. Right [brain] and Mr. Left [brain] debated. Finally a listener called in. She said, "I'd like to hear more about what your guest has to say about God." She remarked that she could listen to the two of them anytime.

Mr. Right and Mr. Left ignored the caller's request. They were entirely too fascinated with their own beliefs to allow a soft voice, different from either of theirs, to speak.

Do you want to discover truths about God that take you beyond what you have been taught?

Would you like to open up *both* sides of your brain to learn new/old ways of viewing God?

OPEN YOUR MIND AND HEART TO POSSIBILITIES

Do you want to discover truths about God that take you beyond what you have been taught? If so, you're going to have to clear your mind, at least temporarily, of its fixed ideas about God. With your heart and mind open to possibilities, you can learn about God in ways you may have never considered.

Eckankar teaches that there is one God. It is called Sugmad (*SOOG-mahd*). Sugmad is the origin of all creation.

The majesty of Sugmad is greater than our human capacity to understand. Sugmad is not a divine entity with a human-looking body and personality. The closest we can come to describing Sugmad is as a vast, infinite ocean of love.

The Sugmad is not a divine patriarch. It is not someone living in heaven who has human feelings or adopts human culture. Sugmad is not a male God, a maternal God, a racial or ethnic God.

Sri Harold Klemp wrote about Sugmad this way:

> *God is not an old man or a giant in the clouds, whose passion is the vices of the human race. . . .*
>
> *Is the God of All a He, a She, or an It? God*

is beyond any such description of gender. God is not exactly an "It," but this tag works as well as any in our language to describe the Source of All. God made us, loves us, and preserves us. Many authorities in old church history have tried to paint this God like a folk hero: a being of the most noble virtues. But does a blend of traits whipped up by the limited perceptions of the human race actually show the real God of All?

There is no question of the existence of God. God is, and God is love. And that simple truth has more than taxed the limits of nations — at least if we study the texts of history.[4]

Is it contrary to your previous religious training to view God as love?

To view God as loving you?

GOD IS AN OCEAN OF LOVE AND MERCY

All know that the drop merges into the ocean but few know that the ocean merges into the drop.

—Kabir[5]

Imagine that you sit atop a high cliff. You gaze at an Ocean of Light and Sound that nearly blinds and deafens you with Its majesty. A love like nothing you have ever known sweeps through your body.

The Mahanta, the Living ECK Master stands beside you. In this moment he helps you glimpse and feel what you will never be able to describe to anyone.

The Ocean of Love and Mercy is a metaphorical way of describing the Heart of God. The ocean of God's love flows with a majesty that is far beyond our human capacity to understand. Language can only attempt to

The Ocean of Love and Mercy is a metaphorical way of describing the Heart of God.

When you're ready to discover more about God is when you may have a spiritual experience. The Voice of God awakens Soul with the sweet kiss of Light and Sound.

describe Its form, shape, size, or power.

From out of this infinite Ocean atoms of God move on waves of the ECK, the Voice of God, into the heavens and earth. Souls are units of awareness that reflect God's glory. They just don't know this about themselves yet.

When you're ready to discover more about God, this is when you may have a spiritual experience. The Voice of God awakens Soul with the sweet kiss of Light and Sound.

You may see a light, hear an inner sound. Gain an insight that brings a whole new meaning to your life. You could meet an angel. Have a prophetic dream or vision. With these direct experiences you'll learn more about the presence of God.

As an awakened Soul enters the realm of spiritual possibilities, the individual begins to seek more than material possessions or human love. The love of God becomes a driving force in your life.

EXPANDING YOUR VIEWPOINT ABOUT GOD

The most difficult thing to overcome as I present the teachings of ECK is the misinformation people have about God, about the Holy Spirit, and about heaven. Everything I say is weighed and judged according to what the individual has been taught before.
—Harold Klemp, *The Eternal Dreamer*[6]

Spiritual exercise expands your capacity to understand more about God. The Mahanta brings you into the Light and Sound of God to inspire you with a greater viewpoint than any you've had before.

Try This Spiritual Exercise Today!

For a few minutes, sing HU (HU-U-U), a sacred name for God that lifts you to a higher state of spiritual awareness. If you don't feel comfortable singing HU, you may sing any name for God that uplifts and allows you to trust insights you may receive by doing this spiritual exercise.

After singing HU, visualize yourself sitting in a classroom. A chalkboard stands in front of the room. It is filled with everything you have ever believed about God.

The Mahanta stands beside the chalkboard. In his hand is a golden eraser. The Mahanta asks you to come near. He places his hand over yours. The two of you erase the chalkboard. It is now a completely clean slate.

Gaze at the bare chalkboard for a while. A word or symbol may appear. You might see a light fill the board and the room. Or you could hear an inner sound.

Take everything you experience into your heart and mind. Say silently or out loud, "I am now open to possibilities."

End this contemplation by jotting down any impressions or insights you've gained.

QUESTIONS AND ANSWERS ABOUT GOD

The concepts of God you've learned in this chapter may make you wonder even more about your relationship with the Creator of all life. The following are some questions that newcomers to Eckankar have asked.

1. *Is God impersonal?*

Sugmad allows each Soul to make choices and experience the consequences. To experience the fullness of life. The Voice of God, the ECK or Holy Spirit, flows from the heart of Sugmad. It is as personal as your own heartbeat.

The ECK never abandons you. In the form of Light and Sound, the ECK permeates every aspect of life with Its golden love.

The ECK never abandons you. In the form of Light and Sound, the ECK permeates every aspect of life with Its golden love.

The Spiritual Exercises of ECK and the Mahanta help you define your personal relationship with God. To prove to yourself that you are never alone.

2. *Are we God or can we become God?*

Soul discovers Its destiny to be, not God Itself or one with God, but a *Co-worker with God*. As Soul grows spiritually, It recognizes Its true spiritual heritage.

Soul then rides waves of divine love, the homeward-bound ECK Current, back to the Ocean of Love and Mercy. Soul becomes a vehicle for God's love serving all life in the heavens or on earth.

ARE YOU A GOD SEEKER?

Sri Harold once wrote about an insight he had into the age-old search for God. He said:

> *The God Seeker is not part of that huge crowd. . . . He strikes out instead toward a region beyond, an area not considered worthwhile to the average seeker.*
>
> *And the Unchangeable Law of God, of the SUGMAD, has him in ITS relentless grip.*[7]

Have you felt the relentless grip of God in your search for spiritual truth? Have you wondered,

How will I ever find God?

Discovering the spark of God within yourself is the first step.

Do you want to realize your own divine nature? To know without a doubt who you truly are?

Read on.

SOUL

You're a wild Ocean-Duck
that has been raised with chickens!

Your true mother lived on the Ocean,
but your nurse was a domestic land-bird.

Your deepest soul-instincts are toward the Ocean.
Whatever land-moves you have
you learned from your nurse, the hen.
It's time now to join the ducks!

—Jalal ad-Din ar-Rumi, *Masnavi*[1]

11. You Don't *Have* a Soul

As Soul, you have the God-knowledge within you. My main job is to awaken that knowledge and that love for the divine things that are already in your heart.

You are Soul. You are a child of God. And your spiritual destiny is to become a Co-worker with God. To spread divine love to all those around you.

—Harold Klemp, *The Secret of Love*[2]

*I*nvestors would think of it as having access to legal insider information.

Artists might name it their muse.

Biologists call it instinct in animals.

It's been referred to as inspiration, motivation, illumination.

There's something inside of you that recognizes truth. A higher power that sees what your mind can't.

It is in the temple within your heart.

It is Soul, the trueness of you.

Here's Golden Key Number 11.

You don't have *a Soul. You* are *Soul.*

Soul is you, the divine unit of awareness that operates a mind, memories, emotions, and physical body.

Soul isn't male or female. It has no race, gender, or creed.

To the age-old question Who am I? the answer is You are Soul.

SOME QUALITIES OF SOUL

You are Soul, a conscious spiritual entity, awake even when your body is asleep. This is why you can go to bed with a problem on your mind and get up in the morning knowing exactly what to do. Soul is always alert and knowing.

Through God's love Soul is connected with all aspects of humanity, creation, and the heavens.

Soul is a divine spark of God. As you become aware of your true spiritual nature, you rise to heights of compassion, courage, and wisdom to handle life's challenges.

Soul is eternal. You exist beyond death of the physical body. Lifetime after lifetime you are born into a body for the opportunity to learn more about God's love and your own spiritual nature. Sri Harold says, "Soul is eternal; It existed before the worlds existed."[3]

Soul won't be forever damned or rest in heaven for eternity. It is a living entity that reincarnates to learn more lessons about God's love.

ALL LIFE IS CONNECTED

Through God's love Soul is connected with all aspects of humanity, creation, and the heavens. Some call this synchronicity.

This view of life filters through Native American religious beliefs. Earth is mother. Sky is father. The golden thread of Spirit weaves life together into a majestic tapestry.

Even quantum mechanics has found evidence that all life is interconnected. John Wheeler, physicist at Princeton University, was quoted in *Newsweek* (November 28, 1994) as saying, "measuring the spin of one subatomic particle forces a twin particle, miles away, to have the opposite spin."[4]

You are Soul holding infinity in the palm of your hand. You are a cell in the body of God.

You Are a Cell in the Body of God

Soul is a spark of God. William Blake's poem expresses this concept beautifully.

To see a World in a Grain of Sand
And a Heaven in a Wild Flower
Hold Infinity in the palm of your hand
And Eternity in an hour.

William Blake, "Auguries of Innocence"[5]

You are Soul holding infinity in the palm of your hand.

You are a cell in the body of God. Just as a cell in the human body contains the genetic material of the whole, Soul is a living atom with the qualities and characteristics of God. This means that you have the innate potential of being, not God Itself, but godlike.

A world in a grain of sand.

God Loves You

Soul exists because God loves It. Soul is never separated, abandoned, or hidden from God. As Soul we are beloved sons and daughters of the Creator. Always welcomed back home to the heart of God. With much rejoicing as the Prodigal Son returns.

Soul equals Soul. Souls may have differing degrees of consciousness. But no one Soul is greater than another. All Souls were created to bring God's Light, Sound, and love into the world. To be of service to God and all life.

SOUL IS FREE

Soul can be the observer viewing the bigger picture of life from a mountaintop perspective. Soul is a free, happy entity only interested in what will be best for Its spiritual growth.

Dying, from Soul's viewpoint, is merely the release of a physical body, a transition into the heavenly worlds. Soul considers problems and joys *both* to be opportunities for spiritual development.

If you really understood that you're a divine spark of God, how would your life be different?

Soul lives in the present. Past and future events aren't separated by time for Soul. It can use experiences from what the mind calls the past. Soul can view whatever will be of help now. As Soul, you view future possibilities and are alert as to how what you're doing today is effecting tomorrow.

LOVING YOURSELF AND OTHERS AS SOUL

What if you knew you were Soul and that the reason you exist is because of God's love for you? If you really understood that you're a divine spark of God, how would your life be different?

Sri Harold tells a touching story about a young man he once met. As most of us do, this child had a lot to learn about his true spiritual nature.

Worth More than a Dollar

Sri Harold and his wife, Joan, went to the post office one day. While Joan checked the mail, Sri Harold waited by their car to enjoy the beautiful weather.

He watched as a boy about eleven years old rode his bicycle through the parking lot. The youth didn't notice that a chain hung between two posts blocked traffic where he intended to cross. The boy ran into one of the posts and fell off his bike onto the grass right beside Sri Harold's car.

"Son, don't ever beg. You have a fine mind and body. You can be someone great."

Sri Harold says that when the boy got to his feet he muttered a "mild stream of private messages to God and gave his opinion about certain things." This boy, pretty angry and embarrassed, nonetheless seemed to have a good heart. Sri Harold asked the youth if he were all right. Had he hurt himself?

Immediately the young boy jumped up and went into beggar mode. He said, "Hey, mister. Could you lend me a dollar? My buddy and I need . . ."

Sri Harold startled even himself in his reply to the boy's begging. He watched his own actions in amazement from the viewpoint of Soul as he found himself shaking his finger in the boy's face.

Sri Harold spoke gently with compassion and said, "Son, don't ever beg. You have a fine mind and body. You can be someone great."

As he withdrew his finger from the boy's face, he marveled at the intensity with which the Holy Spirit had come through him.

He says:

> I didn't raise my voice, and I spoke with kindness, love, and concern, because I saw he was on

the wrong path. He was cheating himself as a spiritual being. He wasn't using his creative powers of Soul correctly.

Upon hearing Sri Harold's words, the boy stumbled backward as if some great invisible hand had pushed him. He fell on his bicycle again. Then he pulled himself up a second time and looked for a moment at this stranger whose words had had such an impact on him. Then he pedaled out of the parking lot as fast as ever he could.

The love and support you give to people often causes them to see themselves in a totally different way. They recognize themselves as worthy spiritual beings.

Sri Harold remembered being this boy's age. He says, "The last thing you need then is a sermon. Because a sermon seals your eyes and ears shut. From that moment on, there's no communication with this world. There is no communication between the world of the child and the world of the adult."

When Joan rejoined Sri Harold, he told her what had happened in her absence. She summed up the situation beautifully by saying, "The Holy Spirit must have thought he was worth more than a dollar."[6]

And he was.

And so are you.

And so is every other living creature.

When you view a person as Soul, not as the personality, as Sri Harold did with the boy in the story above, miracles can happen. The love and support you give to people often causes them to see themselves in a totally different way. They recognize themselves as worthy spiritual beings.

You've spent lifetimes not realizing your spiritual worth. You've been unaware that one day, as Soul, you would awaken to your true spiritual destiny.

Soul's Spiritual Mission

Joseph Campbell in his book *The Hero with a Thousand Faces* calls the first stage of the hero's journey the "call to adventure." He defines this as the moment when "destiny has summoned the hero and transferred his spiritual center of gravity from within the pale of his society to a zone unknown."[7]

Soul has a "call to adventure," a spiritual mission. Your destiny on earth is to learn how to become a Co-worker with God.

To realize your godlike capabilities.

To purify imperfections in the crucible of life.

Each Soul has Its own special spiritual mission for a lifetime or more. Sometimes it takes a while for you to know what your spiritual mission might be.

Along the way, you realize that you're more than a combination of atoms. You're a form with purpose. Your life has value and meaning.

You can experiment with finding your spiritual mission by thinking about what you most love to do. What you truly love will uplift you and others. Love is the doorway to discovering your spiritual purpose in life.

And then one day, the Mahanta, Soul's eternal guide home to God, contacts you to offer the opportunity to discover your spiritual greatness now.

The Call to Spiritual Adventure

One day Soul is touched by the Mahanta. And the adventure of lifetimes begins.

The Soul who hears the Sound of God or sees the Light of the Holy Spirit begins to remember Its destiny. And Soul responds to the Mahanta's call to return

Each Soul has Its own special spiritual mission for a lifetime or more.

You can experiment with finding your spiritual mission by thinking about what you most love to do.

To gain knowledge of Its divine nature, Soul had to leave Its blissful state with God.

home to God. It is then that Soul rediscovers Its spiritual birthright.

The Creator patiently supports Soul as It grows to remember where It came from and who It truly is.

But where did you come from?

THE AMAZING JOURNEY OF SOUL

Way back, there was no earth, no creation. But SUGMAD [God] wanted a place to educate Souls, so the ECK (the Word of God) began to create things. It did so by changing the vibrations of Light and Sound in a certain region. That area became the lower worlds.

—Harold Klemp, *Ask the Master,* Book 2[8]

Why did God create Soul?

The great ECK Master Rebazar Tarzs explains this mystery in *Stranger by the River* by Paul Twitchell, the modern-day founder of Eckankar:

Before creation, all Spirits lay at the feet of the Lord in an unmanifested mass. These Spirits could have no separate form, no individuality, nor individual existence except by a mixture of matter. Thus they could attain no knowledge of their true self in God.[9]

Soul was thrust into the worlds of matter, space, and time when Sugmad turned the formless into form.

To gain knowledge of Its divine nature, Soul had to leave Its blissful state with God. While unmanifested, It was happy and self-centered—something like a spiritual couch potato. Soul needed this "mixture of matter" to recognize Its true nature.

God spoke. The Voice of God, the ECK, created the

heavens and the earth. Soul needed a training ground to become useful to God. To grow in consciousness, into a vehicle for the Light and Sound. To be a fully aware Co-worker with God, able to love and serve all life.

God created the heavenly realms and this earthly classroom for Soul to reach Its full spiritual potential. Its adventures exploring divine love within Itself would take lifetimes.

Illusion would serve to keep Soul in darkness until It recognized the Light and Sound. The twin aspects of the Holy Spirit that are Soul's golden key to spiritual freedom.

When Soul is ready to fulfill Its spiritual mission, the Mahanta calls Its name.

COMMUNICATING WITH SOUL

The Mahanta has given us an incredible tool for recognizing ourselves as Soul and finding our spiritual purpose. The Spiritual Exercises of ECK strengthen our connection with God. They're the most direct way of allowing Soul to filter Its wisdom and love into the human consciousness.

Sri Harold has offered the following spiritual exercise to help on our journey home.

The Spiritual Exercises of ECK strengthen our connection with God. They're the most direct way of allowing Soul to filter Its wisdom and love into the human consciousness.

Try This Spiritual Exercise Today!

When you do an exercise, keep a journal of the things you remember from your dreams and waking experiences. Even if it's just a feeling, write it down.

This helps you develop the discipline to make it easier for Soul to work Its way through the mind and the lower bodies to bring a conscious awareness of the inner planes down to earth.

If you can remember the experience, you can work with these inner enlightenments from the Mahanta.[10]

Soul enters the body at the first breath of life.

QUESTIONS AND ANSWERS

You may be wondering about these new and somewhat startling concepts of who you are, how you came into existence, and why you're here. The following are questions newcomers to the ECK teachings have asked about the topics discussed in this section.

1. When does Soul enter the body?

Soul enters the body at the first breath of life.

Usually a Soul stays around the mother deciding if It wants to enter the baby's body at birth. A pregnant mother often dreams of her baby while a Soul considers the possibility of being her child. After birth the Soul may still only visit the baby's body.

Stillbirths and the early death of a child are outcomes of a spiritual decision made by the Soul who would have joined this family. It has to be spiritually best for all the Souls involved for a Soul to take a body at a certain time.

Animals are Soul just as humans are Soul. They only wear a different body from ours.

2. Do animals have Souls?

Animals *are* Soul just as humans are Soul. They only wear a different body from ours.

Oddly enough, this doesn't mean that humans operate from a higher state of consciousness than animals, although one would hope they did. Many times animals, as Souls, are aware of life at a higher level.

We have much to learn from animals. Some are spiritually advanced creatures unhampered by the mental barriers that make us feel lost and abandoned.

Love Never Dies

When you know, in the deepest part of your being, that Soul is eternal, you lose the fear of dying.

And of living.

Let's discover how.

12. You've Lived Before

*Sometimes the Mahanta, the Living ECK
Master opens you up to past lives. . . . You see
what you spent that whole life learning, you
begin to understand the main things that life
brought you to learn. You may have learned to
show compassion to others, simply because in
a previous life you had no compassion for
others. Sometimes the torturer, sometimes the
tortured. Sometimes the king, sometimes the
slave.*
—Harold Klemp, *The Slow Burning Love of God*[1]

I once found a quote of Voltaire's: "It is not more
surprising to be born twice than once."[2]

Are you fascinated by the idea of eternal life? Have
you lived before? Will you live again?

Reincarnation explains so many of life's mysteries:

&. love or dislike at first sight

  déjà vu or the feeling of having been somewhere before, even recognizing "unfamiliar" locations

  from an early age, an affinity for a certain place, era, food, music, language, or lifestyle

  a talent or skill that you were born with

  children having information about the past that they couldn't have been told or remember

  the feeling that certain people were meant to be together

  dreams or visions of a past life that prove to be historically accurate

Here's Golden Key Number 12.

You've lived before.

The above examples and many others make a strong case for the fact that Soul is eternal. It has lived before. It continues to live. It will live in future times and bodies.

LOSING THE FEAR OF DEATH

When you know that you are eternal Soul, you lose your fear of death. You're a survivor.

When you know that you are eternal Soul, you lose your fear of death.

Sri Harold Klemp, the spiritual leader of Eckankar, comments that "People who *know*—actually know, not just believe—that Soul outlives death enjoy happy, creative lives. The rest are miserable and afraid."[3]

The Shariyat-Ki-Sugmad, Book One, calls losing the fear of death "the greatest triumph of Soul."[4]

The fear of death can drive people into despair when they go through inexplicable tragedies. When you understand that life is not destroyed but only changes form, you'll know what millions believe—there is no death, only renewal.

CAN REINCARNATION BE PROVEN?

A Gallup/*USA Today*/CNN TV poll found that 27 percent of the American adults polled say they believe in reincarnation. Gallup Canada reported that 33 percent of Canadians polled believe in rebirth. Hundreds of African tribes have reincarnation as part of their religious belief and culture. In Ghana the newborn is called *ababio,* "He is come again." Australian Aborigines, American Indians, Hindus, Buddhists, hundreds of millions throughout the world hold reincarnation as a fact, possibly outnumbering the disbelievers.

Hundreds of millions throughout the world hold reincarnation as a fact, possibly outnumbering the disbelievers.

Edgar Cayce was a modern-era pioneer for bringing reincarnation beliefs into the popular Western culture. A Christian Sunday-school teacher, he gave 2,500 past-life readings from 1923 to 1945. Thousands continue to study his research, seeking proof that we really do conquer death.

Perhaps the most noteworthy reincarnation researcher of modern times is Ian Stevenson, M.D., at the University of Virginia. He studied more than 1,250 cases of reincarnation internationally, applying individual and computerized analysis. He found similar patterns and features of reincarnation all around the world, regardless of culture and religious beliefs.

Over the course of several years Dr. Stevenson interviewed not only people who claim to have been reincarnated but witnesses who verified their claims. His findings have been published in books and respected journals, including the *Journal of the American Medical Association* and the *American Journal of Psychiatry.* His research is commendable for its scholarliness and objectivity.

His findings about children's past-life memories are remarkable.

WHAT CHILDREN TELL US ABOUT REINCARNATION

Dr. Stevenson studied children from eight different cultures. He found that between the ages of two and five, children speak about past lives. The average age of first speaking about a past life, he found, is at about thirty-eight months.[5] They stop remembering when they are five to eight years old.

Children are often old Souls in young bodies.

Sri Harold explains the spiritual significance of children's past lives by saying:

> *There is no reason to talk down to children when you realize that they actually are grownups who came back for another experience that they need on this leg of their spiritual journey.*[6]

Children are often old Souls in young bodies.

If the family a child is speaking to doesn't believe in reincarnation or is afraid of it, they miss out on one of the most fascinating experiences of human life—children remembering who, where, and when they've lived before. Sri Harold describes these children recalling past lives as "spiritual transmitters that are . . . broadcasting in a spiritually dead room."[7]

CHECKER PLAYERS FROM THE PAST

An ECKist named Doug recalled an incident that happened with a family he knew. A six-year-old girl said at a family gathering that she wanted a game of checkers for Christmas. This was unusual because no one thought the girl knew how to play checkers.

When they asked who taught her the game, the girl answered, "Nobody did. We always used to play checkers."

Her three-year-old brother chimed in to agree by saying, "We used to play before, when we were big. . . . Before we came to live here. We were old, older than you."

The curious adults soon found a box of checkers and set up the board for the children. They began to play the game very well.

One person asked if the children had lived together. The girl replied, "My brother and I lived in the same house then. We were married."

She also talked about an uncle who died before she was born and said, "I knew him too! I met him before I came here to live with you!" She gave a perfect description of her uncle.

Even though this family's religion didn't allow them to believe in reincarnation, they had to admit, after this incident, that reincarnation was not only possible, but probable.[8]

If you have children between the ages of two and five or are around them, you might try a little experiment. Sri Harold suggests asking the child, "What did you do when you were big?"[9] You may be surprised at how easily the child answers.

So listen.

If you have children between the ages of two and five or are around them, you might try a little experiment. Sri Harold suggests asking the child, "What did you do when you were big?"

Why Do We Forget Our Past?

As Soul, you enter a lifetime and gradually become unconscious of the lives you've lived before. You're the musician absorbed in the music.

If you remembered all your past lives, how could you possibly go on?

You'd meet someone who hurt you in a previous lifetime and accost this stranger for no apparent reason. There'd be even more crime and violence on the streets.

Every single being in your life is there to help you learn lessons of love.

You'd seek out those you had loved before, depriving yourself of new loves and experiences.

Mercifully, a veil is drawn over the past.

It doesn't begin to rise, like the curtain on the next act of the play, until you're ready. And when you are, you'll find that every single being in your life is there to help you learn lessons of love. Many lessons that you didn't learn together in past lifetimes.

The following story shows how Souls reincarnate together to get things right between them the second or maybe even the tenth time around.

The Second Time Around

Our family adopted Prana, a gentle golden retriever named for the life force, the breath of love she brought to us. Mugsy, our cat, was too jealous to accept Prana's love. He died never knowing what a good friend this dog would have been.

A few years after Mugsy's death, I began to dream that Mugsy was ready to reincarnate.

One day I awoke from a nap and told my husband that we had to get to the animal shelter before it closed. I had a hunch that Mugsy was there.

When we arrived, just before closing, we found a little gray kitten that seemed to want to go home with us. We named him Feisty.

Almost immediately upon coming home, the tiny

kitten climbed the stairs to the second floor of our house. Mugsy had loved to sleep upstairs.

We followed Feisty up the steps. To our amazement, the kitten, without looking anywhere else, ran to an old rocking chair that had been Mugsy's favorite. He struggled to reach the seat and snuggled in the same position Mugsy always had.

For a few weeks Feisty showed many more of Mugsy's traits and preferences including disliking Prana. Eventually, though, Feisty's current personality emerged.

Soon the kitten and dog were playing together. Feisty grew to admire Prana so much that he copied her loving ways, including running to greet us when we returned home from work each day. A very uncatlike thing to do!

As Soul, reincarnating in many lifetimes, you are the sum total of all you've learned over the centuries.

The animals kissed, licked, and shared their food. Mugsy had returned to our family. But Feisty found that love was stronger than the instincts of two natural enemies.

Understanding past lives helps us humans figure out how to transcend illusory barriers too. Past-life memories can improve the quality of your life in a number of ways.

WHY REMEMBER PAST LIVES?

Some people want to know about past lives because they think they were a great historical figure.

Most of the time, they weren't.

Some people wonder if they'll come back as a frog or a prince. *Transmigration* is the belief that Souls return as lower life forms. Normally this doesn't happen. Soul progresses up the spiritual ladder.

As Soul, reincarnating in many lifetimes, you are the sum total of all you've learned over the centuries.

Sri Harold explains how Soul evolves:

You are the best and highest spiritual being that you've ever been. If you take a look at yourself and don't like what you see, keep in mind that this is what you've made yourself. It's the sum of all your thoughts, feelings, and actions from before.[10]

In a previous lifetime, you might have wielded more power or been wealthier, but this life is the highest spiritual consciousness you've ever gained. It's the most you've learned about God's love.

Remembering past lives can help you to solve a present problem.

So, why remember past lives if this is the best you've ever been?

Here are a few of the very good reasons to understand the causes having an effect on your present life.

REMEMBERING PAST LIVES HELPS WITH PROBLEM SOLVING

Remembering past lives can help you to solve a present problem. To find a better, more loving way, you can view a similar past-life experience. And say to yourself, "Been there. Done that. Let's handle it better this time."

A movie that makes this point well is *Groundhog Day*. The selfish, egocentric main character has to live the same day over and over. He tries to escape this nightmare by every means possible. Along the way, he discovers much about himself and life. When he learns how to love himself and others, he finds spiritual freedom.

Remembering past lives helps you to realize that you aren't a helpless victim of fate. You can see the thoughts, words, and actions that led to the life you're living today. The Holy Spirit will show how you created your life today. With this knowledge, you can work to create the future you want.

An ECK writer had a dream about a past life. It helped her finish what she had started.

COPYING A PAST LIFE

"I was working on a project that required a lot of preliminary research. Day after day I pored over library books and took notes. I found the research so fascinating that I became totally absorbed in it.

"All that was well and good. My interest level stayed very high. But I wasn't getting anything written except for pages of research notes.

"One night I had a dream in which I saw myself as a monk in a medieval monastery. My job was to copy pages of scriptures onto parchment using elaborate calligraphy.

"I worked diligently but my superiors weren't pleased with my progress. That's because there wasn't any. I'd be so engrossed in what I read, so in love with the written word, that I'd contemplate for hours on a single passage.

"In that lifetime I never even completed one Bible while others around me copied several.

"When I woke up and wrote this dream in my journal, I realized that the Mahanta had shown me an important past life. If I continued to get sidetracked by too much research, I'd never complete the project I was working on.

"Again."

The Holy Spirit will show how you created your life today. With this knowledge, you can work to create the future you want.

Remembering Past Lives Conquers Fear

Remembering past lives can help you overcome your fears. Do you fear water, heights, suffocation? Many of people's phobias are directly related to past lives in which they died or were severely frightened by what they fear today. When you remember, you can face fear and put it behind you.

You may discover that the deeply rooted reason you love or dislike someone goes far beyond this lifetime.

Fear is often the key ingredient in why relationships fail. Through a past-life memory you may be able to see the situation you were in with Souls you're with now. You may discover that the deeply rooted reason you love or dislike someone goes far beyond this lifetime.

As you remember a past life, the emotional and psychological knots can begin to unwind.

If the Mahanta is your spiritual guide, he might pinpoint exactly where a relationship went wrong in a previous life. And show you how to apply love where you once used power and anger. He could take you through the process of healing from past wounds. Even help you forgive yourself for how you hurt others.

An African ECKist had help from the Mahanta to understand a past life that caused her to love someone she was forbidden to love.

The Freedom to Live and Love Again

A black student from Ghana became friends with a young German man. Her friends started to comment on this relationship, wondering if she were romantically involved with this white man.

The young woman felt torn between wanting to please her friends and the enjoyment of friendship with the German.

To help resolve this problem, she did a spiritual exercise. She asked the Mahanta, "Please give me an insight into what's happening. I don't want to lose my friends on this side; I don't want to lose my friend on that side."

In an instant she observed herself as a person in another life. She stood on a beach holding a baby in her arms. A slaving ship docked on the shore. White slavers stood with whips and chains getting ready to ship blacks they had purchased from other blacks away to slavery.

The white slavers loaded the black people on the ship. Her child cried as the woman watched her husband being taken away.

She asked the slave master, "Please let my husband go. We have a child." The slavers showed no mercy to her.

Before the slaves boarded the ship, the woman's husband said, "If we don't get to meet again in this lifetime, surely we will meet in another."

This man, she realized, was the German student she had befriended. Her strong attraction to him was that of a wife whose husband had returned.

As she thought about this past-life memory, she remembered that she'd noticed how the German student walked and talked like an African. Now the Mahanta had brought these two loved ones back together in this lifetime.

The past-life memory helped the girl resist letting her friends' ridicule destroy her friendship with the man. She managed to stay friends with everyone. She knew the value of her friendship with the German man came from far beyond the limitations of one lifetime and one set of circumstances.[11]

Before the slaves boarded the ship, the woman's husband said, "If we don't get to meet again in this lifetime, surely we will meet in another."

DAYS OF SLAVERY

We've probably all been slaves at some point in Soul's journey. If not physically, we've been emotionally or mentally enslaved to our passions and addictions.

John Newton, a slave trader, had great sorrow over what he had done to deprive others of their freedom. In a moment of deep, heartrending insight, he repented. He later became a minister and wrote such stirring hymns as "Amazing Grace."

We've probably all been slaves at some point in Soul's journey.

This hymn, inspired by the Holy Spirit, was John Newton's tribute to life. His story of love conquering power and fear.

Sri Harold and his wife, Joan, adapted the hymn, which is now in public domain, so it could be sung as a spiritual exercise. They added *HU,* the ancient name of God, to express the true source of John Newton's inspiration—the Holy Spirit, the Sound of God. And they set to right some spiritual misperceptions in the original words. Such as the idea that we are "wretches" in the eyes of God. The result is an uplifting hymn sung to the hauntingly beautiful original melody.

Sri Harold and Joan introduced "Amazing HU" during a worship service at the Temple of ECK in Minnesota. Since then ECKists around the world often sing it at their worship services and Eckankar events.

These are the words:

> *Amazing HU, how sweet the Sound,*
> *That touched a Soul like me!*
> *I once was lost, but now am found,*
> *Was blind, but now I see.*

'Twas HU that taught my heart to sing,
   And HU my fears relieved;
How precious did HU then appear
   The hour I first believed!

Through many dangers, toils, and snares,
   I have already come;
'Tis HU has brought me safe thus far,
   And HU will lead me home.

The HU has given life to me,
   Its Sound my hope secures;
My shield and portion HU will be
   As long as life endures.

The earth will someday pass away;
   The sun forbear to shine;
But God, who sent me here below,
   I'll be forever Thine.[12]

A SPIRITUAL EXERCISE TO FIND FREEDOM

An interesting thing began to happen with ECKists who memorized the verses to "Amazing HU." They started to remember past lives when they'd been slaves. And all the fear, anger, and shame that went with that experience. Wonderful emotional and spiritual healings happened for some people.

Sri Harold offers a spiritual exercise technique that could help you recover from past-life wounds that may be affecting your viewpoint of life in the present.

Sri Harold offers a spiritual exercise technique that could help you recover from past-life wounds that may be affecting your viewpoint of life in the present.

Try This Spiritual Exercise Today!

I want to give you a spiritual exercise to help you reach greater spiritual freedom. It's tied to the song "Amazing HU."

To do this exercise, memorize all the verses of "Amazing HU."

Perhaps it will help you have past-life recalls where you were the slave or where you were the slave master. Where you took from life, and where you gave. Where you used power, and where you used love. The life you took, and the life you gave.

You'll find all this inside you.[13]

YOU'VE LIVED BEFORE

In the next chapter you'll read a fascinating story of one Soul's journey over thousands of years. It took her halfway around the world to meet someone who had loved her when no one else did.

You'll also get some practical pointers on how to remember your own past lives.

13. You'll Live Again

The fear of death usually underlies all the other fears that people have. This is what holds them back in their spiritual life. It is the reason many are failures in their material life. Because of something that happened in the past, maybe in another lifetime, the fear of death lies within the subconscious of the individual.

—Harold Klemp, *The Dream Master*[1]

An understanding of reincarnation helps you realize that fear has no place in your life. The love of God eternally keeps you alive as Soul, a spark of the Divine.

Here's Golden Key Number 13.
You'll live again.

Souls reincarnate on earth and in heaven. Souls reincarnating on earth in human form can reincarnate from any of the vast heavens and most any life-form here on earth. This is God's recycling plan.

Eventually we find the Mahanta. He has the power to lead us out of the endless wheel of life and death to total awareness of God.

Soul takes on many different forms as It expands in consciousness. We've lived thousands of lifetimes through a process that, in the long run, gives us greater gifts and blessings.

Eventually we find the Mahanta. He has the power to lead us out of the endless wheel of life and death to total awareness of God.

EACH JOURNEY IS UNIQUE

Each Soul is on an individual journey. No two are alike. We've lived all over this earth and in some areas of the heavens. We've interacted with other Souls, often leaving business that must eventually be finished.

The bonds of love between Souls span centuries because time means nothing to Soul. A thousand years are a blink of an eye for eternal Soul.

Here's the story of Souls whose lives were rejoined in a love that began centuries ago in ancient China.

A JOURNEY OF THREE THOUSAND YEARS

I was very excited about my upcoming trip to Singapore. I'd been invited to an Eckankar regional seminar there. This was my first trip to Southeast Asia, and I looked forward to discovering a culture I knew very little about. This lifetime.

About one month before my trip, I had a dream. This was followed by an interesting inner vision while I did a spiritual exercise.

I recorded the events in my journal.

In the dream I'm a Chinese peasant woman. I'm young and have married into a family in which my mother-in-law despises me. She criticizes me constantly.

In the dream she's ridiculing the food I've cooked for dinner.

I'm very shy. My self-image is low. My husband is afraid to stand up to his mother.

I'm wearing plain gray peasant clothing. This is a hard and miserable life.

MEETING OLD FRIENDS

A petite Oriental woman dressed in traditional costume appeared inwardly to me during my contemplation. She looked to be about fifty or fifty-five years old. Accompanying her was the ECK Master Lai Tsi *(lie TSEE)*.

The woman introduces herself to me as So Jahn. She says her name is pronounced *SOH zhann*. An image of the spelling flashes into my mind. She explains that she can also be called So Jah.

So Jahn tells me that she is a spiritual guardian who has been called back into service in the physical world.

So Jahn tells me that she is a spiritual guardian who has been called back into service in the physical world. She says that Lai Tsi "took her to the Sugmad" when she was one of his initiates in ancient China.

So Jahn has been serving in the inner heavens for thousands of years. But now that it's time to bring the ECK teachings back out openly in the Far East, she says she has been assigned by the Mahanta to assist with this mission. Primarily she serves as a guardian angel to people in the Orient.

So Jahn smiles warmly at me. Love seems to pour from her tiny body. I notice that her feet are bound; she levitates about six inches off the ground. So Jahn's skin is like porcelain. Her features are strong, yet delicate.

I am curious how a woman received spiritual training in ancient China. From my recollection of history

*So Jahn
studied
secretly with
Lai Tsi for
many years.
When he left,
he would
always give
the father and
daughter a
spiritual
exercise to do
until his
return.*

those were pretty oppressive times for women. So I ask her how she could have achieved such spiritual mastery back then.

So Jahn says that her father was very wealthy. She calls him an "enlightened man." He studied the ECK teachings with Lai Tsi.

Lai Tsi would come to her father's home, a mansion set within a large compound. It was like a small city. He owned much farmland. Her father set aside what he called a "spiritual room" for the Master to stay in while visiting.

Because So Jahn loved Lai Tsi and his teachings so much, her father allowed her to receive the Master's instructions. Although So Jahn should have married, as her sisters did, she asked her father to allow her to stay home. To care for him in his old age.

So Jahn studied secretly with Lai Tsi for many years. When he left, he would always give the father and daughter a spiritual exercise to do until his return. In this way, So Jahn grew spiritually.

So Jahn's father loved her so much that he broke tradition and allowed her to remain with him until he died. So Jahn moved in full consciousness into the inner heavens shortly after her father left this physical world.

ARRIVING IN SOUTHEAST ASIA

I've arrived at C.'s house where I'll be staying in Singapore. When she's helping me carry luggage into her apartment, she mentions that I'll be in what she calls her "spiritual room." My mind immediately flashes back to the "spiritual room" for Lai Tsi in So Jahn's father's house.

I tell C. about So Jahn. She says that as I describe

her, she sees a vision of So Jahn. She accurately tells me about So Jahn's features. Then she fills me in on a little more history.

C. says that in ancient China only wealthy women had their feet bound. This was a sign that they didn't have to walk but had servants to do everything for them.

She also tells me that it was quite a sacrifice for So Jahn's father to allow her not to marry. Wealthy daughters married into wealthy families, increasing the father's fortunes. So Jahn was much less valuable to him single than if she had married. Her father must have loved her very much to allow her to do this.

C. thinks it's very interesting that a Westerner would know such details about ancient Chinese life. Especially since I've never been in this part of the world before and haven't studied it except for what the average American might know about ancient China. Which is very little.

I tell a Chinese ECKist about So Jahn. He asks me to spell the name. He says that the reason I saw the name spelled in two parts is that *So* is the surname. A very common one in China.

C. has suggested that I request another visit with So Jahn. I should ask her what province she was from. Then we could find out what her name means.

A Spiritual Reunion

As soon as I ask to see So Jahn, she and Lai Tsi appear inwardly. I ask So Jahn to tell me more about herself. She says she doesn't like to talk about herself so much. But she'll be glad to tell me about her father and Lai Tsi.

C. thinks it's very interesting that a Westerner would know such details about ancient Chinese life.

So Jahn starts to paint a visual picture for me, and the scenes pop vividly into my mind. I'm right there with her as she describes her life in ancient China.

Sometimes, she says, Lai Tsi would travel to their home disguised as a beggar. In this way he could meet people who were ready for a spiritual awakening. He would give them the Darshan *(DAHR-shahn)*. This spiritual blessing of meeting the Master opened their spiritual eyes and sent them searching for God.

So Jahn starts to paint a visual picture for me, and the scenes pop vividly, into my mind.

Other times Lai Tsi would arrive in a carriage driven by a peasant and drawn by four dark horses.

Her father always had beautiful clothes ready for Lai Tsi to wear. First, the Master bathed and freshened up from his trip. Then he changed into these regal-looking garments. She said that some of the servants wondered why her father dressed this "beggar" in fine clothes.

So Jahn shows me an ornament she wears in her hair. On the back of her dress there appears to be something like a bustle. I can't see it clearly.

Before So Jahn and Lai Tsi leave, I remember to ask her what province she had lived in.

She says that she was Cantonese.

As the contemplation nears a close, Lai Tsi pulls me out of my body into a shimmering column of Light. I go so far up into it that I lose conscious awareness.

When I descend from the Light, he tells me that I now have more of the information I need to understand the Oriental mind. This will help me to do a good job of sharing the ECK teachings with people in this part of the world.

LEARNING MORE ABOUT THE PAST

I tell C. that So Jahn is Cantonese. C. says that *Jahn* means Pearl in the Cantonese dialect. She says this type of name is consistent with practices in ancient China. The wealthy fathers named their daughters after precious jewels.

Today we go to visit a re-creation of an ancient Chinese city. Our first stop is to watch a reenactment of a courtroom scene from ancient China. The actress speaks in the same high-pitched melodic tones as So Jahn.

A wax museum is there. We're like two detectives. We carefully search through the museum trying to find models of people who have facial features similar to So Jahn's. We think we can figure out when she lived. I'd forgotten to ask So Jahn what era she was from.

There aren't many figures of women. These are all emperors and such. As I walk toward one scene, I feel my whole body start to vibrate. It is the Chou (Zhou) dynasty starting in 1122 B.C. We quickly find a book that gives more information. The book says this is an era of peace with an emperor who loves the arts and culture. It was a time when ideas could thrive.

As I walk toward one scene, I feel my whole body start to vibrate.

Sounds like this would have been a good era for Lai Tsi to be traveling and sharing the ECK teachings.

In another part of the museum I find some figures of people wearing peasant clothing. This looks similar to what I wore in the past-life dream.

We look for a model of someone with the clothing and hairstyle So Jahn wore. This is more difficult because I sense that I don't have the clothing quite right. Hair pulled back in a bun was the custom for older women of that era though, I discover.

I go into contemplation and ask to meet So Jahn again.

Outside the museum I find a replica of a horse-drawn carriage, similar to the one that carried Lai Tsi to So Jahn's home.

Inner Confirmation

I go into contemplation and ask to meet So Jahn again. Inwardly I see her sit on the bed next to me while Lai Tsi stands nearby.

She confirms that the Chou dynasty is the era in which she lived. Then she shows me her dress again. I also get a better look at her sweet face.

Her chin and nose are longish. Her face has refined features with dark brown almond-shaped eyes. Her cheeks are full. She has a small, rosebud mouth. Although she's older, her face is relatively wrinkle-free.

She wears her thick hair pulled back. Three wooden hair combs with handles at both ends stick out from the bun. Each handle is inlaid with jewels—emerald, diamond, pearl, opal, jade, and ruby.

So Jahn's dress is blue silk with a blue brocade silk tunic over it. The lapels are decorated with a gold pattern over blue.

She shows me the back of her dress again. It isn't a bustle, as I thought. She wears a wide blue sash inlaid with the same type of jewels as her combs. At the back of the sash is a pocket sewn into the fabric. It bulges a little. She explains that because of her family's wealth, the custom was for women to carry their most precious jewels with them in this pouch when they left their houses. This way the servants wouldn't be tempted to steal the jewelry.

As she begins to tell me more about her life, I'm again there in the scene, reliving it with her.

So Jahn says that she cared very little for jewels. But not wishing to dishonor her father, she wore the costume of the day. Inside her pouch she carried little trinkets the visiting Lai Tsi had given to her. These were things to remind her of the ECK teachings and her love of God.

She also liked sweets and kept little cookies or candies in the pouch.

So Jahn enjoyed going outdoors for fresh air. Servants carried her in a simple open litter to the fields of her father's farm. Her bound feet prevented her from walking but the servants brought her to a large old tree where she would sit to do her contemplations.

She enjoyed these excursions so much that her father had pathways made through the fields so she could move from place to place even when the fields were muddy.

A Lifetime in China

Then So Jahn shows me something that brings me to tears. I'm an observer of this scene but suddenly I'm also in the body of someone far off in one of her father's fields. It's the peasant girl from my past-life dream!

So Jahn says that she had recognized me as a Soul with, as she explains, "the Light of God in your eyes."

She says I was very shy. Filled with fear and self-loathing due to the treatment I received in my husband's home. My mother-in-law's open contempt in front of others filled me with shame.

So Jahn shows me that when she arrived where I was working in the field, she'd have her servants stop, and she would call for me to come to her.

I'd run over to So Jahn with my head bowed very

I'm an observer of this scene but suddenly I'm also in the body of someone far off in one of her father's fields. It's the peasant girl from my past-life dream!

humbly. I'd smile at her and even look into her eyes after working up the courage to do so. She'd tell me gently about God.

She was always very careful not to talk to me where others could see. That would have increased their jealousy and made my life even harder. Her servants, also lovers of God, kept the Law of Silence about our private visits.

After a while I finally began confiding my dreams to So Jahn. I had been meeting with the ECK Master Lai Tsi in the dream state. Because I was a peasant I never hoped to meet him physically. So Jahn would help me to understand the spiritual meaning of my dreams with Lai Tsi, who served as the Living ECK Master at that time.

When our visit would draw to an end, So Jahn always gave me a cookie from her pouch. I would save it to eat later in the day when I'd be very hungry.

As this peasant girl, I could feel immense love for So Jahn and her love for me.

I had been meeting with the ECK Master Lai Tsi in the dream state.

SPIRITUAL BLESSING

So Jahn helped me remember how Lai Tsi had once come to her father's house dressed as a beggar. I'd only seen the beautiful carriage that he arrived in on other visits. I didn't recognize the old beggar as Lai Tsi.

Yet one day, Lai Tsi, dressed as a beggar, had stopped in the field where I worked. He looked very tired. I felt great compassion for him.

As hard as it was to do, I reached for the cookie So Jahn had given me. I went over to give it to the old man. I sensed that he needed it more than I did.

When I performed this act of kindness, Lai Tsi looked into my eyes. He gave me the Darshan. It was then that I recognized him as the Master from my dreams.

As So Jahn concludes her story, I sit with tears streaming down my face. She tells me how happy she is to once again see her shy, little peasant girlfriend, serving the Mahanta in his mission of bringing Souls home to God.

So Jahn says that she hadn't told me everything about herself because she wanted me to learn Chinese history. Otherwise, I would have been the typical tourist, just glancing at things and remembering very little. She says she'd enjoyed watching me rediscover details about our past life together.

Lai Tsi has been quiet until now. He motions me to kneel at his feet. I do this.

Then he touches my forehead and says, "I open your heart and mind to receive more of the Light and Sound of God."

Before I leave Singapore I note in my journal that So Jahn is doing her new job well. This is the largest attendance at an Eckankar seminar in Singapore! And it feels as if I've lived in this part of the world all my life. The food, sights, sounds, smells, and customs are all so familiar.

I'm very grateful to Lai Tsi and So Jahn for showing me my spiritual connection with the ECK teachings, spanning over three thousand years. And that my spiritual journey this lifetime includes reconnecting with the Far East.

I'm very grateful to Lai Tsi and So Jahn for showing me my spiritual connection with the ECK teachings, spanning over three thousand years.

HOW CAN *YOU* REMEMBER PAST LIVES?

Not everyone has as vivid or detailed past-life memories as I did in the story above. But it's easy to remember past lives.

You're remembering them all the time. When you meet someone for the first time and instantly feel attracted or repelled, this could be due to an unconscious past-life memory. When you prefer a certain food, music, or clothing, often past-life memories are filtering through your subconscious mind.

It's easy to remember past lives. You're remembering them all the time.

Would you like to try a simple spiritual exercise to help you contact your own hidden treasure trove of past-life memories?

Try This Spiritual Exercise Today!

A study of dreams can help people learn the spiritual reason their life is as it is, and what they can do to improve their lot.

A way to heal oneself begins with a spiritual exercise. At bedtime, sing the word HU [pronounced "hue"]. Softly sing this ancient name for God for five to ten minutes. Also create a mental picture of your problem. See it as a simple cartoon. Beside it, place another image of the condition as you feel it should be.

The second week, if you've had no luck seeing a past life, do this dream exercise for fifteen or twenty minutes. Take a rest the third week. Repeat this cycle until you succeed.

Keep a record of your dreams. Make a short note about every dream you recall upon awakening. Also be alert during the day for clues about

your problem from other people. The Holy Spirit
works through them too.

So be aware and listen.[2]

QUESTIONS AND ANSWERS

Perhaps your questions are similar to those of others who have been introduced to Eckankar's perspective on reincarnation.

*1. Would a belief in reincarnation make suicide seem
more appealing?*

What would be the point of committing suicide? As
Soul, you'll need to return and face the same type of
problem until you find the spiritual gem of love embedded in it.

*2. Do I have to be regressed or hypnotized to remember
a past life?*

Absolutely not. Remembering past lives is a very
natural process. The Mahanta can show you, as in the
story above, through dreams and contemplations exactly what you need to help you understand your life
better today.

SPIRITUAL BEINGS WHO HELP
MAKE OUR LIVES BETTER

The story in this chapter introduced you to the ECK
Master Lai Tsi. He and other ECK Masters work along-
side Sri Harold to help Souls who have earned and need
the blessings of God.

The next chapters will give you some unique perspectives on angels, masters, spiritual guides, and

*The Mahanta
can show you
through
dreams and
contempla-
tions exactly
what you need
to help you
understand
your life better
today.*

miracles. You probably won't find these ideas in the popular best-selling books.

The ECK teachings can show you what secrets angels are *really* trying to share with us.

ANGELS AND MASTERS

"Open thine eyes, O man, and look steadily for love. Then you will learn the secrets as have I; the bright angel of the true Home will stand before you in a glorious robe. He will give you the secrets of love as never before imparted."

Rebazar Tarzs speaking to the seeker
— Paul Twitchell, *Stranger by the River*[1]

14. You're in Training to Become More Than an Angel

If you've taken as much trouble as you need to bear, the spiritual hierarchy sends someone to help you in your hour of need. It will be either man or woman, and you can call this individual a guardian angel.

—Harold Klemp, *Stories to Help You See God in Your Life*[2]

Angels are one form the Holy Spirit uses to communicate with us. They bring blessings and messages to those who have earned them. Angels are also growing spiritually.

Here's Golden Key Number 14.
You're in training to become more than an angel.

You can learn to be a Co-worker with God.

Sri Harold explains a concept not covered in most teachings about angels:

There are thousands of forms a Soul can take.

> *But finally, Soul drops all the outer forms and*
> *becomes the pure Light and Sound of God. That's*
> *the Soul body. It's a far higher form than that*
> *of any human, ghost, or angel.*[3]

Angels
can show us
our own
possibilities.

Although angels are heavenly beings, they're still learning about God. At some point in their spiritual development, angels too meet the Mahanta, who helps them take the next step on their spiritual journey.

WHAT CAN ANGELS DO FOR YOU?

Angels can show us our own possibilities. They aren't doing anything that we can't eventually do for ourselves—and others.

Does that statement surprise you? You've read wondrous stories about magnificent beings of light. But can only spiritual giants perform such miraculous feats?

Spiritual
greatness is
within your
grasp; it is
within your
own heart.

You are Soul, a divine spark of God. Think of yourself as Soul, operating your body.

When the Mahanta becomes your spiritual Wayshower, you're guided by the purest, highest consciousness of God. You have an inner source of godlike wisdom, creativity, strength, and love.

The ultimate goal in Eckankar is not to *see* an angel or being of light, although we certainly are grateful when we do. The true goal is to realize ourselves as spiritual beings and become Co-workers with God. To be able to love as God loves. Spiritual greatness is within your grasp; it is within your own heart.

YOU'RE IN TRAINING TO BECOME MORE THAN AN ANGEL

How do you become more than an angel?

Love is the driving force behind being an angel.

And to receive this love, you must first give it. Each morning sincerely say: *Show me love. Help me to be a vehicle for God's love in the world.*

Devote yourself to spiritual service. The following personal experience is an example of some of the amazing things that can happen when you ask the Mahanta to help you earn your wings by giving love and service to life.

The Mahanta gave me a glimpse of what it means to go on spiritual assignments. One morning I was partially awake when I floated out of my body and began a series of divine tasks. This was not a dream. I had full use of my senses of touch, smell, sight, and hearing.

The Mahanta gave me a glimpse of what it means to go on spiritual assignments.

The experiences began in an inner version of my physical-world office. I was standing looking out a window. Sri Harold walked in and stood behind me. He gently put a hand on my shoulder, and my heart opened to his presence.

Divine love coursed through my being.

For that moment, I became the ECK. There seemed to be nothing left of me, only Light and Sound. I shone and hummed with divine love. If only I could find words to describe the majesty of these sensations!

An Angel with Wings

Instantly I was in the room of a young African-American child. To him I appeared as an angel with wings. He lived in Indianapolis in a very poor neighborhood. While he knelt at his bed saying his prayers, he suddenly saw me. A big grin splashed across his face.

Then he put his head down on the bed because he could no longer get himself to say his memorized prayers.

His oldest sister, who was babysitting him, came in. She saw that he wasn't praying as he was supposed to be.

She raised her hand to strike him. I put out my arm, and she hit it instead of him. She couldn't see what had stopped her, but her little brother could. He grinned with delight. She backed off, shocked. Then she looked at him, and something changed in her.

She realized that he had been praying in his own way and God had protected him from her anger. She backed out of the room. It was as if I could hear her thoughts. She was deciding never to hit him again.

The boy asked, "Are you my guardian angel?"

I smiled and said, "Maybe we'll meet again someday."

A NUN THAT MADE SENSE

I then appeared behind a young woman who was about to commit suicide by running into oncoming traffic. I was in a light body that looked like me and appeared to be physical, but wasn't.

I touched the girl's arm as she contemplated suicide. I said, "I'll cross this street with you."

The resolve seemed to drain out of her. She slumped against me, and I walked her over to a bench. It was on a large grassy area outside a religious school. As we sat there, I reviewed a previous lifetime with her.

In that life she'd been a novice at this school which was a convent then. An older nun had befriended her. The novice never saw the nun except when they sat together on this bench.

The novice had been very depressed during that lifetime because she had lost faith in her religion. She confided in the older nun, who encouraged her to leave

I was in a light body that looked like me and appeared to be physical, but wasn't.

the convent and make a life for herself. Instead, the novice had committed suicide.

Having glimpsed this past life, the young woman now realized that she was at the same crossroads. She could make changes and live. Or succumb to the depression and repeat her suicide.

I encouraged her to think about the past life she'd just seen. Because, after all, she hadn't really died. She was here again faced with the same choice. Would she choose to be grateful for the gift of life this time?

She looked at me and suddenly saw me as the older nun from her past life. She called me her angel.

I smiled and gave her a warm hug. Then I disappeared. I felt as if she'd choose life, but I wasn't attached to her choice. Only filled with love for her.

Throughout these experiences I didn't read people's minds but I knew what was in their hearts. There was no separation between the Life Force in them and me.

I was completely flexible as a vehicle for the Mahanta's love. I noticed that I was in every blade of grass. I was the sunlight. And the sky. Able to change shape, form, or consciousness instantly to meld into the situation. Yet I maintained an individual personality which could serve in whatever way was needed—the ultimate chameleon.

I noticed that I was in every blade of grass. I was the sunlight. And the sky.

AN INVISIBLE GIRLFRIEND

The last episode found me in England of the 1920s.

I was waiting for a young woman.

The woman was a secretary in a company, but she never fit into the group of people who worked there. Someone had invited her to a party with the rest of the young staff. She went because she had a crush on one of the men from her office.

I walked with the woman and said I knew this area. I'd help her find the house where the party was.

When she walked in the door, I became invisible to her and to everyone else.

No one paid attention to this unfortunate girl or seemed happy to see her. In fact they sneered behind her back. They'd invited her only because she'd overheard them planning the party and the rest of the office staff was coming.

She stood in a corner and watched the man she loved. He had his back turned to her. Finally, she got up enough courage to talk to him. He answered her politely but then made a joke about her when she moved away. The group of people around him laughed at her. She felt totally humiliated.

All this time, she didn't see me. But I was aware of her thoughts. It was as if I knew what she intended to do before she did.

I wanted to show her what could really happen if she carried out her plan. In Soul body we viewed the consequences.

She thought of a plan to get the young man's attention. There was a river behind this house. She'd jump into it, pretending to have fallen. The current would start to sweep her away, and she'd cry out. Enough people were outside to rescue her. When they carried her into the house, the man would realize his love for her now that she'd almost died.

It was a naive schoolgirl fantasy. The next thing that happened, she thought was mostly a daydream. I wanted to show her what could *really* happen if she carried out her plan. In Soul body we viewed the consequences.

People would go into the house as soon as she came outside. When she "fell" into the river, instead of being rescued, she'd drown.

Then we watched another scenario. She'd meet a man who really loved her and marry him. They'd have children. She'd forget about these people and live a happy life.

Back in her body, she decided not to bother with this man or these shallow people. She left the house and went home.

Living Life as a Spiritual Assignment

Now, here's the most startling thing about all these experiences. They happened simultaneously. My mind attempted to comprehend them in sequence. But actually I was in all of these places at once!

As Soul I would place my attention on something within the experience. Soul moved instantly from scene to scene.

I was conscious during this entire experience. When I reentered my physical body, it was as if I were putting on a robe.

In my daily life the Holy Spirit, the ECK, shows me things I need to know to help people. I try to quietly fill their needs without their ever knowing I did anything.

I thank the Mahanta for these incredible experiences. They're teaching me things about serving God I'd never imagined. They keep me going when things get rough and I fall into old selfish habits and responses. They inspire me.

Angels in Our Midst

Have you ever thought about dedicating yourself as a spiritual light in a world of darkness?

Have you ever thought about dedicating yourself as a spiritual light in a world of darkness?

If you do, you too may be given spiritual assignments. These will come in the form of guidance that
places you in exactly the right place at the right time
to give service to life.

An ECKist named Walt who is a U.S. Coast Guard
officer took a step toward earning his spiritual wings
by serving on the battleground of life.

ANGELS ON THE BATTLEFIELD

Walt and his wife were eating dinner together one
night. On the other side of the world Iraq had defied
the United States' demand that it withdraw from
Kuwait.

Walt found himself feeling as if he were in the midst
of a battlefield. He seemed to be surrounded by explod-
ing bombs.

Walt went on spiritual alert. As Soul, he went beyond his physical body (in Eckankar this is called Soul
Travel). He traveled to a situation happening in a distant
part of the world. From the calm viewpoint of Soul, he
viewed a horrifying battle scene.

When Walt returned to his physical body, he looked
at his wife. She didn't know that her husband had been
anywhere but at the kitchen table. So she must have
been a little startled at his announcement.

Walt told her that the war in the Persian Gulf was
now in progress. A few hours later, the couple watched
televised news reports. An announcer confirmed
Walt's statement.

Walt immediately enlisted in what he called his
"spiritual tour of duty." He had not been called physically to serve. But for the next few months scenes of
the war filled his thoughts, dreams, and prayers. Often

You too may be given spiritual assignments. These will come in the form of guidance that places you in exactly the right place at the right time to give service to life.

Walt immediately enlisted in what he called his "spiritual tour of duty."

what he saw inwardly was later verified through news reports.

Walt noticed that Souls from many faiths had been called into spiritual service. With love and compassion, they helped others cross through the veil between this life and the afterlife. Working invisibly, these angels of mercy brought comfort to soldiers. And to their families waiting for them at home.

With the guidance of the Mahanta, Walt completed his spiritual tour of duty. He was grateful for the experiences that showed him a new way to give love to life.[4]

CONSCIOUS SERVICE TO LIFE

Were the Souls from other faiths aware of their spiritual assignments too? Many of them probably had dreams, daydreams, or visions that flashed into their minds. If they inwardly saw themselves walking through war-torn areas, they may have thought they were imagining these experiences.

Walt served as a *conscious* co-worker with the Holy Spirit. His religion taught him how to accept the reality of his inner experiences. With awareness he worked more effectively.

Instead of being a soldier who mechanically followed orders, Walt was a well-trained spiritual officer. He could fully experience and appreciate his spiritual assignment.

WOULD YOU LIKE TO CONTACT A GUARDIAN ANGEL?

Some people are paying others to contact an angel for them.

This is unnecessary.

Walt served as a conscious co-worker with the Holy Spirit. His religion taught him how to accept the reality of his inner experiences. With awareness he worked more effectively.

Your connection with God is not mysterious. God constantly communicates with you via the ECK, the Holy Spirit. The ECK is the voice of God. Often the ECK is seen as Light. Or is heard as Sound. The ECK appears in visions and dreams — and in encounters with guardian angels.

These profound spiritual experiences happen naturally. When you've earned them. When you need them. You only have to fill your heart with love and sing HU, the love song to God.

As you sing HU, pose this request to God: If it is for my spiritual good, I'd like to see an angel or spiritual guide who is working with me now.

Try This Spiritual Exercise Today!

To contact a guardian angel, go to a quiet place. For about five minutes sing HU (pronounced like the word *hue*) with love in your heart. HU is the sacred Sound of God that flows through all life.

As you sing HU, pose this request to God: If it is for my spiritual good, I'd like to see an angel or spiritual guide who is working with me now. Then release your request to the ECK, the Holy Spirit.

Gaze into the spot between your eyebrows. This inner screen may fill with images that show the answer to your prayer. Contemplate silently for five to ten more minutes.

Be open to insights and experiences. You may or may not see an angel with wings. It could be a spiritual being who looks like a person but shimmers with light. You might meet a deceased relative who lets you know that you're always loved and protected. Or you may see nothing.

Later you may find that you're beginning to make better decisions and see positive changes in your life. After you do this spiritual exercise, or sometime in the future, you may be helped in a dream by a spiritual being or an inner guide.

During the day, become an angel. As often as you can, perform an act of kindness without expecting a return. This will keep your heart open to receive more of God's blessings.

QUESTIONS AND ANSWERS

People often come to workshops to hear the Eckankar perspective on angels and spiritual guides. Here are a couple of questions they ask about this topic.

1. *How do you know that an angel or spiritual guide is from God?*

Many people fear the spiritual world. Their scriptures and spiritual leaders tell them that evil angels and entities lure the unsuspecting off the path to God.

It's true that there are both positive and negative sides of life. But you're always in charge of and responsible for your own thoughts, words, and actions.

No negative entity can separate you from God. You might be persuaded by the lure of power to experiment with the negative forces of life. You have the free will to accept or reject God's protection.

When people use psychic means to contact the supernatural, they unknowingly invite a psychic energy into their lives. These psychic forces are very unstable. They shift without warning from positive to negative.

One way to tell if a spiritual visitor is from God is to apply this test.

A Test You Can Use

One way to tell if a spiritual visitor is from God is to apply this test. Do you feel unconditional love coming from the spiritual being?

Fill yourself with love and sing HU, the holy name of God. You can also sing the word *God* or the name of a spiritual master or holy figure you trust. This opens your heart to the purely positive spiritual force, the ECK. Singing HU connects you directly to the loving, protective presence of God.

No negative power is stronger than the love of God. As you grow spiritually, you become more self-reliant. You know that you have the inner resources to face anything life brings to you.

The next time you hear children talking about their invisible friends, try this approach. Ask, "What did your friend tell you?" Then listen.

2. *Do children have more experiences with angels?*

A baby is the physical body for a Soul that has recently arrived from heaven. Soul remembers Its spiritual friends and helpers.

The next time you hear children talking about their invisible friends, try this approach. Ask, "What did your friend tell you?"

Then listen and appreciate nuggets of spiritual wisdom. Many youngsters haven't learned to discount their experiences with spiritual beings.

COULD YOUR GUARDIAN ANGEL BE AN ECK MASTER?

You're going to meet spiritual masters of the Light and Sound of God. They teach others about the Holy Spirit in the physical and heavenly worlds. They serve as vehicles for God's love.

You'll soon discover the important role they play in our lives today.

15. ANCIENT SPIRITUAL MASTERS ARE WITH YOU TODAY

*ECK Masters . . . are the guardian angels we
sometimes hear about today. It's a popular
theme. ECK Masters are guardian angels. But
not all guardian angels are ECK Masters.
There's a difference.*
—Harold Klemp, *The Secret of Love*[1]

People who've had near-death experiences (NDEs)
report seeing a bright light form into a *being
of light* whose presence makes the person feel
deeply and totally loved.

Beings of light, guardian angels, heavenly religious
figures, and helpful strangers who suddenly appear all
have something in common.

Here's Golden Key Number 15.
Ancient spiritual masters are with you today.

Sri Harold, who as the Mahanta often appears as
a being of light, said this about angelic visitations:

Whether it appears as a guardian angel, Christ, the Inner Master, or anything else . . . the Holy Spirit takes on a form that fits your state of consciousness, so that It can make Itself known to you in the form of someone you feel comfortable with and have learned to trust.[2]

Some of the guardian angels people see are ECK Masters.

MEET THE ECK MASTERS

A sacred band of highly advanced God-conscious beings guide, protect, and love all Souls. In Eckankar, these spiritual miracle-workers are recognized as the ECK Masters — Co-workers with God.

ECK Masters coach us here on earth and in the heavenly worlds. You don't have to be troubled or near death to meet ECK Masters. You can work and study with them anytime to learn their special skills and wisdom.

ECK Masters have become one with the ECK, the Holy Spirit. They live in the full consciousness of God. They are never unaware. ECK Masters have presented the teachings of the Light and Sound of God since and before the beginning of life on this planet.

AN ANCIENT ORDER OF ECK MASTERS

ECK Masters belong to the Ancient Order of the Vairagi, also known as Vairagi (*vie-RAH-gee*) Adepts. *Vairag* is a Sanskrit word meaning "detachment." The Vairagi Masters have spiritual freedom from the illusions of this world.

Many of these ECK Masters served as the Living ECK Master of their times. They were responsible for protecting and evolving the ECK teachings of the Holy

A sacred band of highly advanced God-conscious beings guide, protect, and love all Souls.

Spirit. Now they serve in the spiritual hierarchy under the direction of the current Living ECK Master.

When a Soul masters the teachings of the Light and Sound of God and receives the Ninth Initiation in ECK, he or she is eligible to join the Order of the Vairagi. (More about initiations in chapter 21.)

Sri Harold writes about the order of ECK Masters:

The Vairagi Adepts [are] people whose only mission is to help others. The ECK Masters work not only on earth but in other worlds to help people find out about the Light and Sound of God. Their only mission, their only purpose is to help people make their own way home to God.[3]

ECK Masters specialize in music, art, health, carpentry, computers—almost any interest you want to pursue. All life offers lessons about your relationship with God.

What Do ECK Masters Do for Us?

ECK Masters love and serve all life by using their skills and talents. For example the ECK Master Prajapati *(prah-jah-PAH-tee)* has the special mission of helping Souls in the animal kingdom.

ECK Masters specialize in music, art, health, carpentry, computers—almost any interest you want to pursue. All life offers lessons about your relationship with God.

The following story shows how you might meet one of the ECK Masters who aren't written about in the Eckankar literature, but who quietly serve life.

On the way home from an Eckankar seminar quite a few years ago, I was deep in thought about my business. I hardly noticed when a slim, blond-haired man sat next to me on the plane. We soon struck up a conversation.

My companion turned out to be a business consultant. The man told me that his area of expertise was negotiations. He said that he'd observed many differences in the way men and women in business communicate.

For the entire flight, I quizzed him. He had amazing insights. This topic, many years later, would be the subject of best-selling books about male and female communication styles. Toward the end of our conversation, I realized that I hadn't even asked the man's name. When he told it to me, I found it to be unusual but oddly familiar. He spelled it for me twice.

Everything the man told me was so useful. What a miraculous gift Divine Spirit had given to me when I needed help with my business.

Everything the man told me was so useful, I went back to work and told my partner all about it. I couldn't seem to get this man and his insightfulness out of my mind.

One day I did a spiritual exercise. With the Mahanta's help I connected the dots to realize what a miraculous gift Divine Spirit had given to me when I needed help with my business.

After two years of membership in Eckankar you can request the Second Initiation. During this initiation you receive a special personal word or mantra that fine-tunes your vibration to receive more of the Light and Sound, the love of God. My children had recently gotten their Second Initiations and new spiritual word.

As I began to contemplate, an image of the helpful businessman I met on the plane popped into my mind. Then the Mahanta seemed to say to me, "What was his name, again?"

I remembered that the man spelled his name for me. It was only then I realized that his name and my children's initiation word were the same!

Inwardly the Mahanta's soft voice explained that my "business consultant" had been sent to help me. The advanced and unique insights he offered were the result of his God-Conscious state. I'd been visited by an ECK Master.

Before this, I thought of ECK Masters as lofty, inaccessible beings who floated in the ethers somewhere. I hadn't realized that they truly are Masters of the Life Force. They have fully realized spiritual, physical, personal, social, even business awareness. And they use their special talents to help people.

This ECK Master, I was told, is an expert in the business field. I realized then that the Life Force uses every aspect of daily life to give us lessons of love. Business can be as much an avenue for spiritual awareness as anything else. Maybe more.

They truly are Masters of the Life Force. They have fully realized spiritual, physical, personal, social, even business awareness. And they use their special talents to help people.

WHAT ARE ECK MASTERS LIKE?

Each ECK Master has a unique personality and teaching style. Some are very direct. Others guide gently by providing nudges and clues to help people find their own answers to problems.

ECK Masters teach spiritual lessons in subtle, dramatic, and even humorous ways. They may catch our attention by doing the unexpected, such as pretending to smoke a cigar. Or appearing disguised as a beggar.

ECK Masters work with us every day. Vairagi Adepts, while on earth, may have been leaders or revered teachers of religious groups. Others served quietly in their communities and villages with neighbors, family, or friends never realizing that these mild-mannered Clark Kents were really Supermen and Superwomen.

ECK Masters are pure Light and Sound working in a physical form which can be either male or female.

FEMALE ECK MASTERS

Throughout history and even into modern times, people report meeting female spiritual beings. They may be identified as angels, the Virgin Mary, or some other holy figure.

Descriptions of these ECK Masters sound similar to modern-day visions of the Virgin Mary.

Two female ECK Masters mentioned in the Eckankar literature are Kata Daki *(KAH-tah DAH-kee)* and Simha *(SEEM-hah)*. You may be fascinated to find that descriptions of these ECK Masters sound similar to modern-day reported visions of the Virgin Mary.

CAN A WOMAN BE THE LIVING ECK MASTER?

Soul has no limits on the experiences It can explore. It also has no gender. Although ECK Masters are male and female, the Mahanta, the Living ECK Master chooses a male body in the lifetime he will become a candidate for this position.

A Soul won't be the Living ECK Master in the lifetimes It chooses a female body. But then neither will most of the males. There's only one at a time.

The Living ECK Master has spent many lifetimes as male and female. Soul needs the whole gamut of life experiences to even be considered for this position.

ECK MASTERS ARE RACIALLY AND ETHNICALLY DIVERSE

ECK Masters come in all shapes, sizes, and skin shades and from all ethnic backgrounds.

ECK Masters come in all shapes, sizes, and skin shades and from all ethnic backgrounds. The Holy Spirit is definitely an equal-opportunity employer.

Meet, for example, Towart Managi *(TOW-wahrt mah-NAH-gee)*. He was an African ECK Master who taught in Ethiopia when it was known as Abyssinia. Towart Managi, and other ECK Masters, made the teachings of the Light and Sound of God part of the African spiritual heritage.

ECK MASTERS AMONG US TODAY

Artists have drawn their visions of some Vairagi Adepts who were the Mahanta, the Living ECK Master of their times. And of course we have photos of modern-day ECK Masters Paul Twitchell and Harold Klemp. (See the photo section in the middle of this book.)

These Vairagi Masters may appear as guardian angels to people today.

Following are brief histories of Vairagi Masters who may appear as guardian angels to people today. These spiritual Adepts are sent on assignments by the Living ECK Master. In the heavenly worlds, most of them are guardians of Golden Wisdom Temples.

Gopal Das *(GOH-pahl DAHS)*. Gopal Das lived in Egypt about 3000 B.C. He founded the mystery schools of Osiris and Isis. He was later responsible for the writing of *The Egyptian Book of Dreams*.

Yaubl Sacabi *(YEEOW-buhl sah-KAH-bee)*. Yaubl Sacabi served among the Mycenaeans. He was a leading figure among the ancient Greek mystery schools.

Fubbi Quantz *(FOO-bee KWONTS)*. Fubbi Quantz served in India as the Mahanta, the Living ECK Master during the time of Buddha, about 500 B.C. He is the guardian of the Shariyat-Ki-Sugmad, the holy scriptures of ECK, at the Katsupari *(kaht-soo-PAH-ree)* Monastery in northern Tibet.

Lai Tsi *(lie TSEE)*. Lai Tsi served in ancient China. The son of a wealthy family, his father was physician to the court of the ancient kingdom.

Lai Tsi taught a contemplation seed which he created upon his return from the heavenly worlds.

ECKists today reflect on this inspiring poem in hymns and contemplation.

Lai Tsi's Prayer
Show me Thy ways, O Sugmad;
Teach me Thy path.
Lead me in Thy truth, and teach me;
On Thee do I wait all day.
Remember, O Beloved, Thy guiding light
And Thy loving care.
For it has been ever Thy will,
To lead the least of Thy servants to Thee![4]

Rebazar Tarzs appeared to Paul Twitchell to begin his education in the ECK teachings and to help him found Eckankar in the modern world.

Rebazar Tarzs *(REE-bah-zahr TAHRZ)*. Rebazar Tarzs was born in 1461 in the mountain village of Sarana in northern Tibet. He taught ECK in the physical world for seventy-five years. He now continues to serve life as a Co-worker with God in an immortalized body.

Rebazar Tarzs appeared to Paul Twitchell to begin his education in the ECK teachings and to help him found Eckankar in the modern world.

Rebazar Tarzs is responsible for passing the Rod of ECK Power from each Living ECK Master to his successor.

Peddar Zaskq *(PEH-dar ZASK)*. Peddar Zaskq is the spiritual name of Paul Twitchell, the modern-day founder of Eckankar.

With untiring love and devotion Paul brought the ancient teachings of Eckankar to the modern world in a way that they would fit into anyone's lifestyle. (More about Paul Twitchell in chapters 31 and 32.)

Harold Klemp. As mentioned in chapter 3, Sri Harold has been the Mahanta, the Living ECK Master and spiritual leader of Eckankar since 1981. He keeps the teachings of ECK pure. As Inner and Outer Master he links Souls directly to the Light and Sound of God.

Encounter with an ECK Master

Many people today report how they've been helped by ECK Masters. Here's a timely dramatic story from an ECKist who received ECK blessings from Rebazar Tarzs.

"Many years ago my husband and I traveled to a large city to meet with a longtime member of Eckankar. We had become very interested in Eckankar after my husband had found an ECK book in our local library.

"Now we wanted to talk to someone who had experience with it.

"When we arrived, we were met with much love and warmth. We were shown to the ECKist's living room. On the wall was a large painting of a man with black hair and short beard wearing a maroon robe. He was standing with one foot in a small boat and the other foot on the rocky shore. His hand reached out, as welcoming as his wonderful smile."

Many people today report how they've been helped by ECK Masters.

The woman recognized him at once. She had known him during her childhood and searched for him ever since. Now, twenty-five years later, here was a painting of him.

Old memories she had long forgotten started coming back. Her heart was pounding with excitement.

As soon as they were back in the car, she asked her husband who the dark-haired man in the painting was.

"He's Rebazar Tarzs, one of the ECK Masters. Why?"

"That man saved my family's lives during the Korean War," she replied, as the memories came flooding back.

It was so exciting, as if it had happened only a few days ago.

The war had been going on for months. The family was trying to get away from the North Korean soldiers and stay away from the combat zones. She and her brothers and sisters were constantly hungry. Sometimes the family walked for days and days without food, hoping to find a safe place to rest.

"All the rules of our society had changed, and we just didn't know how to survive in this new arena of war."

"At last we made our way into the south," the woman recalled, "away from the fighting. There were so many people and no food or water. My parents soon found their money was worthless. Those who had extra food wanted clothes or blankets in exchange.

"During the bombing of our home, we had had only enough time to dress and take our soon-to-be-useless money with us. A blanket or coat would have been worth much more.

"We were all alive and together, but slowly starving and unbelievably tired. All the rules of our society had changed, and we just didn't know how to survive in this new arena of war. Our hunger forced my parents to go out on longer and longer searches for food and water or things that could be traded for food. One day I felt I needed to go with my mother on her daily search. She told me to hold on to her skirt and not to let go, no matter what happened."

Everywhere they went, there were people and children crying. The girl grew tired, but her mother told her that if she fell the people would take her away. She didn't know how far they walked, but that fear kept her going.

By the end of the day, she was so weary she stumbled and almost fell. When she looked up, she saw two big boots in front of her. Then she gazed into the eyes of a big dark man in a strange uniform.

"For a moment fear clutched me. But the love from his eyes was so beautiful and peaceful," the woman said.

"A smile spread across his broad face. My weakness disappeared. As we stood in war-torn Korea, he said, 'You will be all right.' It was in a strange language, yet I understood each word. Who was this man? My mother, unmoving and silent, stared in awe. The man took off his jacket and handed it to me. 'Trade this for the food you need,' he said. I nodded my understanding, took my mother's hand, and headed back to our family.

"As we walked away, I turned to look once more at his love-filled eyes. But he was gone! He was too tall to disappear so quickly among the people around us. Yet he was nowhere to be seen. I remember having such a deep sense of loss—for someone I didn't even know.

"Since my childhood, I had often wondered about that wonderful man. Now after finding Eckankar I can visit with him again from time to time.

"I know that Divine Spirit and the ECK Masters have been protecting and guiding me for a long time. They have been there for me not only in times of suffering but also in times of joy."[5]

HISTORICAL FIGURES WHO WERE ECK MASTERS

ECK Master Pythagoras *(pi-THAG-ehr-uhs),* the sixth-century mathematician and philosopher, founded a Greek mystery school. There he taught out-of-body travel, initiation rites, and reincarnation.

Milarepa *(mi-lah-REH-pah)* is identified in the ECK writings as an ECK Master. According to Lobsang P. Lhalungpa who translated a biography of the eleventh-

"The man took off his jacket and handed it to me. 'Trade this for the food you need,' he said."

century Tibetan saint and poet, Milarepa was "the true embodiment of the highest that man can aspire to and attain" and "the master of sound." Lhalungpa writes that Buddhist master Milarepa received "secret oral teachings of the Compassionate Masters" and "unequaled spiritual blessings."[6]

Shamus-i-Tabriz *(SHAH-muhs-ee-tah-BREEZ)* served as the Mahanta, the Living ECK Master over seven hundred years ago. This Sufi holy man befriended and taught Jalal ad-Din ar-Rumi *(jah-LAHL ahd-deen ar-ROO-mee),* a thirteenth-century Persian and magnificent Sufi poet.

Although not an ECK Master, Kabir *(kah-BEER)* was a Hindu mystic poet and follower of ECK who lived in the fifteenth and sixteenth centuries. He taught Soul Travel (how to move out of the body). His followers, both Muslims and Hindus, harassed him about openly teaching what had been secret.

Would you like to meet an ECK Master?

If you're interested in learning more about ECK Masters, look in the index of any book by Sri Harold in the Mahanta Transcripts series. Look under "ECK Masters" or the name of a particular ECK Master. Two other sources of information are ECKists' adventures with these highly evolved spiritual beings. They are the books *In the Company of ECK Masters* by Phil Morimitsu and *We Are Not Alone* by Robert Marsh.

WOULD YOU LIKE TO MEET AN ECK MASTER?

The following spiritual exercise can help your heart open to the possibility of meeting one of the ECK Masters you've read about in this chapter.

The Vairagi Adepts use a spiritual blessing which reflects their unconditional love for all life. When

Sri Harold finishes his public talks, he raises his right hand to give the ancient blessing of the Vairagi ECK Masters: May the blessings be, or Baraka Bashad *(bah-RAH-kah bah-SHAHD)*.

This blessing doesn't direct the will of God. It reminds us that when we include others in our prayers or bless them, we must be detached from the outcome. We release the situation to God's infinite wisdom and ask for help to understand the workings of the Holy Spirit.

As you go through your day, silently say with love in your heart to each person or animal you meet, "May the blessings be."

Try This Spiritual Exercise Today!

As you go through your day, silently say with love in your heart to each person or animal you meet, "May the blessings be."

Then closely observe life around you. Is it changing in any way? Are your attitudes readjusting? Are small miracles happening?

At bedtime imagine that you're visiting with the Vairagi Adepts. Quietly chant their ancient blessing as you slip off to sleep.

You can recognize an ECK Master in dreams, visions, prayers, or even in waking life by the total unconditional love you feel in his or her presence.

MORE SECRETS IN HEAVEN AND ON EARTH

The next section will show you the secrets of heaven and of earth. You'll learn how your inner and outer lives connect.

ECK Masters live multidimensionally.

So do you. You just may not be aware of it.

HEAVEN AND EARTH

The ECK teachings give you enough spiritual geography to explain where you have been and why. This allows you to put your mind to rest. The reason people without the ECK background are often upset by their inner experiences is because they have no way to fit them into anything society considers normal. They cannot relate them to what we in ECK know is spiritually normal.

—Harold Klemp, *The Dream Master*[1]

16. You Live in Parallel Dimensions

Heaven is not a place as much as it is your state of consciousness.

—Harold Klemp, *The Dream Master*[2]

A woman we'll call Cindy faced a life-threatening medical condition. After Cindy fell asleep in her hospital bed, the Mahanta, her spiritual guide, took her into another dimension to view what was really happening.

Cindy found herself in a Roman coliseum where gladiators fought each other. The sound of clashing blades and the sight of dust and blood convinced her that she was facing a battle for her life.

One night while she was still in the hospital, Cindy moved into a higher state of consciousness. The Mahanta took her to a meeting with several ECK Masters.

One of the ECK Masters said to Cindy, "Your body's very sick. And we're looking at what your spiritual duties can be in the other worlds."

He asked, "What is your goal in life?"

Cindy answered, "To serve God."

The ECK Master said, "You're ready to drop this body. You can go on into the other planes."

Cindy thought about her life on earth. Her daughter was in her early twenties and would grieve over losing her mother. So Cindy said, "I would like to go back."

The ECK Master told Cindy that she had earned the right of choice. She'd grown spiritually and was becoming a Co-worker with the Mahanta and at some point would become a Co-worker with God. Cindy had earned the right to choose where she wanted to serve God.[3]

When she faced death, Cindy had a firsthand experience with the benefits of expanded awareness. She knew that her experiences were real.

Unlike most people who have near-death experiences, this ECKist knew where she was, who she was with, and that she had the freedom to make this important choice. She even knew the consequences. She'd only be dropping the physical body. As Soul she'd live on in the heavens to learn, serve, and love some more.

What a gift this awareness is!

Do universes exist, parallel but separate from our own? The answer is yes.

ETERNAL QUESTIONS

Are there other dimensions?

Do universes exist, parallel but separate from our own?

The answer is yes. Not only are there invisible beings—spiritual masters, guides, and angels. There are invisible worlds.

We operate on many levels all the time.

Here's Golden Key Number 16.

You live in parallel dimensions.

Soul, the eternal spark of God, experiences life on many levels of consciousness. When the body dies, Soul lives on in higher states of awareness that we call the heavens.

WHERE DO WE GO AFTER DEATH?

Soul continues to live after the physical body dies (or *translates,* as dying is called in Eckankar). Soul makes Its home in the level of heaven It has earned. At some point, It may reincarnate back on earth. During dreams or in visions some people see Souls who have translated.

Sri Harold explains these visions like this:

At the base level the physical body dies. People then take up existence on the Astral Plane [the first level of heaven]. It's pretty much the same as here on earth, except they may take on a younger appearance. . . .

This explains why you see your loved ones or even pets in your dreams after they have passed on.[4]

THE LEVELS OF HEAVEN

The worlds of inner reality are usually invisible to the human senses. They can only be perceived by expanding your consciousness. Often this means seeing beyond most people's concept of the afterlife.

In the New Testament Paul said that he knew a man, whether in the body or out of the body, he did not know, who was caught up to the third heaven (2 Corinthians 12:2).

When the body dies, Soul lives on in higher states of awareness that we call the heavens.

Buddha spoke of three worlds.

Paul Twitchell's accounts in his books published by Eckankar and more information by the spiritual leader of Eckankar, Sri Harold Klemp, reveal that there are many levels of heaven. In Eckankar we also refer to them as planes of existence.

Although we tend to look upward when we think of heaven, heaven is not in the sky.

Although we tend to look upward when we think of heaven, heaven is not in the sky. All the universes of creation exist simultaneously at different vibratory levels. As a radio tunes in to higher and lower frequencies, we can expand our consciousness to tune in to other realities.

LOWER AND HIGHER WORLDS

For simplicity, these planes can be divided into the lower and higher worlds. The lower worlds are of matter, energy, space, and time. Thus the mind can define experiences as happening in the past, present, or future.

The higher worlds are composed of pure positive Light and Sound.

YOUR SPIRITUAL BODIES

To live in the different levels of heaven, you must have a body that vibrates at the same rate as that level of heaven. Otherwise, you wouldn't be able to interact with others and have experiences there.

People who've been out of their physical bodies during near-death experiences often mention having a spiritual body. These spiritual bodies can go through doors, move rapidly, and seem to be timeless. As Soul you operate bodies like these all the time.

Now that you know there are other planes of existence, how can you visit them consciously? You can sing sacred words, other names for God, to gain conscious access to the planes of heaven.

THE PLANES HAVE IDENTIFYING COLORS AND SOUNDS

Your experiences on other planes may begin by seeing the Light of God. It can appear as almost any color, green, red, orange, blue, violet, and lighter shades of yellow, even pure white. This spiritual Light emanates from God.

Each plane also vibrates with the Sound of God. The sounds are often similar to those in nature or music, and each level of heaven is associated with certain sounds.

Now let's learn more about the levels of heaven. You don't have to die to experience them. Heaven is here and now.

When you visit heaven consciously, you may be able to see departed loved ones. You might view future possibilities.

When you visit heaven consciously, you may be able to see departed loved ones. You might view future possibilities.

The following brief descriptions offer a few highlights of these planes of existence. As the Mahanta guides you to explore these planes more thoroughly, their rich vastness will continually amaze you.

THE PHYSICAL PLANE

We live on the Physical Plane to learn in God's classroom. But did you know that there's much more to the Physical Plane than planet Earth? Exploring the Physical Plane includes visiting other levels of the physical universes.

If the Mahanta guides you inwardly to see these vast worlds firsthand, they may be some of the most exciting spiritual adventures you'll ever have!

Between the Astral and Physical Planes

Sri Harold has described the sub-Astral, or supra-Physical, area. Beings there are at a higher level of vibration than the physical world and can walk through doors and solid objects.[5] This can be a purgatory. A midpoint between heaven and earth.

Dr. Ian Stevenson, past-life researcher at the University of Virginia, says that some subjects he's studied remember events that happened between their earthly lives. After dying they hovered near where they had lived. Some even attended their own funerals. In their next incarnation, they showed people where the person they had been was buried.[6]

You can visit vast astral libraries to research ancient or advanced material about most any subject.

Those who haven't yet made the transition to the Astral Plane often appear to loved ones to comfort them before completing their journey to the other side.

Then most Souls enter the first level of heaven.

Life on the Astral Plane

The Astral Plane is probably the one you're most familiar with through dreams, especially lucid dreams. It is the first level of heaven. People here eat, drink, talk with each other, attend schools, and live much as they did on the Physical Plane, only on a grander scale.

On the Astral Plane you'll find many great museums. These include a museum that contains the prototype of every invention that will ever be discovered on the Physical Plane. Inventors go to this Astral Plane museum, as Edison did, and draw on it. Sometimes they remember, sometimes not. You can also visit vast astral libraries to research ancient or advanced material about most any subject.

People sometimes use psychic or occult practices to

visit the Astral Plane, the home of psychic phenomena. Psychic energy is an unstable force which can seem very good but quickly turn evil. Psychic or astral projection can easily create an imbalance.

It's important to ask the Mahanta to show you the natural, safe method—Soul Travel—to visit the heavens. (More about Soul Travel in chapter 20.)

As vast and beautiful as the Astral Plane is, the next level of heaven holds even greater fascination.

LIFE ON THE CAUSAL PLANE

The Mahanta can show you how to view your Akashic (ah-KAH-sheek) records stored in the Hall of Records on the Causal Plane, the second level of heaven. This can help you understand how past lives are affecting your life today.

You might see past-life events more fully with all the nuances you didn't observe when you lived before. You may even hear the thoughts and reactions of others who were part of the experience. You can begin to understand what role you played in creating the situations you're in and, more importantly, how to keep from creating unpleasant ones.

From the Causal Plane you enter the third level of heaven.

LIFE ON THE MENTAL PLANE

The Mental Plane is the third level of heaven that Paul referred to in Corinthians. It's home to most religions, although many followers of these religions don't reach the Mental Plane for lifetimes. They may go to the Astral Plane and find a shadow of the true teachings of their religion. Yet they may think they're in the highest heaven.

The Mental Plane is the third level of heaven that Paul referred to in Corinthians.

On the Mental Plane is the Universal Mind Power. This mind energy forms illusion by creating thought molds.

The mind, operating from the Mental Plane, believes that what it experiences is real. Eventually Soul gains enough experience to be able to see through the illusion of the mind and the Mental Plane.

On the Mental Plane the Light of God is often perceived as a blue color.

When you slip into a passion of the mind, life is sending you the message that love has been lost.

THE PASSIONS OF THE MIND

At first glance you might think that the mind would be a wonderful tool for Soul to use, but often the mind can be difficult to work with. It is very susceptible to what are called the five passions of the mind. Any one of these passions can captivate the mind.

The passions of the mind can be counteracted by the five virtues. When you slip into a passion of the mind, life is sending you the message that love has been lost.

Look at the following passions and virtues. When you feel hopelessly lost in the clutches of one of the passions of the mind, try counteracting it with the corresponding virtue.

Passions (Fear- and Power-Based)	Virtues (Aspects of Love)
Attachment	Detachment
Greed	Discrimination
Lust	Contentment
Anger	Forgiveness/tolerance
Vanity	Humility

Life on the Etheric Plane

The Etheric Plane is the higher part of the Mental Plane. It is the home of the subconscious, or unconscious, mind. The source of primitive, instinctual thought.

You'll also find the censor on the Etheric Plane. It serves to keep the conscious mind from knowing more than it can handle.

Now you'll move into a dimension that many people believe is the ultimate. This is where Soul seems to melt into a great abyss.

Between the Etheric and Soul Plane

Although there are smaller voids between each of the planes mentioned above, there is a larger and more well known void between the Etheric Plane and the Soul Plane. Buddhism teaches that this void, experienced as Nirvana, is where consciousness ceases to exist. Actually, consciousness continues, but the worlds of matter end here.

For some, this experience can be the dark night of Soul, so vast it seems as if you've plunged into eternal darkness.

But consciousness hasn't ended. This area is the last hurdle for Soul before It enters into the worlds of pure Light and Sound.

Life on the Soul Plane

The Soul Plane is the first of the true worlds of God above the worlds of time, matter, space, and energy. It is a world of light without darkness. Here Soul experiences the Holy Spirit, the ECK, by direct perception, without interference from the mind, memory, emotions,

The Soul Plane is the first of the true worlds of God above the worlds of time, matter, space, and energy.

or physical senses. This leads to Self-Realization. You discover your true purpose in life. (More about Self-Realization in chapters 27 and 28.)

The levels of heaven aren't really stacked upon each other like pancakes. They exist simultaneously.

A MAP TO GUIDE YOU

The following diagram is one you can use to help chart a course through the heavens. It's a primitive attempt to put something magnificent and vast into a digestible form for the mind. The levels of heaven aren't really stacked upon each other like pancakes. They exist simultaneously.

A Soul Traveler's Guide to the Worlds of God
Higher Worlds—Pure Positive Worlds of Spirit

Worlds above the Soul Plane

Experiences

Dwell in Ocean of Love and Mercy
God-Realization
Dance in pure Light and Sound of God
Ever-expanding consciousness and
   service

Sounds

HU, music of wooodwinds,
violins playing,
deep humming,
heavy wind

Planes	Words to Sing	Sounds	Aspects	Experiences
Soul	SUGMAD (SOOG-mahd)	Single note of a flute	Pure Light and Sound	Direct perception, spiritual freedom, Self-Realization

Lower Worlds—Matter, Space, and Time				
Planes	Words to Sing	Sounds	Aspects	Experiences
Etheric (subconscious mind)	Baju *(BAH-joo)*	Buzzing bees	Stored effects of past lives, unconscious attitudes	Respond to intuition and hunches, learn workings of unconscious and subconscious mind
Third Level of Heaven				
Mental (conscious mind)	Aum *(AHM or Ah-UM)*	Running water	Source of ethics, philosophy, morality; Universal Mind Power; passions of the mind; heaven for most religions	Solve, analyze problems, work in present; learn to control passions of the mind; acquire the five virtues
Second Level of Heaven				
Causal (memories)	Mana *(MAH-nah or Mah-NAY)*	Tinkling bells	Akashic records, Hall of Records	Find past-life memories affecting your life today
First Level of Heaven				
Astral (emotions)	Kala *(kah-LAH)*	Roar of the sea	Psychic phenomena; Astral museum, libraries, and vast jeweled cities; heaven, hell, and purgatory	Flying, lucid dreaming, range of emotions, heal emotional scars
Physical (five senses)	Alayi *(ah-LAH-ee)*	Thunder	Earth, other planets and universes	Use physical senses; live in classroom for Soul, visit other planets

HOW TO LEARN MORE ABOUT THE GOD WORLDS

For a fuller description of the planes, see the "God Worlds" chart available from Eckankar. Two good spiritual geography books include *The Tiger's Fang* and *The Spiritual Notebook* by Paul Twitchell.

Start keeping a journal of your worldly and otherworldly explorations to find the connections between them.

Also, in each book by Sri Harold Klemp in the Mahanta Transcripts series, you can look in the index under "Planes" to find fascinating information about these planes and how to explore them. After all, they're yours. These worlds are your own inner worlds of consciousness. You'll experience them as only you can.

The planes of heaven continue to infinity and are ever-expanding. The journey to explore them is a never-ending adventure.

WOULD YOU LIKE TO VISIT ONE OF THE HEAVENS?

Now you can try the spiritual exercise below to visit the planes of heaven. Pay attention to your dreams and the experiences of your life. Start keeping a journal of your worldly and otherworldly explorations to find the connections between them.

Try This Spiritual Exercise Today!

Before beginning a spiritual exercise to visit the planes of heaven, say, "God, please let me experience whatever will be best for my spiritual good." Know that you're always guided and protected by the Mahanta, agent of God in all the heavenly worlds.

Sing one of the spiritual words on the chart above until you feel the nudge to be still.

With eyes closed, gaze lovingly at your inner screen. Watch images and colors appear. Listen for the sounds of the planes. Visualize scenes unfolding. Imagine you're there. (With practice, you will be!)

Stop the exercise after twenty minutes. Repeat the exercise once a day until it's easy for you to explore these planes. Record your spiritual-exercise and dream adventures.

Learning the Secrets of the Spiritual Planes

In the next chapter you'll look at the interwoven tapestry of your life. The parts you know about now and the hidden aspects yet to be discovered.

17. You Can See and Change Your Future

In ECK, prophecy has a broader definition than just seeing the future. It also includes having the awareness to perceive the spiritual truth in a situation, or to understand the relationship between yourself and another person in a way that no one else can.

—Harold Klemp, *The Eternal Dreamer*[1]

You don't have to be a victim of the past or allow fate to rule your life.

Here's Golden Key Number 17.
You can see and change your future.

The following personal experience gives some clues about how to manage life instead of just letting it happen to you.

THE PLAY OF THE FUTURE

I was very angry at my parents because of pain I'd suffered while growing up.

The process of writing caused me to rise above the pain.

As an adult, I was drawn to the theater and playwriting. Soon after starting a career as a dramatist, I won a grant to write and have a reading of a play about my childhood.

A few weeks before the play was due, I decided to go to a mountain cabin to finish the play. This required me, scene by scene, to relive my youth. The process of writing caused me to rise above the pain. Even to find humor in past situations that seemed tragic at the time.

One night after working on the play, I dreamed that my mother confronted me. She asked, "How would you like it if your children ran around with tape recorders in their heads and exposed *you* onstage at your worst moments?"

I awoke, troubled by the dream. Each time I had questioned if I should be doing this play, the Mahanta, my inner guide and spiritual writing coach, advised: Keep writing!

I decided to sit in a chair in my cabin and contemplate on the dream. When I finished my spiritual exercise I had no new insights. But when I opened my eyes, I was in for quite a shock.

A three-foot-wide ribbon of tiny black insects streamed from the interior wall of my cabin!

When the maintenance person answered my call for help, he said that these creatures were termites. He explained that they'd hidden in the interior wall during the winter. Now as a springtime ritual, they'd eaten their fill of wood and were escaping to the outdoors through the window at the other end of my cabin.

Moved to another cabin and determined to finish my play, I resumed writing.

After stopping for the day, I went for a long walk in the mountains. I thought about all the grievances that had been eating away inside of me for years.

Tears streamed down my face as the Mahanta guided me to release the webs of anger that tied me to the past.

And then something startling happened.

I began to feel faint stirrings of love. I remembered the positive things my parents had done. For the first time, I admitted that these two people had raised me as well as they knew how.

For the things they didn't understand, for the consequences they hadn't anticipated, I forgave them.

TIME TO WRITE THE PLAY

The next morning I prepared to write the final scene of my play. Since I was traveling, I had brought only my computer. I planned to print out the work at home. I'd carefully saved each scene in computer files and made a separate backup disk for safety.

I recognized the anger, pain, and blame that had eaten away at my love and creativity.

When I turned on the computer, to my amazement, all the files were gone. Quickly I inserted the backup disk. It too was completely blank!

It felt as if the room were reeling. I left the desk and fell on the bed. An entire year's work had vanished. And, by not meeting the terms of the grant, I'd have to pay back the money. I cried out to the Mahanta, "Why did you tell me to keep going on this project?"

A soft inner voice said, "Now you can write your play."

I remembered the thousands of termites marching away from the rotted wood. It was then that I recognized the anger, pain, and blame that had eaten away at my love and creativity. These termites of the mind had been destroying the love I needed to be a better writer—and a more compassionate human being.

The ECK-Vidya *(EHK–VEE-dyah)* revealed the future, spread out before me like the scenes of my play. Now that the termites were gone, I could fill my hollow heart with unconditional love. This writing project and trip to the mountains would change the course of my life.

The Mahanta showed me the spiritual roots of my problem.

By writing the play, my confidence and writing skill had grown. If I had to return the money, I realized, it would be a small price to pay for a writing course taught by the Holy Spirit.

When I returned from my mountain retreat, I called the grant officer and told him what had happened. He said, "The grant was to help a promising artist grow professionally. You don't have to repay the money. You've learned a valuable lesson about writing—and about life."

The Mahanta showed me the spiritual roots of my problem. The ECK-Vidya, the ancient science of prophecy, had opened for me, revealing the connections between my past, present, and future.

The ECK-Vidya is a system for gaining total awareness.

That's what the ECK-Vidya can do for you too.

WHAT IS THE ECK-VIDYA?

The ECK-Vidya is a system for gaining total awareness. Only the Mahanta, the Living ECK Master and the ECK Masters in the Ancient Order of the Vairagi can lead you to this source of eternal knowledge.

You study and learn about the ECK-Vidya mainly by doing the Spiritual Exercises of ECK. You also interpret your dreams to help you see how the past and future are interacting in the present.

Simply stated, the ECK-Vidya is an incredible spiritual tool for understanding how life works.

In his book *The ECK-Vidya, Ancient Science of Prophecy* Paul Twitchell describes the ECK-Vidya as a way to rise above time and space, to see connections.[2]

Sri Harold explains the ECK-Vidya with these words:

> *I'm trying to help you develop your spiritual awareness, to bring you to the realization that all life is a series of interconnected wheels. Very little can happen to you that isn't known by you beforehand. All you have to do is learn to be aware.*[3]

INTERCONNECTED WHEELS

We don't live in a vacuum. Each of our thoughts, words, and actions cause equal and opposite reactions in ourselves and others.

Eckankar teaches that the ECK, the life force, weaves as a golden thread through creation. When we tune in to the ECK, we become more aware of these connections which span the course of time. Viewing the ECK-Vidya reveals Soul's relationship with the Sugmad (God) and with life.

Each of our thoughts, words, and actions cause equal and opposite reactions in ourselves and others.

You can learn how your present is affected by people and events from the past or the future.

A crucial key to understanding this ancient science of survival is to recognize the cycles of life.

LIFE FLOWS IN CYCLES

The evolution of man began millions of years ago. It was during these early years that the Ancient Order of the Vairagi, the ECK Masters,

*learned there was a rhythm of life cycles, which
had great influence on mankind.*

—Paul Twitchell, *The ECK-Vidya,
Ancient Science of Prophecy*[4]

The four seasons. Birth, death, rebirth. The ebb
and flow of the tides. The rising and setting of the sun.
All are cycles that operate with natural precision.

The ECK-Vidya reveals that all life runs in cycles.

Two major types of cycles are those that appear in
cycles of three or twelve.

*Throughout
our lives, cycles
of three are
more powerful
than most of us
realize.*

Throughout our lives, cycles of three are more
powerful than most of us realize. People naturally use
them, sensing their powerful effect. Usually it takes
three repetitions to get our attention. Often stories and
jokes are constructed around the principle of threes.

Watch for cycles of three in your daily life and
dreams. They're a clue that the Holy Spirit is trying
to communicate something very important to you.

CYCLES OF TWELVE

*Soul
experiences
twelve major
cycles on the
Wheel of Life.*

One of the most important cycles of life, though, is
the cycle of twelve. Soul experiences twelve major cycles
on the Wheel of Life, a symbolic depiction of the phases
in Soul's development.

Soul accumulates karma and reincarnates through
twelve major phases until It is ready to get out of Its
prison and find spiritual freedom.

When a baby is born, some of the distinct characteristics of that moment in time begin to play upon a
person's life. Planetary, national, community, and family karma (causes and effects) combine with Soul's
individual karmic debits and credits.

A way to understand the cyclical changes in your life is to look at certain periods as beginnings or endings of twelve-year cycles. Look at peak experiences in your life to decide what started a cycle of twelve and when it's likely to end.

You can analyze the cycles you're in now and predict and prepare for new ones.

The ECK Masters can show you how to review your spiritual records.

How Can You See the Past and Future?

The ECK Masters can show you how to review your spiritual records. They're stored within the planes of heaven, especially the Astral, Causal, and Soul Planes. The Soul Plane contains all records of Soul's many lifetimes. On the Soul Plane you can also see possible future events.

Sri Harold explains how he guides Souls to understand the ECK-Vidya:

> *Once we establish an inner bond, which can only occur through agreement between you and me, we can work one-on-one. It requires your saying yes to the invitation. Then I can take you into past lives, and I can show you the future if needed.*
>
> *But these things are not as important as showing you how to live in the present moment.*[5]

Akashic Records

A large number of past-life memories are stored on the Causal Plane. These past-life records are known as the Akashic records.

Some people view the Akashic records as a series of slides or photographs. You may find yourself in a dream or inner vision sorting through index cards on which records of your past lives are stored. Others say that past lives unfold before them like a computer printout.

Often past-life dreams seem like scenes from a movie. As Soul you view the event as an observer. You may also participate in the scene as the main character. You may even know what the other characters are thinking.

If you have a past-life dream, contemplate on it in the morning. Ask to be shown how this past life is affecting you in the present.

Holy Spirit, the Light and Sound of God, communicates to us all the time about what lies ahead.

SURVIVAL TOOLS FOR THE FUTURE

Holy Spirit, the Light and Sound of God, communicates to us all the time about what lies ahead. In a U.S. Gallup poll, 39 percent of those surveyed said they believed that God speaks to them through other people.[6]

In Eckankar this is known as the Golden-tongued Wisdom. It's an aspect of the ECK-Vidya which Sri Harold calls "a Chinese fortune cookie from the ECK."[7]

Life provides you with guidance from the Holy Spirit. Here are a few examples of how the Golden-tongued Wisdom works.

Let's say you're struggling with a problem. You turn on the radio and catch a few words that give you insight into how to resolve the situation.

Or you go to a restaurant. The server unknowingly says something that may appear to be very ordinary to everyone else but offers a missing puzzle piece for you.

These are examples of the Golden-tongued Wisdom. It's not mediumship or channeling but happens naturally because all creation is connected through the ECK. The written or spoken words light up, giving people the information they need.

The ECK is constantly loving and supporting each of us in these amazing ways.

WAKING DREAMS

The waking dream is yet another fascinating aspect of the ECK-Vidya. This is an event or series of coincidences that happens while you're awake, giving you the guidance of the Holy Spirit.

The waking dream is often an unusual occurrence that catches your attention.

The waking dream is often an unusual occurrence that catches your attention. In the story that opened this chapter the termites were an example of a waking dream. They signified the anger that was eating away inside me. When a waking dream happens, you wonder, *What does that mean?*

You can interpret waking dreams as you would symbols in a sleeping dream. Some people consider waking dreams as signs from God either warning them or steering them in a direction that is best for them and everyone else.

Waking dreams can also confirm that you're on the right track.

For example one ECKist was working on a project, and she wondered if she were getting too heavy-handed with it. As she tried to decide what to do, a little statue of an angel that was on top of a bookshelf over her desk fell to the floor. There was nothing to cause the angel to topple.

She interpreted this as a waking dream, a message from the ECK. It influenced her to decide that she didn't want to be a "fallen angel" by using power instead of love. She decided to try a lighter touch with the project.

If you're interested in knowing more about this

aspect of the ECK-Vidya, look in the index of one of Sri Harold's books in the Mahanta Transcripts series under "waking dream." Also, *The Secret Language of Waking Dreams* by Mike Avery is available from Eckankar and contains valuable information on how to interpret and use symbols in your waking life as you do with dreams.

Soul can place Its attention anywhere on the Time Track, in the past, present, or future.

GETTING ABOVE THE TIME TRACK

The Time Track is the linear progression of events in time. But Soul is above the Time Track. Soul can place Its attention anywhere on the Time Track, in the past, present, or future.

Spiritual exercises help us become more conscious of this. Sri Harold offers the following spiritual exercise to help us find the practical benefits of working with the ECK-Vidya.

Try This Spiritual Exercise Today!

Spend a day or a week paying close attention to unusual incidents the ECK brings you. Things happen as the ECK guides you to take a step, to make something work out right. Anything that grabs your attention may be an aspect of the Golden-tongued Wisdom. Working with this is just a matter of awareness.

Sometimes the ECK gives you warnings. An alarm going off, for instance, might not be for the most apparent reason. It could be the ECK signaling you to be alert, be aware, be on the lookout for other things. Even a sudden birdcall may be a hint that you should be careful, hurry up, or pay attention.

> The worlds of ECK in the lower regions inter-
> lock like puzzle pieces. With expanded awareness,
> you are able to take in more and more of these
> interlocking worlds of ECK, so that when some-
> thing happens to you or around you, you know how
> it fits in and what it means to you.[8]

QUESTIONS AND ANSWERS

The storehouse of knowledge hidden within the
inner worlds is vast. We've only touched on a few key
aspects. For more information on the ECK-Vidya, refer
to *The ECK-Vidya, Ancient Science of Prophecy* by Paul
Twitchell. In Sri Harold's books look in the index under
"ECK-Vidya" to learn how he has continued the evolution of this intriguing yet practical aspect of the ECK
teachings.

Meanwhile, here are some questions people new to
Eckankar ask about the ECK-Vidya.

The storehouse of knowledge hidden within the inner worlds is vast.

1. *How is the ECK-Vidya different from psychic read-
    ings?*

Even the best psychic readers can only look at the
Akashic records on the Causal Plane. Because they
offer an incomplete reading at best, they can't see the
underlying spiritual roots of your problems. Many
psychic readers can't verify whether they are reading
your records or someone else's.

Such psychic methods as astrology, numerology,
channeling, or past and future readings are often a
person's first experiences with the power of invisible
forces.

But these aspects of the spiritual life can become a trap. It's easy to misuse unstable psychic forces. Or become so immersed that you lose sight of your true purpose in life—to become a Co-worker with God.

The ECK-Vidya takes you far beyond the psychic worlds to the Soul Plane. There you receive a more comprehensive view of all Soul's incarnations.

When you have a revelation through the ECK-Vidya, you must learn how to use the information in your life. Will you use it for power and control?

Sri Harold writes:

> *Thus the paradox is that one who gets the gift of prophecy is not able to tell anyone about it. He must follow the Law of Silence. Otherwise, the road to unfoldment stops right there.*[9]

Past-life memories aren't static. Soul lives in the present and experiences these powerful images as happening now.

2. *Should I ask someone to take me back into a past life?*

A licensed health professional may use hypnosis or past-life regressions to help a person who is in a program of therapy. He uses the information from a past-life memory to help the patient overcome current fears.

But in the wrong hands or used for amusement, to satisfy curiosity or for power, past-life regressions and hypnosis are risky.

Past-life memories aren't static. Soul lives in the present and experiences these powerful images as happening now. When Soul relives the experience, the mind remembers the past image and its emotional, mental, and physical consequences.

The Mahanta can guide you to remember only what is best for you right now. Sri Harold explains one of the dangers of remembering past lives without the help of the Mahanta:

> *The tangles of past karma are tied in with the memories of past-life experiences and must be dealt with so carefully. The hypnotist often lacks the spiritual training to deal with karma and pass it off into the Audible Life Stream. That's also one reason, in a parallel case, that the suicide rate among psychiatrists is so great.*[10]

Sri Harold illustrates this point by telling the story of a psychiatrist who regressed a woman to a past life. It greatly disturbed the woman. She remembered living during World War II when she had been a prisoner in a German concentration camp. This woman saw things she couldn't begin to handle emotionally and went into severe shock.[11]

During past-life regressions or hypnosis neither the therapist nor the patient are in control of what will be remembered.

That's the problem. During past-life regressions or hypnosis neither the therapist nor the patient are in control of what will be remembered.

Ancient Secrets of Survival

The ECK-Vidya is as ancient as creation. It is part of the ECK teachings. The ECK Masters can show you how to use this valuable knowledge for greater insight and awareness into your own life.

Within the ECK teachings you'll find the ancient laws and principles that silently, invisibly govern all life. The spiritual laws of ECK are underlying principles that lead to success in every aspect of life.

The next chapter will show you how to use spiritual laws to master your own universe.

18. Spiritual Laws Bring Harmony to Your World

In the worlds of ECK, everything fits together.
Everything is in its proper time and place.
When the conditions are right, when the ECK is
flowing cleanly, everything works in harmony.
It may not happen often, but when it does, hope-
fully we can recognize it as one of the golden
moments of truth, a golden moment of life.
—Harold Klemp, *The Dream Master*[1]

*L*ife is pretty basic.
If you want to succeed in the game of life, you have to learn the rules. If you want to scale the heights, you need the proper tools and equipment. If you want to master your destiny, you have to understand how the heavens and earth connect.

Eckankar teaches the spiritual laws of ECK. These laws are embedded in the teachings of ECK.

You can find explanations of the spiritual laws of ECK in the written and spoken teachings of Eckankar. However, it's only through the secret teachings that you begin to really understand how the spiritual laws apply to you personally.

Unlocking their mysteries leads to wonder. The moment of insight. The thrill of discovery.

Here's Golden Key Number 18.
Spiritual laws bring harmony to your world.

As you gain deeper understanding of the spiritual laws of ECK, you naturally become more balanced, loving, joyful, and wise. You face life with courage and confidence.

The Difference between Spiritual Laws and Commandments

The spiritual laws of ECK show how to live a balanced and abundant life. You aren't commanded to obey certain laws or rules. Consequences are the teachers that show you when you have ignored or forgotten a spiritual principle.

The spiritual laws of ECK show how to live a balanced and abundant life.

You don't have to memorize the spiritual laws. You discover them through dreams, moments of heightened awareness, and during the Spiritual Exercises of ECK.

Then you apply them.

The story below takes us to a store and a pizza parlor where an ECKist named Rosa gained some new insights into spiritual law. One of the ten commandments is "Thou shalt not steal." But the Mahanta, Rosa's Inner Master, used the spiritual Law of Karma (cause and effect) to give Rosa a lesson she would remember.

Rosa bought a lawn chair. When the cashier rang up the sale, she didn't notice that the price was $14.95. Instead, she charged Rosa $4.95.

Rosa didn't mention the mistake. She left the store thinking she'd just saved $10.00.

As Rosa walked out the door, a lady dropped a bottle of milk. It spilled all over Rosa's shoes. This caused Rosa to wonder if maybe the ECK was giving her a sign to think about her deception. But Rosa was too happy with her good fortune to pay attention.

The chair wasn't worth what she was now paying for it in back pain.

The first time Rosa sat in the new chair, she wrenched her back trying to get up. Finally she got the message. The chair wasn't worth what she was now paying for it in back pain.

Rosa drove to the store to pay the $10.00. On the way three cars in a row pulled in front of her. They all had license plates with the letters E-C-K. Rosa recognized that the Mahanta drew her attention to these waking-dream experiences to assure her that the Holy Spirit was guiding her to do the right thing.

Rosa paid the manager the extra ten dollars. She left the store thinking that everything was now in divine order.

But when Rosa arrived at the pizza parlor where she worked as a waitress, the lesson continued. Two customers ordered spaghetti dinners. Both times she wrote $4.95 on their tickets when the actual price was $14.95.

Both times Rosa had to pay the extra $10.00 out of her earnings. She complained, "Gee, you know, they could have said something."

Suddenly she remembered the chair. It was Rosa who hadn't pointed out the cashier's mistake.

Rosa concluded her story by saying, "I ended up paying for that chair three times! Well, I guess that's a lesson well learned."[2]

Through these experiences in her daily life, the Mahanta brought Rosa a greater understanding of spiritual law. The consequences taught her more about how life really works than preaching could ever have done.

Ignorance of spiritual law isn't bliss.

But not everyone knows about these spiritual laws. Does that mean spiritual law doesn't apply to them?

WHAT IF YOU HAVEN'T HEARD OF THE SPIRITUAL LAWS?

Ignorance of spiritual law isn't bliss.

Bending the spiritual laws by using black or white magic only shows a lack of awareness. This includes trying to make things happen that are contrary to the natural cycles and rhythms of life.

It takes many lifetimes to understand how the spiritual laws operate. The Mahanta teaches you the spiritual laws by helping you gain insight into your experiences. He shows you the patterns and cycles of life.

It takes many lifetimes to understand how the spiritual laws operate.

Understanding spiritual law helps you to realize that there's nothing capricious about how God's creation operates. You also find life's shades of gray.

THE DIFFERENCE BETWEEN RIGHT AND WRONG

The human mind is very good at bending and misinterpreting spiritual law, commandments, and moral and civil law to justify actions.

But the spiritual laws of ECK are clear and precise. They hold us to the highest ethical and moral standards. One who is knowledgeable of and abides by spiritual law is honest, trustworthy, loving, and fair in dealing with others.

Sri Harold has recommended a book written by Richard Maybury. He refers to Maybury as a contemporary thinker who researched the moral and ethical laws of religions and philosophies. Maybury distilled the laws and principles he found into a set of natural guidelines.

Maybury's book *Whatever Happened to Justice?* presents two basic laws expressed in only seventeen words. Maybury asks that these laws be quoted exactly.

---

(1)   Do all you have agreed to do, and

(2)   Do not encroach on other persons or their property.[3]

Maybury's laws are simple, effective, and spiritually correct.

Now, let's take a look at two spiritual laws that affect all of us. Yet they're often the least understood laws of life.

THE LAW OF LOVE

Pain and the past are nothing more than love's chrysalis, its shell, its seedbed, in which these necessary nothings release such wonders, such as the comforting thrill of God's hand on one's shoulder.
—Paul Twitchell, *The Key to ECKANKAR*[4]

It is the love of God, not the fear of God, that will bring you into the fullness of life.

An ECKist found on a long overseas flight how the Law of Love supersedes all else.

It is the love of God, not the fear of God, that will bring you into the fullness of life.

"On a very crowded plane I had a choice," she said. "I could sit in a row of cramped seats. Or move to the last two seats of the plane where I could stretch out and relax.

"Unfortunately, the last two seats were in the smoking section. And cigarette smoke made me sick.

"Secretly I also harbored a lot of judgments about smokers. I considered them to be lower on the spiritual ladder than those like me who didn't indulge in such a filthy habit. I conveniently forgot about all my own habits as I sat in judgment on smokers.

I realized that although I disliked smoke, each smoker was a Soul who deserved love and respect.

"I decided to take my chances and sit in the last row. Only after I had settled into my seat did I discover that the seat beside me would be occupied. The flight attendants directed anyone from the nonsmoking section who wanted a smoke to sit next to me!

"As a procession of smokers sat beside me puffing happily, I fumed.

"Finally I realized my attitude wasn't helping. I remembered the Law of Love. So I decided to look for the love in this situation.

"Then I realized that although I disliked smoke, each smoker was a Soul who deserved love and respect. I decided that when the next person sat beside me, I would fill myself with love instead of rage.

"In a few minutes, a young man moved into the seat next to mine. I closed my eyes and silently sang HU, a holy love song to God. My heart opened with compassion.

"The man lit his cigarette and considerately turned his body so smoke wouldn't blow in my face. He decided not to even finish the cigarette but snuffed it out halfway through.

"After the man left, no more smokers sat next to me. I rested contentedly for the rest of the flight. I'd learned a valuable lesson in the Law of Love. It applies to everyone, not just those I approve of."

Although Eckankar doesn't tell you how to live your personal life or what lifestyle choices to make, smoking is strongly discouraged. Smoking can harm your body and fog your consciousness.

No law is greater than the Law of Love.

The ECKist in the story above learned that having rigid opinions causes us to lose the love that could heal any situation. No law is greater than the Law of Love.

THE LAW OF KARMA

People are not equal when they come to this world at birth. Everyone has a different load of karma coming into this lifetime.

But most people have no idea how to work this off, or that it even exists. And so they live within their human shells, too afraid to live and yet too afraid to die. Wanting heaven, because earth is hell, and afraid to go to heaven, because you have to die to get there.

It's this big spiritual problem.

—Harold Klemp, *How the Inner Master Works*[5]

The Law of Karma is probably one of the least understood of all the spiritual laws. The word *karma* has been bandied about in popular culture. Most people think of karma as a harsh system of retribution and punishment.

The Law of Karma is probably one of the least understood of all the spiritual laws.

Instead, karma is a balancing of accounts with life. It is the Law of Cause and Effect. The Law of Karma is God's divine plan to help Soul grow into the loving spiritual light It was always meant to be. Each time you choose power over love, for example, you must eventually perform an act of love in repayment. Each act of love earns a blessing in return. That's the Law of Karma simply stated.

The physical laws of the universe mirror the Law of Karma: Action leads to reaction; what goes up comes down. The Law of Karma reveals that life is logical, predictable, and fair. It makes sense out of what appears to be chaotic.

People often wonder why there is so much pain and suffering in life. Why are there wars, disasters, and other catastrophes?

IS KARMA UNCARING?

Yes and no. Karma is as impersonal as the law of gravity but it's also no more vindictive than the physical laws that govern nature.

Soul yearns for spiritual growth. Your mind, body, and emotions don't always recognize the jewels of opportunity embedded in each experience. But Soul does. Each person has a unique relationship with Divine Spirit. Although placed in identical circumstances, people deal with events in their own way.

People often wonder why there is so much pain and suffering in life. Why are there wars, disasters, and other catastrophes? But where some find despair, others find hope.

Some Souls go through experiences like these and strengthen their godlike characteristics — compassion, courage, unconditional love. They may save strangers from suffering or even give their lives for others. Each Soul has Its unique relationship with life and with God.

Even the cruelest of experiences can help people recognize that Soul survives anything. Soul is eternal.

Soul is not eternally damned. Nor is It branded from birth with unearned burdens.

THE DIFFERENCE BETWEEN
KARMA AND ORIGINAL SIN

Original sin is a concept that says you're spiritually bankrupt at birth. It's used to explain the need for salvation.

Eckankar teaches that you're not spiritually guilty or saved because of the actions of another. Instead, you're responsible for every aspect of your life. You've earned your karma.

Also, releasing karma isn't what some call being cleared. You can't hire another person to clear your karma away. Your debt is with Divine Spirit.

THE DIFFERENCE BETWEEN
BEING SAVED AND BEING TAUGHT

Before Thoreau died, his aunt is reported to have asked Henry if he had made his peace with God. His reply was, "I don't know that we ever quarrelled."[6]

The deathbed is not the place to make things right with God. You need to start a bit sooner. Confessing or repenting of sins may comfort a person. But it is life itself that teaches you better. And debts to Life must still be repaid.

The Mahanta doesn't save you from the effects of your sins or take away your karma. What would you learn? You would still have to repeat the experience to understand the spiritual law you broke.

Instead, the Mahanta does something even better. He shows you how to keep from doing harmful things to yourself and others. He takes you to the karmic causes of your problems today, gradually opening the wounds of the past so they can be healed in the Light and Sound of God.

Confessing or repenting of sins may comfort a person. But it is life itself that teaches you better.

THE SYSTEM OF KARMA

The more karma you create, the more lifetimes it takes to reap the consequences of your thoughts, words, and actions. This cycle of lives is known as the wheel of karma.

When you become aware of being on this wheel, you begin to wonder how to get off of it.

You long for spiritual freedom.

When Sugmad (God) created the lower worlds It established the Law of Cause and Effect, which is the Law of Karma. This system is administered by spiritual beings known as the Lords of Karma. Impartially, they keep track of what we've sown and what we'll reap.

Camus said, "Don't wait for the last judgment—it takes place every day."[7] You don't rot in a grave and then reunite with your physical body on a final judgment day. Instead you go through a life-review process after each incarnation.

THE LORDS OF KARMA AND THE LIFE REVIEW

After dropping your physical body at death, you have a life review with the Lords of Karma.

After dropping your physical body at death, you have a life review with the Lords of Karma. These spiritual beings look at your Akashic records, the accounting of good and bad karma you've accumulated over your lifetimes. The Akashic records help them to see where you're still lacking in spiritual awareness.

The Lords of Karma prepare a plan for your next lifetime based upon what you've learned and earned. They assign your next life whether in heaven or on earth.

Although the Lords of Karma may allow you to make choices such as which body to incarnate in or which set of Souls to incarnate with, their system is pretty impartial.

They don't care much about your feelings or desires. Their only interest is in what's best for you spiritually. What will most efficiently help you learn the lessons of divine love you haven't figured out so far?

But once you have earned the blessing of meeting the Mahanta, something wonderful happens. The Mahanta can free you from the wheel of karma and lead you to spiritual freedom!

THE MAHANTA BECOMES YOUR KARMIC BANKER

When the Mahanta, the Living ECK Master accepts you as a spiritual student, he takes over management of your karmic account. When a karmic debt must be paid, he guides you to the time, place, and type of experience that will cause the least amount of wear and tear on you. Sometimes you can repay karmic debts in dream experiences and not have to go through them physically.

Right now the Mahanta can start helping you on a daily basis to free yourself from the bondage of karma and reincarnation.

At your physical death, the Mahanta will meet with you to guide you through the transition from life on earth to life in heaven. The Mahanta will escort you past the Lords of Karma directly to the heavenly home you've earned.

Right now the Mahanta can start helping you on a daily basis to free yourself from the bondage of karma and reincarnation.

HOW CAN I LEARN MORE ABOUT SPIRITUAL LAWS?

To learn about more spiritual laws, refer to *The Spiritual Laws of ECK* and *The ECKANKAR Dictionary.* Also Sri Harold's writings, especially the four volumes of ECK parables, *Stories to Help You See God in Your Life,* are filled with examples of spiritual laws at work in daily life.

Below are some other spiritual laws. They cover a wide range of everyday experiences.

The spiritual laws of ECK include the laws of: Noninterference, Silence, Gratitude, Plenty, Economy, Harmony, Reversed Effort, Detachment, Attitude, and Consciousness.

Life goes easier when you have a higher perspective of what is going on and why.

Understanding the Spiritual Laws of ECK Can Change Your Life

When you begin to understand and follow the spiritual laws of ECK, you'll notice subtle, and sometimes dramatic, changes for the better. Life goes easier when you have a higher perspective of what is going on and why.

Here are a few things one ECKist has learned about the Law of Silence.

"While gaining an understanding of the Law of Silence, I have discovered that if you speak of something before it is time, it's like an ice cube that has not frozen all the way through. You poke it with your finger, and the ice cube breaks. It is not yet strong.

"If I have an inner experience that nobody needs to know about, I have learned to keep quiet. If what I learned in the inner experience would benefit another person, only then can I release the information. The ECK comes through strongly to let me know what I should talk about.

"One year, for example, I planned to apply to art school. I prematurely talked to a friend about my plan. Suddenly I felt I had lost the energy of my plan and became worried that it wouldn't manifest.

"On the day I went to apply at the art school, however, I got off the bus at an earlier stop and began walking. During this walk I felt the energy return.

"I asked myself, *What's happening?*

"I saw the image of an aircraft on a runway. It needs time to gather force and lift off.

"In walking from the bus stop to the school and realizing the importance of the Law of Silence, I again picked up the energy to apply for admission by the time I got to the art school."

Another ECKist tells how she uses the spiritual laws of ECK at her job in a large corporation.

"I sat down once with a book of the spiritual laws of ECK," she said. "I wanted to see which ones I applied to my job. By the time I got to the end, I realized that I use every one of them.

"When I plan a project, I consciously use the Law of Economy. I understand how to apply it to the piece of work I'm doing.

The ECK can open your heart to receive the blessings of life.

"When I'm training or coaching people, I understand how the Law of Noninterference comes into play. And the Law of Love."

BREAKING THE BONDS OF KARMA

In his book *The Spiritual Exercises of ECK,* Sri Harold gives many techniques to help you gain a better understanding of yourself and the spiritual laws. Let's try a spiritual exercise from this book to help you balance your karmic account by bathing in the Light and Sound of God. The ECK can open your heart to receive the blessings of life.

Try This Spiritual Exercise Today!

Find a comfortable position and relax. Shut your eyes, and look at the inner screen. Imagine you are watching a movie screen. Sometimes it will be black, sometimes white, sometimes gray. There may even be times when you can see a scene or a moving picture.

At first, try looking straight at the screen. After a while this may not work, so let your inner vision stray to the left or right about ten degrees. Suddenly, out of the corner of your eye, you may notice that something has appeared on the screen. Begin to look for the Master.

In a relaxed way, look obliquely, knowing that your attention is really to the center. Begin singing HU or chanting your secret word [a word given by the Inner Master during an ECKist's initiation].

As you do this spiritual exercise and sing HU to yourself, it begins a purifying, cleansing action on Soul. Old habit patterns—the gossip, the idle chatter, the dishonesty with oneself—start to fall away.[8]

The spiritual laws of ECK serve as guideposts to help you live in abundance and harmony with the ECK.

MORE LOVE THAN YOU'VE EVER KNOWN

The spiritual laws of ECK serve as guideposts to help you live in abundance and harmony with the ECK.

The next chapter will introduce you to the most powerful tools available for living a life filled with joy, peace, purpose, and love.

Sri Harold Klemp
The Mahanta, the Living ECK Master

Sri Harold at home in his study doing research for the ECK works, May 1994.

Sri Harold speaks at an Eckankar seminar.

Sri Harold and his wife, Joan, at the Temple of ECK, November 1994.

ECKANKAR—A WORLDWIDE RELIGION

"This is the largest ECK seminar that has ever taken place."
—Sri Harold Klemp, Lagos, Nigeria, July 1991.

Sri Harold Klemp, the Mahanta, the Living ECK Master is cheered by a crowd of ten thousand who came to hear "The Living Word," theme of the 1991 ECK African Seminar.

For upwards of five minutes, there was an unprecedented applause, in appreciation of a dear friend, whom we had always longed for. —Asifo Brume-Ezewu, *The Truth Magazine.*

Peter Skelskey, president of Eckankar, speaks at the 30th Anniversary World Festival of the Unity-and-Diversity World Council, sponsored by the United Nations.

Near right: In an official ceremony on September 7, 1993, Juan Antonio Santesteban accepts the certificate of registration for Eckankar Mexico from the Secretary of the Interior of Mexico. Far right:

Juan Antonio, RESA of Mexico, and his wife, María Gonzalez, president of Eckankar Mexico, receive the Mexican flag at a special ceremony on September 14, 1993. Eckankar was honored to be one of sixty religious associations, chosen from eight hundred registered groups, to be invested with the Mexican flag at this special ceremony.

ECK students from China, Hong Kong, England, Ghana, and Nigeria sing HU on the Great Wall of China, April 11, 1992.

On Sunday, April 18, 1993, a group of U.S. Army Reserve chaplain's assistants toured the Temple of ECK to learn more about Eckankar. Afterward, the chaplain's assistants presented Peter Skelskey, president of Eckankar, with a certificate of appreciation. The tour was arranged with the help of ECKist Nick Vlcek, a chaplain's assistant in the U.S. Army Reserve.

ECKists Serve Their Communities

Photo by John Harriz

Members of Eckankar in Delaware County, Pennsylvania, participate in the local "Adopt a Highway" program to be of service to the community.

As a community project, ECKists in Minneapolis brought food-shelf donations to the Temple of ECK. Toni Lucas, project coordinator, and Michael Chandler delivered items to the food-shelf warehouse on December 21 for distribution.

Photo by Allen Anderson

Photo by Ardi Keim

The Temple of ECK Choir from Chanhassen, Minnesota, led by choir director Rich Miller, performs at nursing homes and other public places.

Licensed ECK health professionals give freely of their services on a sixteen-day trip to Ghana following the 1993 ECK European Seminar. Paul Van Camp, M.D., was honored to be made a chief of welfare and progress in Nsabe. Above, second row, from right to left: Paul Van Camp in traditional regalia for the "outdooring" of a new chief; his wife, Johane Van Camp, R.N.; Bob Rountree, M.D.; and Paul's sister, Cathy. Right: The paramount chief of Nsaba accepts the Van Camps' gift of ten sewing machines for a vocational training center in Nsaba.

Eckankar Is for Youth of All Ages

Photo by Robert Huntley

Young ECKists find a youth study book, *The ECK Teensie Discourses,* in the seminar bookroom.

Photo by Ursula Maydell

ECK families share their love for God during a monthly ECK family hour at the Edmonton ECK center.

Parents celebrate the consecration of their child. ECK High Initiate Anne Pondorf officiated at this first ECK consecration ceremony in Latin America.

Photo by Michael Pondorf

ECK Eighth Initiate Lyn Crawford was second runner-up in the 1993 Colorado State Fair Silver Queen Contest. With her carved wooden walking stick in hand, she read two of her poems in the talent competition.

Photo by Robert Huntley

Cubmaster Doug Sumner and Cub Scouts at a weekly meeting at the Temple of ECK.

THE TEMPLE OF ECK—SPIRITUAL HISTORY IN THE MAKING

The Temple of ECK is the starting place for Soul's dream of reaching God.

> —Sri Harold Klemp,
> *The Temple of ECK*

Sri Harold checks final architectural plans as he surveys the Temple site prior to the ground breaking.

After donning the commemorative helmet for the ground breaking, Sri Harold turns the first shovelful of earth at the site of the Temple of ECK on Monday, September 11, 1989, at 10:30 a.m. This spiritually significant moment marks the beginning of the next era in the history of Eckankar.

Photos by Stan Burgess

Giving the ancient blessing of the Vairagi ECK Masters, Sri Harold completes the transfer of the ECK Seat of Power from Sedona, Arizona, to Chanhassen, Minnesota, at 12:00 noon, October 22, 1990.

People of
all faiths
worship at
the Temple of
ECK.

Photo by Robert Huntley

The Temple of ECK is both a Golden Wisdom Temple and a local community church. It is a place for all people who love God.
—Sri Harold Klemp

Photo by Larrie Easterly

Visitors enjoy
walking the Temple's
contemplation trails.

Tours are
regularly
scheduled
year-round.

Photo by Robert Huntley

In the vestibule of the Temple, the natural daylight floods in through golden-framed glass doors and through the skylight above. ᘖ symbols adorn three sides of the stairwell railing. Above the stairwell is a twenty-foot-wide octagonal skylight.

The stained-glass blue star in the sanctuary ceiling represents the Blue Star of ECK.

At the east end of the sanctuary is the chapel with curved rows of seventy-eight upholstered seats. The chapel features a three-tiered ceiling with a fully curtained, curved back wall. Weddings, consecration ceremonies, and other special events are held here.

The eight-hundred-seat sanctuary in the Temple of ECK.

A cantilevered staircase leads downstairs to the fellowship hall.

Photo by Sharmaine Johanson

Spring at the
Temple of ECK

Summer at the
Temple of ECK

Photo by Robert Huntley

Autumn at the
Temple of ECK

Photo by Allen Anderson

Winter at the
Temple of ECK

Photo by Robert Huntley

Photo by Bree Renz

Joan Klemp sings "Amazing HU," accompanied by flutist Bettine Clemen at the Temple of ECK, on May 5, 1991. At this Temple of ECK worship service, Sri Harold introduced the ECK version of the public-domain song "Amazing Grace" that he and his wife adapted for ECK use. He said it is a song that can open the heart and be used as a spiritual exercise.

The Temple of ECK is located west of the Twin Cities in Chanhassen at 7450 Powers Boulevard. It is one-third mile north of Minnesota Highway 5 on Highway 17.

Photo by Joan Klemp

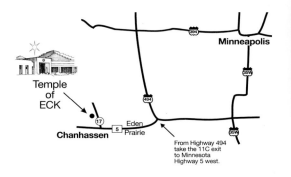

Sri Harold Klemp, the spiritual leader of Eckankar, welcomes you to the Temple of ECK.

ECKANKAR SEMINARS ARE SPIRITUAL CELEBRATIONS

Speaking at the 1992 ECK European seminar in Paris, France, Sri Harold tells how to turn stumbling blocks into stepping-stones on the path home to God.

"So as you go home today, I would like to say I love you. May the blessings be." At the 1992 ECK Worldwide Seminar in Minneapolis, Minnesota, Sri Harold Klemp, the Mahanta, the Living ECK Master gives the ancient blessing of the Vairagi Masters, known as the Eagle-eyed Adepts.

Sri Harold gives the Darshan, the gaze of the Master.

Photos (l-r) by Marianne Thomas, Bree Renz, Bernard Chouet, Bree Renz, Robert Huntley, and Bree Renz

ECKists from around the world share keys to spiritual freedom they found in ECK.

Youth celebrate the theme "The Grateful Heart" by creating a HU heart as a gift for Sri Harold. Seminar highlights included talks by Sri Harold, music by saxophonist James Lott and others, fun at the ECK dance, and many other special moments.

Photos (l-r) by John Maritios, Sandra Rosen, and Larrie Easterly

Some ECK Masters of the Ancient Order of Vairagi

Gopal Das
Taught in Egypt
about 3000 B.C.

Lai Tsi
Served as
Living ECK Master
in ancient China

**Yaubl
Sacabi**
Taught among
the Mycenaeans
and ancient
Greeks

**Fubbi
Quantz**
Taught during
time of Buddha
in India

Rebazar Tarzs
Born in Tibet about five
hundred years ago, he
taught the modern-day
founder of Eckankar, Paul
Twitchell.

Fubbi Quantz and Lai Tsi illustrations by Helen Baird, Yaubl Sacabi by Connie Kassal.

PAUL TWITCHELL — A MAN WITH A MISSION

Portrait by Betsy McCabe

Paul Twitchell, the modern-day founder of Eckankar

Paul Twitchell autographs a copy of *The Tiger's Fang,* the story of his journey into the heart of God.

SPIRITUAL ECSTASY

When I say joy, ecstasy, *and* rapture, *these words aren't sufficient to say what life beyond this world is.*

Harold Klemp, *The Drumbeat of Time*[1]

19. You Need to Know the Most Powerful Prayer

When people come to ECK, they sometimes find their lives speed up. Life becomes more adventurous and exciting. Sometimes they say, "Please, I don't want any more excitement." But if you let it, your life will move progressively forward. And it all begins with the singing of HU.

—Harold Klemp, *The Drumbeat of Time*[2]

Y ou're about to discover the most powerful holy word ever known.

Here's Golden Key Number 19.
You need to know the most powerful prayer—HU.

Singing this simple one-syllable sound can bring joy, ecstasy, and rapture. Singing HU can bring the experience of God.

HU is an ancient, once secret, holy name for God. The sound of HU is God's love as it pulses within the rhythm of life.

233

Sri Harold Klemp, the spiritual leader of Eckankar, expresses the vastness of HU with these words:

Listen for the love.

> *People singing softly to each other, the song is of the HU. People laughing, the laughter is of the HU. And even when there are people crying, the crying is of the HU. . . . And the birds, and the wind. These are all of the sound of HU.*[3]

Listen for the love.

SING HU

Whenever I face tough situations, I try to remember to sing HU. I do this as a love song to God, to bless the situation for the good of all concerned.

One night a few weeks after we brought them home, our two baby cockatiels, Sparkle and Sunshine, squawked and flapped their wings. They looked very distressed.

My husband placed the birds on my shoulders. Sparkle, gray and yellow wings held tightly against her body, pressed against my cheek. The bird trembled and appeared to be trying to communicate something.

I began to sing HU. This sound soothed the birds. Then I remembered reading a book, *Stories the Animals Tell Me* by Beatrice Lydecker. The author explains that it's possible to communicate with animals by catching mental images of what they're thinking. Then you speak back by returning images.

I sang HU and quieted my mind. Immediately I saw an image from Sparkle. She was in a robin's dead body lying on the floor of a forest. I felt Sparkle communicate that thunder made her remember her last lifetime. A big wind had come along and knocked her off a branch.

With a spring storm raging outside, this was the first time these two domesticated birds had ever heard thunder.

I used mental images to calm Sparkle. I tried to communicate that she hadn't really died. She's alive in a new body. Now she's an inside bird with people who love her. The storm is outside. And the wind can't blow her away."

As I sang HU, the two birds started imitating me by making little HU-HU-HU sounds too. I told them to listen for HU in the thunder, that HU is in all of God's creation.

Then Sunshine began to tell his story. He puffed up his little yellow feathers, and the orange spot on his cheeks glowed. He said that birds in the forest warn each other when a bad storm is coming. He'd been trying to tell us that they were all in danger!

I thanked him for the warning. Then we all sang HU again.

After this conversation, both birds were quiet for the rest of the evening even though the storm continued.

This experience showed me that HU is truly recognized by all of God's creatures. Singing HU helps us communicate Soul to Soul because HU opens us to God's love connecting all life.

You can hear more stories about these delightful birds and the spiritual lessons animals teach us on the audio- or videocassette of Sri Harold's talk at the 1994 ECK Worldwide Seminar. It is titled "Sunshine and Sparkle."

Singing HU as a love song to God spiritualizes your attention, raises your consciousness, and brings you

HU is truly recognized by all of God's creatures. HU opens us to God's love connecting all life.

direct experiences with the ECK. HU is prayer in pure form.

HU, THE MOST BEAUTIFUL PRAYER

What opens the heart? A number of holy words and prayers can, but one of the best that I've found is the word HU. *I offer it to you and the world today. So offer it to others in the spirit of love.*

—Harold Klemp, *How the Inner Master Works*[4]

A survey conducted by the Gallup organization and published in the March 1994 issue of *Life* magazine reported that nine out of ten Americans say they pray. Ninety-five percent believe their prayers have been answered.

Nondirected prayer is true prayer. It doesn't attempt to change God's mind, other people, or situations.

The Spindrift organization in Lansdale, Pennsylvania, conducted one of the most dramatic studies of prayer. Dr. Larry Dossey, a physician who has practiced medicine for twenty years, reported the findings in the March/April 1994 issue of *Natural Health* magazine.

The group proved that prayer is effective. But they wanted to discover which type of prayer is most beneficial—directed or nondirected. The study defined directed prayer as praying for something specific. Nondirected prayer doesn't try to control the outcome. The study showed that nondirected prayer is more effective. Nondirected prayer is true prayer. It doesn't attempt to change God's mind, other people, or situations.

Sri Harold explains why nondirected prayer is so powerful:

There is a true way to pray, and that way is

*simply to say, "Thy will be done." Because it will
be done anyway. Even better, perhaps, is to be
silent and let God speak to you.*

*What a novel idea: prayer in which you let
God speak to you. To some people it may even
seem* revolutionary.[5]

And life-changing in the most unexpected ways.

Sing HU to Heal a Broken Heart

Singing HU or another holy name of God with love
in your heart is nondirected prayer. Sing HU. Then go
into quiet contemplation.

HU is a holy sound that people of any faith can use
to expand awareness and gain a spiritual perspective —
the mountaintop view of Soul. Try adding HU to your
prayer life. It may help you hear the answers God is
giving.

The story below shows how singing HU brings
comfort during life's most painful experiences.

HU Comforts the Grieving

An ECKist named Mike was asked to speak to a
support group for grieving parents whose children had
died. The night Mike spoke, a Roman Catholic couple
from Ireland attended. They were suffering over the
loss of their daughter. Far away from home, they needed
the comfort of being with others.

Mike taught the group how to sing HU. He led them
through a spiritual exercise in which they imagined
that they entered a river of Light and Sound.

The Catholic couple tried the exercise again at home.
They sang HU together while falling asleep that night.

The wife dreamed that she went to a hospital to be

*Try adding HU
to your prayer
life. It may help
you hear the
answers God
is giving.*

told that her daughter was gone. She interpreted this to mean that her daughter wasn't in pain anymore.

Then the woman saw her daughter with other children. She said to her mother, "I'm fine. I don't hurt anymore. I feel happy, and I have a job to do, working with these children. It's just wonderful here."

Her mother wanted to bring the girl to her father, but the daughter said she couldn't leave. She belonged there. But she invited her mother to visit anytime.

The woman asked how to do this. The girl replied, "Just do what you did to get here. It will bring you here again."

The next morning the woman told her husband and their other children about the dream. Soon the whole family was seeing the girl in their dreams.

The couple were so happy about how singing HU had helped them that they told their Bible-study class. They wanted to share HU with everyone because they had direct experience with this powerful healing tool.[6]

HU was once a secret name for God.

Remarkable. Life-changing. Heart-opening HU.

THE HISTORY OF HU

HU is an ancient name for God, and the sound of HU is one of the sounds of the ECK, the Light and Sound of God. The ECK is the Voice of God that pulses through all creation.

HU was once a secret name for God. The ECK Masters, known as the Ancient Order of Vairagi Adepts *(vie-RAH-gee AD-ehpts)* have reintroduced HU to the modern world.

The Sufis sing HU. There are mentions that some Native American religions sing HU as a form of prayer song.

One of the most fascinating reports of HU is from Africa. ECK Masters taught in Africa thousands of years ago. And many African tribal religions have retained portions of the ECK teachings such as a knowledge of reincarnation, the Light and Sound, and the HU. Knowledge of HU has been passed from generation to generation.

HU is used by many Africans. Whenever people go to the farms or they're at sea, if they need help, they shout HU.

Sam and Irene, two ECKists from Ghana, explain why so many African people have responded favorably to Eckankar and the HU. Sam tells how HU is used by many Africans. He says, "Whenever people go to the farms or they're at sea, if they need help, they shout HU. The idea is that somebody will know that you are in trouble."

The person responding to the call for help will immediately also sing HU to let the distressed one know that help is coming. The two people sing HU to each other while neighbors follow the sound of HU to rescue the person in trouble.

Sam says, "They just know, when you sing HU, help always comes. But they have forgotten that this is really calling on God."

Irene says that in Ghana mothers tell their children to sing HU when they're frightened. They don't know why HU brings such peace, but singing it comforts the babies.

Sam tells a story to show how knowledge of the HU was once a secret.

"I Know about This HU"

A young ECKist had moved to an African city. His father still lived in the country. The young man worried that his father would disapprove of Eckankar. Yet he wanted to share the HU with his father before he died. His father was quite ill.

When the son finally worked up the courage to talk to his father, the old man said, "Wait a minute. I know about this HU."

He explained to his son that whenever any person of royalty died, he was buried in the family grove at night. Mourners formed a procession and carried torches. They entered the grove which was said to be otherwise inaccessible.

Often when Africans learn more about Eckankar, they discover the history of their rituals.

They believed that only light and singing HU would give them access to the grove. These two elements were thought to raise the vibrations of the royal person. Then he could enter the grove of heaven and penetrate the curtain between life and death.

The father was shocked to find that his son knew about HU. It had always been kept secret.

Sam says, "Wherever this tradition came from, it represents the Light and Sound which has been forgotten. But they still do the ceremony."

As Sam and Irene note, often when Africans learn more about Eckankar, they discover the history of their rituals.

Their lost spiritual heritage is restored.

When you sing HU, you tune yourself in to the purest love within life.

SINGING HU FOR PROTECTION AND INNER GUIDANCE

When you sing HU, you tune yourself in to the purest love within life. I had a firsthand experience with the power of HU to protect.

A public parking lot is adjacent to my garage. One afternoon as I drove up and pressed the button for the garage door opener, it didn't work.

This puzzled me. The opener had always worked.

When I got out to open the garage door myself, a man who had been sitting in a car in the parking lot jumped out and rushed toward me.

I heard an inner voice I recognized as the Mahanta, my spiritual guide, give clear commands: "Get back in the car. Lock the door."

I immediately did as I was told.

The man swerved to run in another direction. He seemed to be pretending that he wasn't really pursuing me.

I again pressed the button to open the garage door. This time the door slid up easily.

I parked the car. Got out. Checked behind me. Then pressed the button to close the garage door. I hurried out the side door of the garage and rushed across the yard to my house.

As I tried to unlock the door, I saw the man run into the yard. I froze. No one else was around. Evil seemed to ooze from him. I knew he intended to hurt me.

I began to sing HU very quietly. And I called upon the Mahanta for help.

A field of clear light had surrounded me, and he couldn't see me at all! I was invisible!

My pursuer looked directly at me. But a field of clear light had surrounded me, and he couldn't see me at all! I was invisible!

The puzzled man kept looking my way. He had been watching and knew I had to be there. He actually turned in circles, amazed at not being able to see me where he knew I must be. Finally he ran around the house to find me.

As he searched for me, I moved and hid on the side of the garage. I watched as he returned to his car, jumped in, and sped away.

Stunned and shaken by the experience, I rushed into the house.

Within one minute, my husband arrived home from work early. I ran to tell him about the man chasing me.

My husband said that he had been working when suddenly the Mahanta urged him, with a strong inner nudge, to go home right away. He dropped everything he was doing and ran out to his car, sensing that I was in some kind of danger. If the man had succeeded in attacking me, my husband would have been home in time to help.

We hugged each other and thanked God for this powerful gift of HU and the loving protection of the Mahanta.

When I filed a police report on the incident, I told about everything but becoming invisible. I didn't think the officer would believe that part. But it happened. And that stalker is probably still wondering how his intended prey disappeared.

You can sing HU right now for more love, peace, guidance, and protection in your life.

You don't have to wait until you're frightened to sing HU. You can sing it anywhere, anytime.

A Love Song for Any Occasion

You can sing HU right now for more love, peace, guidance, and protection in your life.

Eckankar offers two audiocassettes in a set, *HU: A Love Song to God.* Tape one features Sri Harold Klemp explaining the benefits of singing HU. Tape two has a recording of three thousand people singing HU. You can play this tape while working, exercising, going to sleep, or at any quiet time.

Try singing HU with the recording when you do a

spiritual exercise or pray to God. It may remind you of the spiritually uplifting Gregorian chants that still touch the hearts of many today.

Watch for subtle or even dramatic changes in your dreams—and in your waking life.

Sing HU to Open Your Heart to God

Here is a spiritual exercise you can use now. Sri Harold shares it in *The Spiritual Exercises of ECK.*

Watch for subtle or even dramatic changes in your dreams— and in your waking life.

Try This Spiritual Exercise Today!

Close your eyes and look to the Spiritual Eye [between your eyebrows]. Sing HU, an old and secret name for God. It is one of the most powerful words for spiritual upliftment that I can give you.

As you sing HU, listen for the Sound. The Sound may be heard in any number of different ways. It can be like a train going by, a bird, buzzing bees, sometimes a flute, or even guitars. The way you hear It just depends on where you are.

These sounds are the action of the Holy Spirit, the ECK, as Its atoms vibrate in the invisible worlds. The Sound you hear is the vibration at the particular level to which you are attuned at the time.

Imagine the Sound purifying you, removing the impurities of Soul. It will bring you an understanding of how your actions have caused your problems. It will also give you an indication of what you can do to unfold and how to figure out the way to do things right.[7]

Questions and Answers

Often people want to know about singing HU. Here's a couple of questions newcomers to the ECK teachings have posed.

The sound of HU origi- nates from the heart of God.

1. *Is it better to sing HU or Om?*

Try singing either sound from time to time. See which one works best for you. Om originates from the level of heaven known as the Mental Plane. The sound of HU originates from the heart of God.

2. *Is there a right or wrong way to sing HU?*

The most important thing to remember while sing- ing HU is to feel love in your heart. You can sing HU as a melody or as a single drawn-out note. Sing it softly for about five to ten minutes, up to thirty minutes. Then sit quietly and listen for sounds. Look for light and colors.

Or as one little boy said: "Sing HU. Get answers."

Sing HU to Visit Heaven Here and Now

Singing HU is at the heart of the Spiritual Exer- cises of ECK and the Soul Travel method for expanding consciousness. The ancient science of Soul Travel has been taught through the ages by the ECK Masters.

In the next chapter, you'll learn basic Soul Travel techniques for gaining heightened spiritual awareness. To live as a vehicle for God's love in a world that sorely needs more love.

20. You Can Soul Travel

In ECK, we don't look for explanations; we look for experience and realization. This comes through Soul Travel, which is simply the separation of the spiritual consciousness from the human consciousness. Through the Spiritual Exercises of ECK, when you are ready, this experience may come about in a number of ways. And once you have this experience, death will never have a hold on you again.

Harold Klemp, *The Golden Heart*[1]

Soul, the real you, can travel or move into a higher state of consciousness where the veil of illusion is lifted. Where you view life with greater perspective. Where you discover your own innate love, courage, wisdom, and God-knowledge.

Here's Golden Key Number 20.
You can Soul Travel.

WHAT'S IT LIKE TO SOUL TRAVEL?

After a vivid, conscious Soul Travel experience, you may struggle for words to tell of your adventures.

An ECKist told about how difficult it can be to describe some Soul Travel experiences.

"I have seen the Light and heard the Sound of God," he said. "But how to convey what happened?

"It might be described as dancing with intense, brightly lit white fireflies going around and through me. It sounded like millions of ice particles hitting glass, with some bouncing off and others crashing through it.

"The Light was the brightest, most intense light. A light beyond the whitest of whites. The roaring sound of the ocean encompassed my total awareness.

"It's possible to go on and on about these experiences, but no human language comes close to describing the actual events."

Access to a higher source of understanding is our spiritual birthright.

HOW CAN SOUL TRAVEL HELP ME?

Soul Travel is useful for achieving the smallest goals or the loftiest. A longtime ECKist remembered one of the first benefits she noticed when learning to Soul Travel consciously. An out-of-the-body perspective enabled her to put on her lipstick without using a mirror!

Soul Travel is a God-given gift that allows us the opportunity to make our lives easier—in the simplest and the most powerful ways.

Access to a higher source of understanding is our spiritual birthright. But first you may need help recognizing when you're Soul Traveling.

How Do People Naturally Experience Soul Travel?

Did you ever drive somewhere, get to the destination, and not remember the interval in between? Somehow your brain and mind were operating the car, but you were somewhere else far away. This movement away from your body is Soul Travel.

Have you ever had a problem at work? You come home tired and frustrated, not knowing what to do? You sit in your easy chair, get quiet, and begin to drift off. Suddenly you have a mountaintop view of the problem and see the bigger picture. You were Soul Traveling at that moment of insight. The mind couldn't help you, but as Soul, your higher awareness did.

Do you remember sitting in a classroom and drifting off into a daydream or fantasy? Your physical body was still there, but you, Soul, traveled into worlds that were much more intriguing than that classroom.

Have you ever awakened with a jolt out of a deep sleep? Every night as you dream, you travel out of your body to visit heaven. Vivid dreams in which you feel as if you're really there are Soul Travel. A sudden awakening signals that Soul is returning to the body very quickly. In these instances you may remember where you've been more easily than when you awaken more slowly.

A sudden awakening signals that Soul is returning to the body very quickly.

Soul Traveling with Your Muse

Here's how Soul Travel worked for Dawn, an Australian ECKist and artist. Tapping into the creative force is an integral part of her work.

One day during Dawn's spiritual exercise, she saw a vision of a winged lion. Afterward, she quickly sketched a rough drawing but couldn't paint it.

So she asked God to show her how.

She described her next contemplation this way:

I saw very clearly a lion walking through a lush rain forest. It had the most beautiful bronzed wings, like the feathery wings of an eagle. The sunlight caught them so that the wings shone golden.

Then I thought, That's fantastic! Now I know about the wings. But how am I going to paint this lion?

Dawn decided to Soul Travel to visit the king of the jungle.

In the city where Dawn lived, there were no zoos with lions. So she decided to Soul Travel to visit the king of the jungle.

Suddenly, as the American Indians describe it, Dawn became the animal. The artist felt her whole body change into a lion's. Her head, chest, and muscles could bear great weight. She had a sense of fur. And a desire to roar!

After Dawn finished her contemplation, she painted the images she had seen — and been. Dawn said, "It was one of the most powerful paintings I've ever done. I called it *The Warrior.*"

When she exhibited the painting at an art gallery, people loved it. The mighty winged lion lumbering through the tropical forest sold very quickly.

Later Dawn continued the winged-lion theme by painting a series she named *The Warrior's Journey Home.*

Soul Travel. Imagination? Fantasy? Visions? Make-believe? What is it?

Imagination, a
Golden Key to Higher Awareness

Imagination is often dismissed by skeptics as a lovely plaything not of much practical use. But the adventure of Soul Travel often begins by using imagination to visualize where you want to go. What you hope to accomplish.

Paul Twitchell, the modern-day founder of Eckankar, referred to Eckankar as the Ancient Science of Soul Travel. He conducted workshops to help people move into higher states of consciousness.

The adventure of Soul Travel often begins by using imagination to visualize where you want to go.

A longtime ECKist named Millie spoke about attending one of these workshops when Paul showed her the role imagination plays in Soul Travel experiences.

Proving the Reality of Soul Travel

Paul Twitchell told the audience attending his workshop that they could decide where they wanted to visit in their Soul Travel journeys.

Millie had always longed to see the pyramids.

She followed Paul's instructions by chanting a sacred word silently while keeping her consciousness focused on where she wanted to go.

She describes the experience this way:

> *The first thing I know, I'm watching this barge that looks like a Cleopatra kind of thing going down the Nile River. And I went off into one of these little trips forgetting all about the pyramids.*

When the spiritual exercise was over, Paul walked around the room and asked people to talk about their experiences.

He came to Millie and asked if she had experienced anything.

She said, "Nope."

Paul looked at her and said, "Mildred!" Then he repeated the question.

Millie answered, "Nothing. I didn't go anywhere."

Paul said, "Well, what were you doing all the time?"

Millie responded, " Oh, nothing. I was just sitting here watching this barge going down the Nile . . . "

Suddenly Millie remembered that the pyramids, where she wanted to go, and the Nile River were connected. So she asked Paul, "Is that it [Soul Travel]? I've been doing that all my life."

He answered, "Well, why don't you admit it, then?"

Millie said, "I didn't know I was doing it. I just thought I was clairvoyant.[2]

When you have a guide, a goal, and a love of learning, Soul Travel becomes an adventure.

THE DIFFERENCE BETWEEN A TOURIST AND A TRAVELER

Millie's story illustrates the difference between unconscious and conscious Soul Travel. You Soul Travel naturally. But when you have a guide, a goal, and a love of learning, Soul Travel becomes an adventure. You transform from a *tourist* into a *traveler.*

The tourist just comes for a visit.

The traveler enjoys new landscape but is motivated by the desire to learn. He studies where he's going. He charts a course but is open to possibilities.

When he gets there, the traveler fits in more easily. He finds the best guide to show him what an ordinary tourist would never see.

With the Spiritual Exercises of ECK and the help of the Mahanta, you can become a conscious Soul Traveler. The Wayshower to the spiritual worlds, the Mahanta, will take you wherever you want or need to go. He's already mastered every state of consciousness you may experience.

Sri Harold describes the value of Soul Travel:

> *We can belong to a group of spiritual beings who operate both in the physical and the invisible worlds.*
>
> *It is quite natural to move back and forth between the planes [levels of heaven] in full consciousness, to see different places, and to converse with beings who have the great wisdom of God. Furthermore, it is a sign that you are moving ahead spiritually in a very fine fashion.*[3]

Getting out of the body is many people's first vivid Soul Travel experience.

MOVING OUT OF THE BODY

Many people who have near-death experiences report that they moved out of their bodies into a realm of light and sound. Sometimes they met beings of light in the form of holy figures from their religion or guardian angels.

Your first out-of-body experience often results in awareness that you are more than a physical body. Moving out of the body can help you to lose your fear of death. You prove to yourself that the real you, Soul, survives without the physical body.

Did you know that you don't have to be near death to move out of your body or to Soul Travel?

But did you know that you don't have to be near death to move out of your body or to Soul Travel?

The Spiritual Exercises of ECK along with guidance from the Mahanta allow you to experience heaven here and now.

Soul Travel with the Spiritual Exercises of ECK

If you know how to love and how to put love into the Spiritual Exercises of ECK, you will then know how to live life correctly. There won't be anything more you can learn about it from reading a book, because at this point you will have the secret of life. The secret of life is love.
—Harold Klemp, *The Golden Heart*[4]

Singing HU is a basic element in many of the Spiritual Exercises of ECK. During Soul Travel people often heal spiritually. They immerse themselves in the ECK. Broken and shattered dreams emerge whole again.

The Spiritual Exercises of ECK are a springboard for conscious Soul Travel experiences. They work on the same principle as physical exercise which increases endurance and helps the body operate more efficiently.

Spiritual exercises increase spiritual vitality, energy, and agility.

Spiritual exercises increase spiritual vitality, energy, and agility. They bring a direct infusion of the Holy Spirit, the ECK, into your being.

Soul Travel Experiences Are Individual

The Mahanta helps you, through the Spiritual Exercises of ECK, to have experiences as you're ready for them. And when they'll help you the most.

Here are some things that may happen when you do the Spiritual Exercises of ECK:

- You see the Light and hear the Sound of God.
- You meet ECK Masters who guide you through the inner worlds of heaven.
- You have a sensation of floating or moving out of the body.

᠄ Your life begins to become more understandable and manageable because you're gaining greater perspective.

᠄ You feel more love than you ever thought was possible.

Is Soul Travel always a dramatic experience?

That sounds terrific, you say. But is Soul Travel always a dramatic experience?

Sometimes you'll feel as if nothing is happening. Not everyone has vivid Soul Travel experiences. At times the experiences are so profound your mind can't remember them.

Other times you'll go through cycles of rest when your inner life is quiet. You can use this period to apply what you've learned.

You may even be one of those who don't need to Soul Travel consciously. Because you're ready for even greater spiritual awareness. Soul Travel is only used in the levels of heaven that are of matter, time, and space.

In dimensions of pure Light and Sound, Soul Travel isn't necessary. You don't have to shift to higher awareness. You're already there.

Sri Harold recommends that you do spiritual exercises daily. They're your lifeline to the love of God.

BASIC ELEMENTS OF THE SPIRITUAL EXERCISES OF ECK

The Spiritual Exercises of ECK is a very helpful book by Sri Harold which gives many different types of spiritual exercises. Some can be done with the eyes closed or open. Others involve applying a spiritual principle to your daily life. *The Spiritual Exercises of ECK* is a tool box for living a quality spiritual life in a material world.

Sri Harold recommends that you do spiritual exercises daily. They're your lifeline to the love of God.

Start with five to ten minutes until you're doing a spiritual exercise for twenty to thirty minutes once each day.

HOW TO DO A SPIRITUAL EXERCISE OF ECK

The following are steps for people of any faith to do a simple spiritual exercise.

Find a time and place where you won't be interrupted. You don't need anything to create atmosphere such as candles, incense, or music. Do the spiritual exercises at the same time every day to establish your spiritual rhythm.

Sit or lie down in a comfortable position. Relax. Take a few deep breaths.

Think of something or someone that makes you feel love. This can be a spouse, child, parent, friend, pet, or an uplifting scene from nature. You also can read a spiritual quote that opens your heart. Fill yourself with the loving presence of God.

Visualize your spiritual master. This can be Jesus, Buddha, Muhammad, or any other holy figure, spiritual guide, or guardian angel. If you want to visualize the Mahanta, use the likeness of the Living ECK Master or envision a blue light or blue star.

Place this image on the inner screen between your eyebrows. This spot is known as the Spiritual Eye or Tisra Til *(TIZ-rah TIL)*. The Spiritual Eye is a doorway to heaven.

Take a few deep breaths. While exhaling, sing HU. You can also chant any holy name for God, the word *God,* or the name of your spiritual master.

After singing HU for about five or more minutes, consider a problem or question. Then sit in quiet con-

Do the spiritual exercises at the same time every day to establish your spiritual rhythm.

templation. Or if you're doing the exercise before sleep, you may drift off into a dream.

Look for the Light. Listen for the Sound. Notice if the image of your spiritual guide speaks to you or you hear an inner voice guiding you in a positive direction. Listen for answers and insights.

Listen for answers and insights.

If you move out of your body, know that you're always protected and loved by God. If your mind drifts and fills with distracting thoughts or fear, sing HU again to focus your attention.

Close your contemplation with the ancient blessing of the ECK Masters, May the blessings be. This is a reminder that you're praying for God's will to be done — not yours.

Write your thoughts, feelings, insights, and experiences in a journal. Over time, you'll be amazed at how you're gaining more clarity, balance, wisdom, and love.

Pay attention to your dreams. Notice the signs life gives you and the words of others that seem specially meant for you. These are all ways God speaks to us.

Be patient. Sometimes nothing dramatic will happen. Daily journal writing helps you to recognize the subtle changes and gifts you're receiving by doing spiritual exercises.

A SIMPLE WAY TO LEARN HOW TO SOUL TRAVEL

You'll find hundreds of Soul Travel techniques in the Eckankar books, particularly those by Sri Harold Klemp.

The following is a spiritual exercise Sri Harold gives to those who want to Soul Travel in full consciousness.

Try This Spiritual Exercise Today!

Just before going to bed at night concentrate your attention on the Spiritual Eye, that place between the eyebrows. Chant HU or God inwardly and silently.

Hold your attention on a black screen in the inner vision, and keep it free of any pictures if at all possible. If you need a substitute for mental pictures flashing up unwantedly, put the image of the Living ECK Master in place of them.

After a few minutes of this, you may hear a faint clicking sound in one ear or the sound of a cork popping. You will suddenly find yourself outside the physical body, looking back at it in the room. Now you are ready for a short journey in the other worlds.

There is nothing to fear, for no harm can come to you while outside the body. Although you may not know it, the Mahanta will be standing by to keep watch over your progress. After a while the Soul body will return and slide gently into the physical self with hardly more than a very light jolt.

If this is not successful the first time, try it again, for the technique works. It has worked for others.[5]

QUESTIONS AND ANSWERS

When people first hear about the exciting prospect of learning how to Soul Travel, they have a lot of questions. Here are a couple of those most frequently asked.

1. *What is the silver cord? Will the silver cord break when you Soul Travel?*

   Or ever the silver cord be loosed, or the golden bowl be broken, or the pitcher be broken at the fountain, or the wheel broken at the cistern.
   Then shall the dust return to the earth as it was: and the spirit shall return unto God who gave it.
   —Ecclesiastes 12:6–7

Sri Harold describes seeing the silver cord when he was a young man in one of his first out-of-body experiences as a "pulsing, luminous cord resembling a plastic garden hose. . . . Its bluish-white glow brightened the dimly lit room."[6]

The silver cord connects the physical body to your inner bodies. At death, the silver cord is severed.

The Bible passage above speaks of when Soul permanently leaves the body at death. But in Soul Travel, Soul temporarily leaves the body, as in going to sleep each night, and the silver cord is not severed. In Soul Travel you are simply expanding your awareness as Soul and learning to live more fully.

In Soul Travel you are simply expanding your awareness as Soul and learning to live more fully.

2. *What's the difference between meditation and contemplation?*

   Another word for contemplation is appreciation.
   —Sri Harold Klemp, *How the Inner Master Works*[7]

Meditation is a valuable spiritual tool on Soul's journey toward God. Many ECKists say that they practiced meditation techniques before learning to contemplate.

Often meditation results in a person's first experience of seeing the Light of God.

Meditators generally combine breathing techniques with stilling the mind and singing a mantra. They passively wait to experience peace, calm, and a state of bliss.

Often meditation results in a person's first experience of seeing the Light of God.

Contemplation, which is practiced in the Spiritual Exercises of ECK, is active prayer. While contemplating, a person can pose questions, visualize scenes, think about a spiritual quote. The result is expanded consciousness and greater love. Soul Travel is one of the results of true contemplation.

SOUL TRAVEL LEADS TO HEIGHTENED AWARENESS

Soul Travel and the Spiritual Exercises of ECK will help you move into higher states of consciousness.

But what is consciousness?

What will happen as your consciousness expands into full awareness of who you truly are?

GOD KNOWLEDGE

Soul in the lower worlds is often asleep. It's asleep with habits which prevent It from walking the direct path to God. We are trying to rise above this level in awareness. We are trying to reach a higher consciousness.

—Harold Klemp, *Stories to Help You See God in Your Life*[1]

21. Expanding Your Consciousness Is the New Frontier

"Knowledge can bring many things, for knowledge comes from mind expansion, but the consciousness of the heart brings love, and love brings all things."

—Rebazar Tarzs to Paul Twitchell,
The Key to ECKANKAR[2]

D o you yearn to transcend the everyday and the ordinary? If so, then welcome to the incredible world of adventures in consciousness.

Here's Golden Key Number 21.
Expanding your consciousness is the new frontier.

Having an expanded consciousness allows you to handle any situation better, to enjoy life more fully. With an expanded consciousness you can achieve your greatest spiritual potential.

WHAT IS CONSCIOUSNESS?

You define yourself and everything around you through the lens of consciousness. Soul is a unit of awareness, a spark of the Divine. Consciousness is what Soul has experienced and realized so far in Its journey back to God.

Consciousness is a Soul's world view, Its store of knowledge over lifetimes. Consciousness affects Soul's capacity to give and receive love. Your state of consciousness defines your world, creates illusions, and fuels the journey to self-awareness.

Each spiritual leader can take his followers as far as he has gone in his state of consciousness.

Even heaven is a state of consciousness.

HOW TO EXPERIENCE HIGHER STATES OF CONSCIOUSNESS

God's love is limitless. It's as impossible for our human state of consciousness to accept the infinite love of God as it would be to pour an ocean into a teacup.

The Mahanta has the highest state of God-Consciousness, and he helps you expand your consciousness to accept more and more of God's love. By expanding your consciousness, you gain a higher level of consciousness.

Each spiritual leader can take his followers as far as he has gone in his state of consciousness. Jesus achieved the Christ Consciousness. Buddha achieved the Buddha Consciousness. Those who follow these spiritual masters and live their teachings of love can aspire to these states of consciousness.

As you have more experiences with the Light and Sound of God, however, your state of consciousness may expand beyond the limits of your current religion. This brings the excitement and change of new horizons.

You'll hardly recognize the person you were—even a month earlier—after you've started to expand your consciousness with the help of the Mahanta. For love will be transforming you into a greater spiritual being.

Expansion of consciousness is the new frontier where science and spirituality meet.

THE NEW FRONTIER

Scientists are developing models for consciousness. Expansion of consciousness is the new frontier where science and spirituality meet. The ancient ECK teachings have been on the cutting edge of this frontier for eons.

A student (chela) of the Mahanta, the Living ECK Master has the opportunity to move beyond the human consciousness, naturally and without the use of drugs or psychic methods.

Some Souls achieve cosmic consciousness. This is a heightened form of human awareness in which one begins to vividly experience the connections within all life. People who have entered cosmic consciousness often think that they've discovered the ultimate consciousness of God.

But there's more. Much more!

CONSCIOUSNESS IS MORE THAN A MERIT BADGE

Using words to describe levels of consciousness we haven't achieved is like naming mountains that we merely dream about climbing. Higher, or expanded, consciousness can't be labeled, much less understood, by those who don't have it.

Expanded consciousness isn't a badge or a title. It's a capacity to love, and a wisdom and an understanding of life that must be won every moment of every day. People can and do slip from higher into lower states of consciousness when they allow the passions of the mind to dull their spiritual senses.

Yet it's impossible to judge someone's state of consciousness. For only God knows what is truly in a person's heart.

OUR WORLD REFLECTS
OUR STATE OF CONSCIOUSNESS

Planets, countries, cultures, and neighborhoods form states of consciousness also. This is known as group consciousness. For the people who share a group consciousness, it colors their view of others outside that group.

Life is about living with our own creations. Our world is shaped and formed by consciousness.

Group consciousness expands too. Nations can become kinder and gentler — or not. Those in leadership positions often reflect the group consciousness of a country or geographic area.

CHANGING YOUR STATE OF CONSCIOUSNESS

Life is about living with our own creations. Taking full responsibility for everything in our universe. It's about realizing that until we change our state of consciousness, nothing else can improve. Our world is shaped and formed by consciousness.

There are two main impediments that keep us from changing our state of consciousness. They create the illusion that we're ruled by the hand of fate. They are the victim consciousness and the social consciousness.

We're cocreators of our own universe. Ignorance of that fact results in the victim consciousness. We forget that our thoughts, words, and actions created the present. When we do not take responsibility for anything in our lives, we become the victim. We feel nothing is our fault; things are done to us, not by us. Yet we can overcome this limited state of consciousness by taking responsibility for the events in our lives, one by one.

The social consciousness causes us to value approval more than a greater awareness of God.

Another key to overcoming the victim consciousness is gratitude. When we look for the love, the gift, in every situation, we open up to greater possibilities.

The second major barrier to changing our consciousness is the social consciousness. It makes us fearful of what others will think.

The social consciousness causes us to value approval more than a greater awareness of God. It's a form of blindness that many Souls stay in for lifetimes.

OVERCOMING SPIRITUAL BLINDNESS

The following story is from an ECKist named Calynn who overcame the snares of victim and social consciousness to experience the love of God.

Calynn always enjoyed going to Eckankar seminars. As she prepared for one that was to be in New York, she realized that it was time for her to face a new challenge. Calynn is physically blind and usually travels with her guide dog Trina. Yet in large crowds, Trina often became confused and distracted. She was also hard to handle on an airplane. Traveling with Trina had become a burden for both of them.

Calynn had made arrangements to share a hotel room with some friends at the seminar. But when she arrived, she discovered that her friends weren't there as planned.

As she sat in her hotel room alone in the big city, Calynn thought of all the worst things that could happen. She fought feelings of panic. Then she called to the

Mahanta by his spiritual name, Wah Z *(WAH zee)*. Instantly, she felt his comforting presence.

Calynn knew that she was facing an important choice. She described her thoughts this way:

> *My old pattern would have been to just sit and wait for someone to come and help me. I began this adventure wanting to challenge those patterns of helplessness and self-imposed limitations.*
>
> *It seemed such an enormous problem. Could I trust the ECK?*

In her anguish and loneliness, Calynn started to sing HU.

SING HU TO CHANGE YOUR STATE OF CONSCIOUSNESS

Singing HU expands the consciousness to allow a person to accept the love of God and see situations from a higher viewpoint.

After a few minutes of singing HU, Calynn decided to take charge of the situation. Her friends might be delayed for hours or all night. She didn't want to sit alone feeling terrified.

And she was getting hungry.

So this blind woman had to pick up the telephone in New York City, call a stranger, and ask for help.

Calynn reached for the phone. She called the front desk, explained her situation, and asked for help. While she waited for someone to come, she inwardly saw the inner image of Wah Z smiling at her.

She said, "I felt at that moment such love and support pouring into me. My hard, fearful heart began to melt. Whatever happened, I knew that I was going to be OK."

Soon a gentleman from the security department knocked on Calynn's door. He helped her go down to the seminar where she connected with other ECKists who would be able to escort her.

Calynn expressed what she learned with these words:

> *My needs caused me to reach out for help, and by doing so I was able to allow others to serve Spirit by helping me.*
>
> *This weekend taught me that being blind and needing a lot of help to get around physically is a way of serving. I had always felt as if I had nothing to give and no way to serve. But I know now that's not true.*
>
> *The ECK has given me a very special way to be a channel [for God's love]. I now can see the true reason and mission I have chosen for this lifetime.*

Calynn had a spiritual healing. The Mahanta opened her heart to receive the love around her.

This is how consciousness expands.

That same weekend, Calynn received another initiation into the Light and Sound of God. Greater awareness and her next initiation went hand in hand.

It often works that way in Eckankar.

THE INITIATIONS OF ECK

You are the hero of your journey home to God. Along the way, with the Mahanta as your spiritual guide, you'll go through tests and lessons. As you experience life and become more aware of who you are and why you're here, the Mahanta increases the flow of the ECK, the Light and Sound of God, into your being.

You are the hero of your journey home to God.

When the Mahanta opens your spiritual vision and hearing to receive a significantly greater level of divine love, this is known as an initiation.

THE FIRST INITIATION

The First Initiation starts a purifying process as Soul begins Its adventures into conscious evolution.

After a spiritual student comes under the Mahanta's care and becomes a member of Eckankar, a miraculous experience occurs. In the dream state the Mahanta opens this Soul to a greater flow of the Light and Sound. The person may or may not remember this spiritual awakening, but it's a sacred time for Soul. This is the First Initiation.

Often the new initiate finds that life speeds up. Over many lifetimes we create debits and credits with life (called karma). The First Initiation starts a purifying process as Soul begins Its adventures into conscious evolution.

THE SECOND INITIATION

After two years of study in Eckankar, a student of the Mahanta may ask for the Second Initiation. This is an inner and outer recognition of spiritual progress.

Inwardly, the Mahanta links Soul directly with the Light and Sound of God. It's a bond of the heart in which the person at last has the opportunity to become free of the chains of karma and reincarnation. To come under the protection and care of the Mahanta who regulates the payment of karmic debt.

By the Second Initiation most people know if Eckankar is the spiritual path for them. The Second Initiate makes a commitment to work consciously with the Mahanta toward Soul's greatest good.

For various reasons, sometimes to keep harmony

in the family, the person may continue to be a member of another religion and privately study the ECK teachings. There are even ministers of other religions who are initiates of Eckankar. Their spiritual calling is to quietly bring the Light and Sound of God to those in their flock.

If the Second Initiate in Eckankar wants to start teaching Eckankar classes, he is now eligible to become a trained Eckankar teacher, or Arahata *(ah-rah-HAH-tah)*.

The second initiation is officiated by an ECK Initiator. This is a member of the Eckankar clergy who is appointed by the Mahanta to perform this sacred ceremony that anchors the initiation in the physical world. The ceremony lasts about thirty to sixty minutes. At the outer initiation, the chela is given a personal word which serves to lift Soul to a higher vibration of the ECK.

A personal word serves to lift Soul to a higher vibration of the ECK.

The inner initiation can happen before, after, or during the outer initiation, but both are necessary to complete the cycle.

Higher Initiations

Initiations are golden keys for expanding one's consciousness to higher and higher levels. Higher Initiates are those who have received the Fifth Initiation and above. They often teach classes about Eckankar and take leadership positions in their local ECK communities.

After the Fifth Initiation and additional training a chela is eligible to become an ordained member of the Eckankar clergy. Male and female clergy, married or unmarried, are trained to perform the four ECK celebrations of life: consecrations (similar to baptism), weddings, memorial services, and rites of passage (similar to confirmations).

A minimum of seventeen years of spiritual study in Eckankar is needed to be eligible for the Fifth Initiation and then training as a member of the ECK clergy. Some Higher Initiates, however, choose not to perform clergy functions. They serve silently in their communities as vehicles for God's love in the world.

Spiritual Aid

A remarkable benefit of having the Mahanta as your spiritual guide is that you can write about your spiritual life or any question or problem you're having in a letter to Sri Harold.

Divine Spirit will often answer your letter whether you mail it or not. After writing the letter, pay attention to your dreams and subtle experiences and occurrences in your daily life, such as the words of others. They can hold clues to answering your question or solving your problem.

The Spiritual Exercises of ECK are also amazing tools the Mahanta offers to bring about spiritual healing. He goes to the root spiritual causes of your problems—even ones that stem from past lifetimes.

The Mahanta is the only one who can help you do this.

Experience it for yourself.

The Mahanta goes to the root spiritual causes of your problems—even ones that stem from past lifetimes.

Spiritual Exercises Expand Consciousness

The Spiritual Exercises of ECK are a treasure whose value we might overlook because of their simplicity. But they are your lifeline to the Word of God. The Mahanta has

*put this key to higher states of consciousness
in your hand.*

—Harold Klemp, *The Spiritual Exercises of ECK*[3]

Want to increase your physical stamina and vitality? Try physical exercise.

Want to increase your spiritual energy and agility? Try spiritual exercise.

The Spiritual Exercises of ECK are your key to having the love, self-discipline, and wisdom to get more out of life than you ever thought possible. As the mainstay of the Spiritual Exercises of ECK, singing HU, the sacred love song to God, opens your heart to expand consciousness by receiving the love of God.

Try This Spiritual Exercise Today!

If you have an uncomfortable experience or dream—or one you don't understand—take it into contemplation. Begin by singing HU for a few minutes. Then rewind the dream or experience, and run it through your mind. Next, visualize a door that opens into golden sunlight. This is the Light of God.

Now take the uncomfortable experience from the darkness; take it from the silence and solitude through the open doorway where it is dissolved by the Light and Sound of God.

This exercise can get you in the habit of looking for a brighter, more creative world, where you can find more inner satisfaction. With the help of the Inner Master, the Mahanta, you are learning to take charge of your life. You are becoming the aware Soul, the creator of your own worlds.[4]

With the help of the Inner Master, the Mahanta, you are learning to take charge of your life.

THE WORLDS WHERE CONSCIOUSNESS EXPANDS

You are about to visit worlds as real as the one in which your physical body lives right now. You move into these universes every night.

Stay aware. You're entering the incredible field of your own dreams.

22. Your Dreams Are Real

Dreams touch every level of our life. They may let us glimpse the future, or give suggestions for healing, or share insights into our relationships. Above all, they can and will steer us more directly toward God.

—Harold Klemp, *The Living Word,* Book 2[1]

*E*verybody dreams.

If you're not paying attention to your dreams, you're missing the other half of your life.

In *Writers Dreaming* author Naomi Epel interviewed successful writers who recounted the dream origins of characters, plots, and style, and how dreams had influenced their work. She calls dreams the "artist in your basement."[2]

Here's Golden Key Number 22.

Your dreams are real.

Dreams are a state of consciousness. They're clay that you, the dreamer of your life, use to sculpt your universe. Dreams are real, vital experiences. At times they have changed the course of history. And they can change the course of your life.

DREAMS HAVE IMMEASURABLY
ENRICHED THE HUMAN CONSCIOUSNESS

Dimitri Mendeleyev napped and dreamed the periodic table of elements. Niels Bohr's sketch of a dream formed the basis for his Nobel Prize-winning work on atomic theory. Einstein's theory of relativity resulted from years of meditating on the meaning of a childhood dream.

Civilization is directly indebted to dreams for its existence.

Civilization is directly indebted to dreams for its existence. The Holy Spirit communicated with primitive life through dream images. Sri Harold Klemp, the spiritual leader of Eckankar, explains how human language originated through dreams.

> We take language for granted. Where do words come from? Our anthropologists would probably run to Africa and trace the genetic tree of one group or another, then make all kinds of suppositions about what point people left off grunting. . . . But it never occurs to people that much of the early information about language came to people from the dream state.
>
> This teaching came through the Holy Spirit, working through Its messengers, the ECK Masters.[3]

Dreams have always been with us. A vehicle for God to guide us to our true destiny of realizing our full potential as spiritual beings.

So, why don't more people recognize the significance of dreams?

LOST DREAMS

Adolescent Plains Indians of North America were sent on a vision quest to meet in a dream the guardian spirit who would protect them for the rest of their lives.

Some dreamers dreamed a song of protection. Upon returning to their tribes, the youth, now a man, sang his song for the rest of the tribe. Dreams belonged not only to the dreamer, but to the dreamer's community.[4]

These people knew that dreams are another way God communicates with us. Dreams are designed to teach us how to love. Too bad most of us have forgotten how important they are.

The ancient Egyptians, Sumerians, Greeks, and Romans all believed that the gods guided them through dreams. The Old Testament of the Bible tells stories of dreams from God that inspired and prophesied. Later writers such as Aristotle and Cicero attempted to debunk the spiritual nature of dreams.

Yet early Christians believed that God guided the fledgling church through dreams and visions. In the fifth century, St. Jerome, according to historian Morton T. Kelsey, mistranslated a Hebrew word that made it appear working with dreams was forbidden by the Bible. Author Wilse B. Webb writes, "As a result, dreams were categorized with witchcraft for more than a thousand years."[5]

Early Christians believed that God guided the fledgling church through dreams and visions.

In other religious traditions only the dreams of the politically or socially powerful were valued. Wise, insightful, prophetic dreams were thought to be beyond the grasp of commoners.

Eventually, in most cultures, dreams were lost as a source of truth. Today we are learning more about the mechanics of dreams.

WHAT SCIENCE TELLS US TODAY ABOUT DREAMS

Modern-day science and psychology continue the fascination with dreams. But in an effort to observe and dissect dreams, the spiritual nature of a dreamer's experience has been overlooked. Dreamers are hooked up to equipment in laboratories where science proves that everyone dreams, including mammals and some birds and reptiles. Our eyes move quickly while we're dreaming. Scientists can detect dreams by observing this rapid eye movement (REM).

During dream time, which is now known to be essential, certain brain cells turn off and others turn on. The brain seems to be processing information in different but equally important ways while dreaming. Adults who are deprived of REM sleep can't function well.

It seems that we're physiologically programmed to perceive dreams as real experiences.

Dreaming is indeed proving to be the other vital half of our lives.

Another interesting discovery is that for the brain, dreams are reality. Our eyes follow actions in dreams as if we were awake, yet our bodies are mostly immobilized so we don't fully react to dream images.[6]

It seems that we're physiologically programmed to perceive dreams as real experiences.

TAKING SCIENCE A STEP FURTHER

Through my study what I have found is that all life is a dream. The dream of everyday living is no more or less a dream than what happens at night during the sleep state. A dream a dream, but it is also reality, as real as everyday life out here.

—Harold Klemp, *How the Inner Master Works*[7]

Eckankar is unique as a modern-day religion which teaches that dreams are real experiences. The only difference between experiences in dreams and those we have when we're awake is that our physical bodies are asleep for dreams. Both the dreaming and waking states are valid realities.

While we dream, we visit heaven!

Dreams are happening all the time whether we remember them or not. Sri Harold explains it like this:

> *We assume that when we go to sleep, we're just starting a dream.*
>
> *Actually we're tapping into the expanded awareness of Soul as It is existing—as we all are existing—on the inner planes, simultaneously with our existence on the earth. . . . Soul is multidimensional. It shares all the aspects of God. Soul can be everywhere at all times, and all places at the same time.*[8]

And where are we when we dream?

In heaven. The afterlife. Areas of higher consciousness. We experience the same vistas people who have near-death and out-of-body experiences find.

While we dream, we visit heaven!

If only we could remember.

WHY WE CAN'T REMEMBER MOST DREAMS

Some brain cells turn on while we dream, and others shut off. Many of the nonfunctioning cells are those that are responsible for memory. This is why, upon awakening, most people immediately forget 95 percent of what they dream.[9]

This physical process of censoring dream information is a reflection of a function of the mind called the mental censor. The mental censor blocks out most dream experiences and keeps us from realizing what we're unable or unwilling to see about ourselves through dreams. This censoring process causes dreams to be cloaked in symbols and images that have to be deciphered. We remember dream experiences with distortions, in fragments, or not at all.

But, why?

Sometimes our egos don't want to know the full truth about hidden motives, actions, and desires. Often we can't bear to remember the roles we've played in creating sad circumstances today through our past actions. So we remember a dream that shows us how someone wronged us, but not the other way around. Only every once in a while does the truth seep through.

Dreams are meant to be doorways to expanded consciousness.

Other times our everyday consciousness could be stunned into inaction or passivity by the beauty, wonder, and love available in the inner worlds. Therefore the censor "protects" us from knowing too much too soon.

Dreams are meant to be doorways to expanded consciousness. So, how do we get past the censor to walk through those dream doors?

MEET THE DREAM MASTER

The Holy Spirit works through the Mahanta to open the human heart to divine love. The Mahanta, the Living ECK Master is the Dream Master. He may at times be perceived by the dreamer as a trusted holy figure or a being of light, but more often he looks just like Sri Harold Klemp does in the physical. At times the Dream Master is simply felt as an invisible presence in dreams coaching Soul to observe something for Its spiritual benefit.

The Dream Master uses your own state of consciousness to shape dreams into lessons, stories, movie plots, or whatever will get and hold your attention. The Dream Master designs each dream to teach you something about yourself and life. About your relationship with God.

BYPASSING THE CENSOR

One of the most remarkable things the Dream Master does is to bypass the censor. By singing HU, you can ride a wave of divine love into states of higher awareness. You can become a dream catcher. Catching dreams in purest form. It's incredibly thrilling to do this!

Your dreams eventually become Soul journeys. At the same time, the images and symbols of dreams stop being obscure. They begin to provide direct access to divine guidance from the Holy Spirit for the most minute and important aspects of your daily life.

Dream guidance may lead to your next job, love, a smarter way to invest your money, clues to better health, or any number of essentials. Eckankar literature is filled with stories of how dreams have led to healings spiritual insights, and journeys into the vast heavenly worlds.

The Dream Master will never enter your dreams without your permission. But just ask, and he'll be there.

IMPROVING THE QUALITY OF YOUR DREAMS

People who begin working with the Dream Master report increased dream memory, vividness, and significance.

People who begin working with the Dream Master report increased dream memory, vividness, and significance.

Author Peter Occhiogrosso wrote of his brief involvement in the dream teachings of Eckankar. His study of these teachings brought an unequaled experience of dreams. Occhiogrosso states that at no other time in his life, including years of standard psychotherapy, had he experienced such abundant dreams, vividly recalled, sometimes in full color, and frequently occurring in otherworldly settings. He also observed subtle changes in himself which he found difficult to explain but "impossible to overlook or to ascribe to accident." He still recalls some of the dreams he had during his Eckankar dream study.[10]

But the Dream Master can also pull the curtain over things we're not ready to face. He serves as a filter to balance the impact of uncensored dreams on our emotional, mental, and physical well-being.

He is the wise tour guide to adventures in your own vast worlds of consciousness. You can expect miraculous changes in your life when you begin working with the Dream Master.

You may have spiritual healings that may lead to improved physical, emotional, and mental health.

BENEFITS OF DREAMING YOUR WAY THROUGH LIFE

Here's a partial list of the types of experiences you may have when you start working with the Dream Master and using the spiritual tools of Eckankar.

- move out of your body into lucid dreaming and beyond to experience parallel universes, to enjoy adventures in multidimensional living
- lose your fear of death
- go on spiritual assignments for the Mahanta to serve other Souls who need assistance
- learn to interpret dream messages from God
- have spiritual healings that may lead to improved physical, emotional, and mental health

- experience the effects of actions (karma) in dreams instead of physically
- meet others and even remember shared dreams
- remember past lives that are affecting you today
- understand why you have recurring dreams
- understand the true meaning of nightmares and how to deal with dreams of intrusion
- see future possibilities through prophetic dreams
- learn to take responsibility for your life by changing the outcome of your dreams and ultimately mastering your own destiny
- discover waking dreams and Golden-tongued Wisdom—how to work with dreamlike aspects by observing signs, symbols, and divine intervention in daily life
- learn to work with daydreams and Soul Travel to move naturally into states of heightened awareness for keener insights and problem solving
- study the secret teachings of the Holy Spirit that are only taught at heavenly schools, Temples of Golden Wisdom

Begin by Learning to Interpret Your Dreams

You're the best interpreter of your own dreams.

Although you may be tempted to buy books that tell you what dream symbols are supposed to mean, remember one size does not fit all, or even most. You're the best interpreter of your own dreams.

You can begin to remember and interpret your dreams by starting with the Spiritual Exercises of ECK and a sense of wonder. It's as simple as having a pen and paper—a dream journal—by your bedside.

Before going to sleep, sing HU to spiritualize your

You'll soon discover that dreams can prepare you for upcoming events.

attention and lead you gently into heaven. When you awaken, even if it's during the night, make notes about your dreams right away.

Dreams usually relate to what's happening in your life now. So, write in your journal about the day's events. What are your fears, thoughts, challenges?

The dream often is telling you how to become more in tune with the high spiritual nature that is your birthright. Reread your journal to see patterns and cycles. You'll soon discover that dreams can prepare you for upcoming events.

THE DREAM TEACHINGS OF ECKANKAR

In addition to your personal inner exploration of dreams, the ECK writings contain a vast treasure chest of absolutely amazing knowledge and insight into dreams.

Sri Harold has written the ECK dream discourses. These are two years' worth of monthly discourses that members of Eckankar can study to help them understand their dreams. By using the Eckankar materials referenced in the bibliography for this chapter, you'll discover some of the most important material ever taught about dreams.

Prove it to yourself.

SPIRITUAL EXERCISES
UNLOCK THE SECRETS OF DREAMS

Now try the following spiritual exercise to help you find messages from God hidden in your nightly dreams.

Try This Spiritual Exercise Today!

At some level Soul knows everything. If there is something that you would like to bring into consciousness, here is a way to get help.

Before you go to sleep, relax and decide that upon awakening you will have an answer to whatever it is that you desire.

When you awaken it will be in the forefront of your thoughts. At the moment of slipping from or into sleep, you are opened to truth and in direct contact with it. It is at this point that you will perceive your answer.

Immediately make note of it in your dream journal.

We know that there is an answer for every situation that comes up in life. There is always a way, somehow. What holds us back is our attitudes.

Learn the value of doing a spiritual exercise just before retiring or upon awakening. It works to your advantage during these times of change in conscious awareness.[11]

At the moment of slipping from or into sleep, you are opened to truth and in direct contact with it.

QUESTIONS AND ANSWERS

You've explored only a tiny corner of your vast field of dreams. But you probably have a lot of questions about them. Here are a few that other dreamers have asked.

1. What are nightmares and why do we have them?

Nightmares relate to something going on in your

Many children are remembering past lives when they're having a nightmare.

life right now. The so-called "bad" dream may be there to help you conquer a fear. Often nightmares are memories. Many children, especially between the ages of two to five, are remembering past lives when they're having a nightmare.

An ECKist named Benjamin tells about what he learned from one of his nightmares.

> *Once I had a bad dream about a tornado. It really scared me. I was in a tornado. Not even spiders are that scary. Nope. Tornadoes are the worst.*
>
> *So, in my dream this big tornado went right through our street. Our house and everything was wrecked.*
>
> *Everyone was badly hurt except for us. We were the only people on the street that weren't really hurt. We had some cuts or scratches, but we didn't have any broken bones or anything. Nothing happened to me. I was completely fine.*

Benjamin had this dream after a tornado swept past his classroom. He and the other children stayed safe in the music room listening to the sirens wail. The whole experience left Benjamin with a lingering sense of fear.

Later Benjamin realized something important. The nightmare showed him that he had been safe during the storm. Benjamin's nightmare helped him remember and understand a little bit more about God's love for him.

This essentially is the purpose of dreams. Even nightmares are trying to tell you something for your spiritual good.

2. How can we have dreams of the future?

When you have a prophetic dream, you as Soul move into possibilities. The dream helps you, from a mountaintop view of higher consciousness, to see that train coming down the track. Then you have a choice of staying for the experience, avoiding it, or altering your actions.

To the Top of the Mountain

Human language inadequately describes what lies ahead on your own journey toward the heart of God. But the next six chapters attempt to provide you with a road map for Eckankar's direct, adventurous, heart-opening path to becoming a Co-worker with God.

LOVE

Love is God.

> —Rebazar Tarzs to the seeker,
> *Stranger by the River*[1]

23. THE KEY TO YOUR SUCCESS IS SETTING SPIRITUAL GOALS

Wayfarer, God has many levels of spiritual attainment, but concern thyself only with the true Home. Be not afraid to see God, for in desiring God thou hast true desire!

—Rebazar Tarzs to the seeker,
Stranger by the River[2]

*D*id you know that you can set spiritual goals? Most people think that their spiritual life just happens. They think they must accept whatever they were taught to believe. What everyone else seems to believe.

Usually it's not until something traumatic happens that people begin to look around and wonder what the spiritual life is all about.

Here's Golden Key Number 23.
You can set spiritual goals today and change your life.

You don't have to wait till life has brought you to your knees. You can begin to infuse your life with more spiritual meaning right now.

In a November 28, 1994, *Newsweek* article it was reported that 58 percent of the people polled said they felt the need to experience spiritual growth.[3]

Are you looking for deeper spiritual meaning? Setting spiritual goals is an important key to finding greater awareness, peace, and love.

It's Time to Break the Illusion

You came forth from the Creator as Soul, a divine spark of God. You were sent by God to this world to gain experience. To learn how to plumb the depths and heights of God's love.

Earth is a schoolroom designed to help you find love in yourself, others, and God. For many lifetimes you have lived with the illusions that kept you thinking the physical world is all there is.

But you're not bound to earth and earthly ways.

You can even find a way, one that has been in existence for centuries, to help you find deeper meaning and more love in your life.

Spiritual Goals and Eckankar

You pick a goal, such as God-Realization. Then you open yourself to the Holy Spirit, the ECK, and make your way directly through life to accomplish the goal. There will be help along the way. You take it as it comes, even though it may not seem to fit into your beliefs up to that time.

—Harold Klemp, *The Golden Heart*[4]

In Eckankar, spiritual goals are based on ancient teachings about how the Holy Spirit operates in our lives. These goals are designed to guide you step-by-step to reach your full potential as a spiritual being.

Whether or not you ever formally become a student of Eckankar, efforts to achieve spiritual goals will improve your spiritual life. In the next chapters of this book, use the information that seems to best fit into your own plan for spiritual development.

Efforts to achieve spiritual goals will improve your spiritual life.

But above all, have a plan.

SETTING SPIRITUAL GOALS
IMPROVES THE QUALITY OF YOUR LIFE

As soon as you begin setting spiritual goals—and getting serious about achieving them—you'll notice subtle, perhaps even dramatic changes for the better.

The story below is an example of how setting a spiritual goal begins to improve the quality of your daily life.

Gloria had an experience that helped her see how fear was ruling her life. One night she did a Spiritual Exercise of ECK (a form of nondirected prayer). She asked the Mahanta, her inner spiritual guide, to help her discover the source of her fears. In a dream following the spiritual exercise, Gloria saw the Mahanta, Sri Harold Klemp. He gave her stacks of paper and said, "Well, you have a lot of fear. Here it is, all catalogued and ready to read."

Gloria told the Mahanta that she didn't want this information. But the Inner Master persisted, saying,

Well, you've been asking about your fears, so I thought you'd appreciate having a copy of them all. Here they are, in chronological order. All the

fear you have ever experienced in all your life-times.

With those words, he handed her the papers.

They passed the papers back and forth between them a few times. Then the Mahanta said, "I'll just leave this here so you can refer to it anytime you want to."

Gloria woke up knowing that she could choose between letting go of fear or staying with her old habits and attitudes. She firmly set a spiritual goal to conquer fear.

At work that week, Gloria found herself having to point out a budget problem to her superiors. They didn't like what she had to tell them. Usually Gloria would have felt insecure if her job performance was questioned. This time, though, she remembered that she had set a spiritual goal to face fear. She stayed calm.

In a tense meeting with her managers, Gloria explained how she had come to her conclusions. When she finished, the person who was in charge of the contract said, "Gloria, I blew it! You did everything that was supposed to be done in this matter."

The meeting broke out into a pandemonium of angry accusations. Again, Gloria remembered to stay composed. In a short time, her manager said, "Gloria, what do you think our true situation is here?"

Now her resolve was getting the ultimate test. No one had ever asked her opinion about such important matters. But she kept up her courage and gave an analysis.

Soon the meeting broke up, and everyone went away to think over the information Gloria had given.

Gloria realized that she had what she described as "an inner peace that far exceeded what my coworkers considered normal. I simply felt a connection within that overcame the hysteria around me."

All of life is designed to teach you about God's love for you.

The next morning when her manager told her that the problem had been resolved, Gloria thanked the Mahanta for helping her through a maze of fear that had been holding her back.[5]

As you can see from the story above, the situations you face in everyday life are the very things that help you achieve spiritual goals. You don't learn about God only in church on Sunday. Or even from holy scriptures. All of life is designed to teach you about God's love for you.

GOING FOR SPIRITUAL GOALS

There are many spiritual goals that you might choose. Here are a few long-term spiritual goals that we will discuss in later chapters.

1. **Spiritual Survival:** To become a spiritual survivor linked directly to the Light and Sound of God.

2. **Truth and Wisdom:** To gain truth and wisdom through direct experiences with the Holy Spirit.

3. **Divine Love:** To become a vehicle for God by giving, accepting, and returning divine love to all life.

4. **Self-Realization:** To gain Self-Realization and spiritual freedom. To know who you are and discover your purpose in life.

5. **God-Realization:** To become one with the Holy Spirit and a Co-worker with God. To have the full capacity to love as God loves.

More about these later.

HELP ALONG THE WAY

The Spiritual Exercises of ECK are designed to help you achieve your own spiritual goals. Try the one below to get started on your journey.

Try This Spiritual Exercise Today!

First choose something you want in your life or pick a problem that needs to be dealt with. Then set clear goals.

First picture the goal clearly— what you want to do or be in life.

Second, ask yourself the following questions. Your goals must pass four tests. (1) Are they specific? (2) Are they realistic? (3) Can the results be verified? and (4) Do they give a date for completion?

Next, of course, you must begin working toward your goals in your daily life. As you do this, you can also use visualization or daydreaming to help you. First picture the goal clearly—what you want to do or be in life. Then fill the picture with unbounded love, because love is the true creative force that removes all limitations.

Practically all famous or successful people in this world have done this. The ECK Masters have set the goal of God-Realization and becoming a Co-worker with God for the chela of ECK. Holding this picture with love can pull you through rough times.[6]

QUESTIONS AND ANSWERS

Now that you've become acquainted with a few long-term spiritual goals, you may have some questions about them.

1. *Why do we need to set spiritual goals? Doesn't our spiritual progress happen naturally?*

Setting goals may seem like a mental process that doesn't quite fit a spiritual prize.

But increasing your spiritual awareness is like anything else in life. It takes effort. It takes commitment, persistence, humility, and a willingness to explore areas that most human beings don't even know exist.

Set clear objectives and receive specific inner and outer guidance on how to achieve your spiritual goals.

Eckankar is unique in that it's a religion that doesn't just encourage people to drift toward God. With the Mahanta, the Living ECK Master as your inner and outer teacher, you are given personalized guidance for spiritual development. Together with the Inner Master you can set clear objectives and receive specific inner and outer guidance on how to achieve your spiritual goals.

2. *Are spiritual goals the same for everyone?*

Each Soul is on an individual journey to God. As you continue with your own personal spiritual development, your goals may change.

Before you continue reading, take a moment to jot down your own spiritual goals now. Do you want more love in your life? Are you looking for meaning and purpose? Would you like to overcome obstacles such as fear or anger that are keeping you from mastering your spiritual destiny?

Whatever your spiritual goals might be, you'll find ways to achieve them if your resolve is firm and your love for God is strong.

Ready? Let's take a look at some spiritual goals the teachings of Eckankar can help you achieve.

24. You Can Master Spiritual Survival Skills

*Man must regain his adventuresome spirit,
and then he will want to live spiritually,
boldly and dangerously. Then he will not be
caught up in a great drive for security. Security? What security? Does anyone have security
without God? Is not the greatest security the
strength of Spirit?*

—Rebazar Tarzs to the seeker,
Stranger by the River[1]

The Goal of Spiritual Survival: *Become a
spiritual survivor linked directly to the Light and
Sound of God.*

M ost people don't know there are such things
as spiritual survival skills.

Here's Golden Key Number 24.
You can master spiritual survival skills.

With spiritual survival skills you do what you can to make heaven your home now, instead of waiting until you die to experience the blessings of God. Living your daily life becomes a spiritual experience. You are growing as a spiritual being in a material world.

Sri Harold Klemp, the spiritual leader of Eckankar, writes about the level of commitment it takes to survive spiritually:

> *Of those who want to walk the spiritual path, I would ask this question: What motivation do you have that is strong enough for you to look for God in every waking moment of your day?*[2]

THE FIRST SPIRITUAL SURVIVAL SKILL

To become a spiritual survivor, the first skill you need is to survive daily life. Sri Harold explains a crucial spiritual principle—the relationship between spiritual and material living.

> *In ECKANKAR, we want to see people develop into strong human beings. This is a path for the strong. The meek shall inherit the earth, but the strong shall go into the highest reaches of heaven.*[3]

THE SECOND AND THIRD SPIRITUAL SURVIVAL SKILLS

The Light and Sound of God are the Holy Spirit communicating with and sustaining all life.

Until you recognize the Light and Sound of God, the ECK, you wander in spiritual darkness. The Light and Sound of God are the Holy Spirit communicating with and sustaining all life. The Light and Sound is the Voice of God, the love of God flowing through creation.

To survive spiritually, you make a direct connection with the Light and Sound of God. This is your second spiritual survival skill.

Here's the choice.

You can occasionally happen upon a stream and slake your thirst for God. Or you can have a pipeline that runs right into your house.

The Mahanta, the Living ECK Master is an agent for God. His spiritual mission is to connect you with the Light and Sound of God.

This allows you to fill yourself with the Holy Spirit every moment of every day. To tune into the highest source of spiritual love and wisdom. To have the love of God coursing through your veins. The initiations offered in Eckankar, given by the Mahanta, link you directly to the Light and Sound of God. The spiritual exercises taught in Eckankar help you keep this connection alive.

Direct experience with the Voice of God is something most religions don't know about.

Instead of the occasional moment of insight or vivid spiritual experience, you have a spiritual lifeline to the Voice of God. The result is steady inner guidance, protection, and the loving presence of God from the highest, purest source. Your spiritual experiences become more intense and comprehensive than ever before.

But you'll have to discover the difference for yourself. Direct experience with the Voice of God, manifesting as Light and Sound, is something most religions don't know about.

What Most Religions Have Lost

The Light was seen in the burning bush from which God spoke to Moses. The Light of God is what Saul saw on the road to Damascus. The Sound is referred to as the Word of God. The sound as of a rushing wind and the tongues of fire that the apostles experienced on the day of Pentecost was the Light and Sound of God.

Most religions have forgotten how to help their followers directly experience the Holy Spirit as their founders may once have done. Dogma, tradition, and ritual have replaced the direct experience of the Light and Sound of God.

SEARCHING FOR WHAT RELIGIONS HAVE LOST

An ECKist we'll call Randy went sightseeing in London. He met a homeless woman sitting outside Westminster Abbey.

She said that he was just like the other tourists. Randy said that he was different because he wanted to understand why religions had lost the Light and Sound of God. The woman was interested in what Randy had to say. She too, sitting in the shadow of spiritual icons, was a seeker.

HU is a spiritual key that most religions have lost.

Randy taught her how to sing HU. Randy knew that when people sing HU as a sacred love song to God, they can often see the Light and hear the Sound of God. HU is a spiritual key that most religions have lost.

After the woman sang HU, she told Randy about her journey.

> *I have been coming to Westminster Abbey to sit on this bench every day for the last thirty years. Every day I have asked God for guidance. I just knew that this would be the place where my answer would come.*

Now that the woman knew about the HU, she had what she'd been seeking all those years.[4]

Having a direct connection with the Light and Sound of God is your second skill for spiritual survival. You can begin to experience these twin aspects of the Holy Spirit by using the third spiritual survival skill—singing the holy love song HU every day.

THE FOURTH SPIRITUAL SURVIVAL SKILL

At some point in your spiritual journey, you'll need a guide who can lead you to God. The fourth spiritual survival skill is knowing to ask for help from a spiritual master who has achieved the goals you're trying to reach.

You may decide to ask Sri Harold Klemp, the Mahanta, the Living ECK Master to help you achieve your spiritual goals. He works with many others as their inner and outer spiritual guide and friend.

This takes trust.

The only way you'll know if the Mahanta is the right spiritual guide for you is to prove it to yourself.

Because so many religious leaders have claimed to have a monopoly on God, it's only natural that we are skeptical of any spiritual leader, teacher, or master.

Yet asking for help on your spiritual journey is an important spiritual survival skill. The only way you'll know if the Mahanta is the right spiritual guide for you is to prove it to yourself.

THE FIFTH SPIRITUAL SURVIVAL SKILL

If you ask the Mahanta to work with you, he'll offer inner guidance using every aspect of your life to help you grow spiritually. The Mahanta, the Living ECK Master has reached the highest consciousness of God. When you ask him to be your spiritual teacher, you're choosing the highest communication with the Holy Spirit.

No one can or should try to convince you of this. You are the best judge of what spiritual teaching, if any, is best for you.

But just as you go to a doctor or consultant and would be wasting your time if you didn't listen to the advice, so it is with the spiritual life. That's why the fifth spiritual survival skill is surrender. Surrender allows you to test whether what you're learning with the help of the Mahanta (or any spiritual teacher) is working for you.

Eventually you'll discover that all you're surrendering are your old attitudes, patterns, problems, and worries. Never your free will, identity, or personal possessions.

Sri Harold explains surrender this way:

All that is asked of him [the initiate of Eckankar] is to surrender his attachment to material things. He may then find enjoyment in the things provided for this life; but should they be lost due to misfortune, he will pick himself up and show gratitude for what blessings he retains. That is the meaning of surrender *in ECKANKAR.*[5]

True surrender is turning your spiritual needs over to a higher power.

TRUE SURRENDER

True surrender goes deeper than just throwing your hands in the air and saying, "I give up." True surrender means getting your ego, fears, and doubts out of the way so the pure love of God can come through as inner guidance. True surrender is turning your spiritual needs over to a higher power.

Guy, an ECKist, told this story of how surrender to the Inner Master helped him face a life-and-death situation.

Guy's family dog, Tabu, an especially sensitive creature, was his almost-constant, loving companion.

One morning while Guy was preparing to give his children a ride to school, he felt tension in the air. It was as if something were about to happen. Then his sons came running into the house screaming, "Daddy, come quick. Tabu has been hit by a car!"

Guy said, "I opened myself completely to the ECK. I focused on the presence of the Mahanta."

Out in the street he calmed his frightened boys. They told Guy that Tabu had been hit in the head. "At that point," Guy said, "I knew it was serious."

In spite of his strong emotions, Guy focused on the presence of the Mahanta and surrendered. He filled himself with unconditional love and began to sing HU. Guy said, "Even though this dog means so much to me, it was in the hands of the Mahanta now."

Gently holding Tabu's head in his lap, Guy opened his heart completely to the unconscious animal.

Guy said:

> Whatever was to be his destiny, if it was his time to go, I wanted him to know I had an ocean of unconditional love in my heart for him. I felt this love pouring from me to Tabu.

After a few moments, blood began to come out of Tabu's nose. Guy kept singing HU and gently wiped the blood from Tabu's nose.

Tabu's eyes opened. When the dog focused on Guy, a look of recognition came to the dog's eyes. Joy rushed through Guy's heart. The whole family watched as life returned to Tabu's body.

Tabu sat up. Guy said, "He looked like a dazed prizefighter as he slowly walked into the house."

Gently holding Tabu's head in his lap, Guy opened his heart completely to the unconscious animal.

Guy feels that his surrender to the Mahanta had saved Tabu's life. He closes his story with these words:

I know that we were given a gift of divine love from the Mahanta. The love and protection of the Master surrounded our home.[6]

LEARNING TO TRUST INNER GUIDANCE

If you're interested in working with inner guidance, try the following Spiritual Exercise of ECK. It's designed by Sri Harold to help you make a distinction between your old ways of making decisions and how things work when you are guided by the ECK.

The mind has the power to make you believe you are always right.

Try This Spiritual Exercise Today!

Everyone wants to make good decisions. But how do you know when you are being guided by the ECK or the mind? Here's a simple way to tell.

If guided by ECK, you are more likely to change your mind when new information comes along. You're quicker to admit that an earlier decision based on sketchy information needs to change.

The mind has the power to make you believe you are always right. That's why a headstrong person acts so smart. He thinks he's always right, though he's often wrong.[7]

QUESTIONS AND ANSWERS

By now you may be wondering how to take your first steps toward spiritual survival.

1. *How can I know if listening to inner guidance from the Mahanta is right for me?*

Sri Harold explains how to take a step-by-step approach to developing trust in your spiritual guide:

> *Don't believe something because I said it or some other member of ECK said it.*
>
> *Prove it to yourself. If it works, take it a step further. And if it doesn't work, let it go.*
>
> *Beyond experience is something much more important, and this is simply learning how to give and receive God's love. And that's not experience. That's a condition. That's being able to open your heart, to open your wings, to accept the gifts of life.[8]*

Prove spiritual truth to yourself.

Here's an exercise you're welcome to try. Just fill in the blanks below. It will help you prove spiritual truth to yourself.

Show Me Thy Ways, O Lord

A. This is something I doubt about inner guidance: _____

B. Here's a question I have: _____

_____

C. These are ways I'll recognize that my question or doubt has been answered: _____

_____

D. Now I release my doubt or question to the Holy Spirit.

E. Results: _____

_____

Be alert to the many ways Divine Spirit is answering your prayers.

When you ask the ECK to prove something, your answer might come as an event, in a dream, through the words of another person, or even on a billboard. Be alert to the many ways Divine Spirit is answering your prayers.

2. *Are people who are not studying Eckankar guided and protected by the Mahanta?*

Sri Harold explains how the Holy Spirit protects those who are Its vehicles for love in the world.

> *Those who have earned the higher states of consciousness have a protection from Divine Spirit that is unknown to the average person. When anger or mockery is directed against one of these individuals—whether a member of the Christian, Hindu, or Buddhist faiths, or of ECKANKAR—there is a white light that surrounds this person and gives protection. The negative thoughts which are directed toward him, like darts or arrows, can only come back upon the sender.*[9]

THE NEXT SPIRITUAL GOAL

Spiritual survival leads you out of the valley of illusion and into the light of truth.

But there is more. Much more.

25. It's Your Right to Discover Truth and Wisdom

Truth is perfect and complete within itself. It is nothing newly discovered, for it has always existed. So I say that Truth is never far away from thee. It is always near. . . . Learn to listen to the Voice within thy own self. In time you will learn that your body and mind will blend in unity, and you will realize the oneness with all life.

—Rebazar Tarzs to the seeker,
Stranger by the River[1]

The Spiritual Goal of Truth and Wisdom:
Gain truth and wisdom through direct experiences with the Holy Spirit.

Direct experiences with the Holy Spirit allow you to discover truth for yourself. When you have your own proof that you are loved—beyond measure—by God, nothing can take it away

*There is no
person, place,
thing, feeling,
thought, or
action that can
ever cause
God to stop
loving you.*

from you. Knowing truth leads to wisdom. The wisdom
of one who finds answers by going to the Kingdom of
God. The wisdom of one who travels a road not taken
by the masses.

TRUTH AND WISDOM
AREN'T WHAT YOU'VE BEEN TOLD

You were probably taught, either this lifetime or in
past lives, that you can be lost or separated from God.
Even that you can be eternally damned by God.

Maybe God's love was even hidden behind the image
of a vengeful and punishing Creator.

As a result, you may have lived in spiritual despair.
Feeling alone and forsaken by God.

Here's Golden Key Number 25.

It's your right to discover truth and wisdom.

Through direct experience with the Light and Sound
of God, the Holy Spirit, you can prove to yourself that
nothing separates you from God. The truth is that you
are constantly sustained by God's love.

Let this truth blaze in your heart. There is no person, place, thing, feeling, thought, or action that can
ever cause God to stop loving you.

Sins, your negative traits and actions, are merely
experiences to teach you more about God's love. The
consequences of your actions (karma) — pain, suffering, joy — all help you recognize and accept God's love
in every experience. You don't have to believe in the
loving presence of God. It's not a matter of faith.

With simple spiritual exercises, you can discover
for yourself the truth about your relationship with God.
And grow wiser and stronger in the process. But it
takes a lot of courage to seek truth and wisdom.

THE SEARCH FOR TRUTH AND
WISDOM BEGINS WITH YOU

The search for truth begins with self-awareness. It takes spiritual stamina and courage to discover truth. It requires facing yourself. And loving yourself.

The first stages of truth-seeking can be challenging for people. The Mahanta, the Living ECK Master offers to help those who want to break through illusions. Bit by bit, at the pace you can handle, Sri Harold, as the Inner Master, helps you become more receptive to truth. More open to receiving the love of God that is all around you.

You weren't meant to live in spiritual ignorance.

Sri Harold explains what truth based on daily life experience can mean to you.

What is truth? Truth is the ability to live life with joy and happiness.

Truth isn't a set of words. Truth is knowing how to live this life, with its troubles and with its joys, and take them day by day. Truth is to love waking up in the morning to face another day, no matter how hard life becomes. If you can do that, you're living truth.[2]

You weren't meant to live in spiritual ignorance.

Only a true friend will help you see what you're doing to yourself or others. The Mahanta is this kind of true but gentle friend.

An ECKist named Nancy wrote a story in which she shared an important truth that she found.

FACING THE TRUTH ABOUT YOURSELF

Nancy married a man with whom she felt both spiritual and human love. She and her husband chose thick silver wedding bands to wear. These rings were to be symbolic of their relationship.

A still voice within me, the voice of the Mahanta, answered, "You have lost compassion for your husband."

Nancy and her husband noticed after the wedding that the bands irritated their fingers. They began taking them off each night. Later they realized that this was a message from the Holy Spirit that the couple needed to allow each other more space.

After eight years of marriage, Nancy's husband told her that he wanted a divorce. She cried out to God, asking for the truth about why her marriage had failed.

Nancy said, "A still voice within me, the voice of the Mahanta, answered, 'You have lost compassion for your husband.' " She sadly realized the truth in these words. Over the years Nancy had stopped giving her husband the freedom he had needed to grow.

Soon the couple separated.

Nancy asked friends about love. One said, "Love is seeing the good in another and letting the rest go." Another friend explained to Nancy that one culture didn't allow the exchange of wedding rings. It was thought to be a sign of ownership.

Nancy wondered, *Did I own my husband? Did I own that relationship?*

The Mahanta inwardly assured Nancy that she would learn a more spiritual way of loving.

Several months later, Nancy and her husband decided to try again. This time though, they didn't wear the wedding bands. The rings stayed in a box on the dresser.

One day Nancy discovered that the rings had disappeared. They were gone for months, then suddenly reappeared. Later she learned that a neighbor boy had stolen the rings—and then returned them.

She said, "Divine Spirit was telling us something.

This time we would make it."

Nancy concluded her story by saying that she learned that the love she once sought with her husband can only be found in God. She now sees "the good within myself, my mate, and all life." She says, "My priorities are now in order."[3]

Nancy and her husband were helped to face the truth about what had prevented them from loving each other. They realized that true love is about sharing, not about owning. Nancy and her husband didn't move to a mountaintop or enter a monastery to discover the truth about themselves. They worked with the Mahanta and applied what they learned in their daily lives.

You gain wisdom through the heart, not the mind.

And truth leads to wisdom.

WISDOM IS KNOWING HOW TO FIND LOVE IN EVERYDAY LIFE

I will whisper to thee, dear ones, this divine secret. Let thine ears become filled with wisdom and thy hearts with understanding. Now it is this: All things will gravitate to thee if ye will let love enter thine own hearts, without compromise.

—Rebazar Tarzs to the seeker and his beloved,
Stranger by the River[4]

Wisdom helps us have more understanding and less fear. Here are some secrets for gaining wisdom.

- You gain wisdom through the heart, not the mind. From loving not intellectual prowess.
- Wisdom enters by listening to the Voice of God, the small still whisperings of the Holy Spirit.
- Wisdom grows by making it a habit to draw from

What people can get from Eckankar is a sense of wisdom. A sense of knowingness.

life the richness woven into each moment.

❧ Wisdom comes to those who learn how to put love into every aspect of their lives.

THE BENEFITS OF WISDOM

Here's how an ECKist expressed the benefits of the wisdom he'd gained through studying the teachings of Eckankar for a number of years.

"What people can get from Eckankar is a sense of wisdom. A sense of knowingness.

"Probably the greatest difficulty that people have is uncertainty. A feeling that they don't know what's going to happen next. That they don't understand why they're here. A feeling that life, somehow, has a meaning which they can't figure out.

"Through the Spiritual Exercises of Eckankar and the information provided in ECK seminars, I've found that I can have a feeling of certainty and comfort. It's absolutely unbelievable.

"And this is genuine wisdom. Not pompous or arrogant wisdom, but a feeling of centeredness. Of knowing that I have a place on this planet and a purpose in this life."

HOW DO I GET THERE FROM HERE?

Wisdom and truth.

It takes tremendous courage and commitment to achieve these spiritual goals. But when you do, greatness is within your grasp.

Try this spiritual exercise. It's designed to help you find the truth and wisdom you've been seeking for lifetimes.

Try This Spiritual Exercise Today!

If you don't know anything about ECK, the main tool you have to work with at this point may be prayer—your communication with God. If you are sincerely interested in truth, in knowing who you are and why you belong here, ask God in your prayers: "Show me truth."

Ask God in your prayers: "Show me truth."

If your heart is pure, the Lord will bring truth into your life. But it may not come in a way that fits your expectations; it may come in a different way. It may come through the gift of a book or by way of a person telling you one small step that you need to take before you can go to the next step.

And so you can pray to God. Just say, "I want truth," or "Dear Lord, give me knowledge, wisdom, and understanding." But the greatest thing you could ask is: "Dear Lord, give me love."

Knowledge, wisdom, and understanding are only the attributes of God. But when you have love, you have the whole thing. We seek first the highest, most divine, most sacred part of something which is nothing other than our own inner being. And with this come the attributes of God and the spiritual liberation, which is something no baptism can ever bring.

When you ask for truth with a pure heart, Divine Spirit will take you one step closer to coming home to God.[5]

QUESTIONS AND ANSWERS

Here are some things you may be wondering by now about gaining truth and wisdom.

1. *How do you know when you have truth? Is there an authority to trust?*

Sri Harold writes:

> *No longer do you have to listen to a man in a pulpit or even to myself standing on a stage and telling about truth. Truth is not the same for any two people. No two people have exactly the same outlook on life. Each one of our experiences is unique; Soul is unique.* [6]

Experiment with learning to listen for inner guidance from the Holy Spirit.

Experiment with learning to listen for inner guidance from the Holy Spirit. Insights and ideas will come through. Test them out gradually. It takes awhile to trust that God is steering the ship.

How can you tell?

When guidance is from the purest source, it will be moving you toward the most loving position or decision for you and everyone else.

2. *Is there such a thing as absolute truth?*

Yes, there is. But each Soul has Its own perception of truth based on Its state of consciousness.

This doesn't mean truth changes. It does mean that as we grow in awareness, we have a better grasp of truth, and greater wisdom.

A SPIRITUAL GOAL TO OPEN YOUR HEART TO GOD

The next spiritual goal is one that the poets write about and the mystics swoon over. Feel yourself facing a warm sun that soothes and heals your heart in ways you never imagined possible.

You are about to discover the power of love.

26. You Can Have the Greatest Love of All

*So I tell thee, my children, this great prin-
ciple. Human love is that which speaks of the
self; a selfish love which demands a return of
the love that pours forth.*

*And divine love is that which has no
thought of anything in return. When ye both
have the love of others, regardless of what
may happen or be done to thee, then ye have
divine love.*

—Rebazar Tarzs to the seeker and his beloved,
Stranger by the River[1]

The Spiritual Goal of Divine Love: *Become a
vehicle for God by giving, accepting, and returning
divine love to all life.*

D o you want to have more love in your life?
Here's Golden Key Number 26.
You can have the greatest love of all.

The way to have more love is to give love—unconditionally.

The way to have more love is to give love—unconditionally. Not only to those who are easy to love. Not only to humans or pets. But to all life.

THE BENEFITS OF GIVING UNCONDITIONALLY

In *The Healing Power of Doing Good* author Allan Luks reported that there are physical, emotional, and mental health benefits to what he calls "the healthy helping syndrome." He says that people who make a habit of serving experience a "helper's high." They feel an increased sense of well-being.

More than half the people Luks surveyed felt better about themselves when they helped someone else.[2]

A member of Eckankar named Allen shows how giving divine love is satisfying to the giver as well as the receiver. He chose a way to give to life that most people wouldn't think offered many opportunities for love. Allen joined the police force in a large American city. His beat turned out to be an area with the highest crime rate. He describes the spiritual growth he gained by giving divine love as a police officer.

THE OTHER SIDE OF POLICE WORK

"I've seen how the flow of love works in many violent domestic situations. I've answered calls where people were hurt, emotions out of control.

"While doing my job in a professional manner, I allowed myself to have love and goodwill toward the family going through the emotional stress. In response to my attitude, people lowered their voices. Negative emotions subsided. And the family began to talk calmly.

"I remember when I decided to work as a police officer. I looked at myself in the mirror that evening and asked, 'How can I be most useful as a vehicle for love in this world?'

"The police work that I've been doing so far shows me that I found the right answer to that question for me."

Giving unconditional love makes people feel good about themselves. Loving others without expecting a return forms a circle of love that includes the giver. But often our previous religious training has instilled a sense of sinfulness and fear that remains rooted in the heart. The person you've been taught to love the least is the one who needs love the most—yourself.

The person you've been taught to love the least is the one who needs love the most—yourself.

Unconditional Love Starts with Loving Yourself

Often people think that to truly love God means to hate yourself.

This isn't true.

God is love. God's love sustains you constantly. You are God's beloved child. To fully love God means to be able to receive God's love too.

Some people believe that they're sinful and unworthy of God's love.

Your true nature is godlike.

Your true nature is love.

And often human love is our first step toward a higher form of spiritual love.

Human Love Can Become Unconditional

First comes loving yourself. Then comes loving others. You give warm love to people who are close to you. But the person who is growing spiritually learns how to give charity to all life. This is a detached love that means having goodwill toward everyone.

Human love can open your heart to the godlike love that just loves. Because God loves. Whether you deserve it or not. And that's how we want to love, if we're to become Co-workers with God someday.

Human love can open your heart to the godlike love that just loves.

HUMAN LOVE LEADS TO DIVINE LOVE

Giovanni, an ECKist from Switzerland, learned how to move from human love to the kind that gives unconditionally. Here's his story.

"I always thought I had a good relationship with my mother. But I had never been able to openly express my love for her. Like many men, I would give her love indirectly and hope she knew. But as I grew spiritually, I wanted to learn more about this reluctance to give love openly to others. I began to look at other people's behavior with loved ones.

"One day I realized that my mother was also rather undemonstrative. As Soul I saw how I had chosen my family in this life. My mother's coolness was nothing more than my own beliefs and behavior—maybe from past lives—coming back to me.

"One way my mother did show her love was through food. In my profession as a TV cameraman, I often work through mealtimes, and sometimes I stop by my mother's house on the way home.

"Even if she is in the middle of doing something else, she immediately asks if I have eaten. If I haven't, she jumps up and starts cooking.

"As I sit at the table to eat, she sits with me to keep me company. A long time passed before I realized how much love these small events contained. Still, in my daily spiritual exercises, I asked my spiritual guide to teach me how to love my mother in a more open, sincere manner.

"Soon an opportunity arose. My mother called and asked me to take her from Switzerland to Italy to open up her other house for a visit. At that moment I perceived the gift. I agreed to accompany her.

"The morning of our trip, I got up and did a spiritual exercise and asked my guide, the Mahanta, to help me make this day truly special for my mother.

"I was determined to start a new cycle. Love was the goal, and I would make myself totally available for anything she needed.

"En route, we talked. I listened to everything she had to say, we laughed, and we also shared moments of silence. At one point I felt the need to hold her hand, something we had never done. I knew this was my golden opportunity to begin a new relationship with her.

"With courage I took her hand gently in mine. My mother looked at me with surprise but then smiled and accepted my gesture. I felt love flowing freely between us.

"As we neared our destination, I invited my mother to lunch, telling her she should order whatever she wanted. We had a wonderful time and shared much laughter. I could tell a great healing was on the way.

"When we got to the house, I opened all the doors and windows and turned on the electricity and water. When I went to ask my mother what my next chore was, I found her outside cutting wood. I told her I would cut the wood so she could work inside. Hours later when I was cutting the last big logs, she came back and offered to help me. As we were sawing the logs, I felt

In my daily spiritual exercises, I asked my spiritual guide to teach me how to love my mother in a more open, sincere manner.

something change. We were having fun, and when our gaze met, there was a new sense of joy and love never before experienced.

"The last log proved extremely difficult to cut. With a big smile, my mother said aloud, 'Oh, there must be a knot.'

"Instantly, I understood this was a bit of Golden-tongued Wisdom in which Divine Spirit was telling me some piece of inner truth. I thanked the Mahanta and said to myself: *Now I understand.* There was a knot of unresolved karma (effects from the past) between us that kept my mother and me from unconditional love. The Mahanta was helping me cut through this knot of past experiences. And my mother was helping me dissolve the old attitude with generous and joyous laughter!

"I realized that old behavior patterns can be completely erased with the help of the Inner Master. This subtle experience helped me open my heart and love others in a new way."[3]

Divine love is always constructive.

Giovanni found a love that was truer and a more satisfying relationship with his mother when he allowed the Mahanta to lead him to divine love. This is the kind of love that never hurts, but always heals.

DIVINE LOVE ALWAYS UPLIFTS

Many times, two people love each other, and it deepens their love for God. Love between people, whether of the opposite or same sex, is often a way for divine love to grow in the human heart through selflessness.

Divine love is always constructive. In so many relationships, people abuse each other and call it love.

Divine love doesn't abuse others.

Divine love transforms the lover into an instrument of God. A vehicle for bringing God's love into the world.

THE GOAL IS TO BECOME AN INSTRUMENT FOR DIVINE LOVE

As you grow in your love for all life, the Holy Spirit sends you on spiritual assignments.

Divine love is miraculous and healing. As you grow in your love for all life, the Holy Spirit sends you on spiritual assignments. You're in training to become a Co-worker with God. Moving in harmony with divine love.

An ECKist told a story about a dramatic experience which showed her how God uses willing vehicles as channels for divine love and healing.

THE LANGUAGE OF LOVE

"After attending an Eckankar seminar, I stayed in the city to visit my sister Miriam.

"Miriam worked in a center that educates and trains disabled babies and preschool-aged children. Miriam told me how she and the other staff members learned to communicate with the disabled children in their program. She said that the children had a kind of intelligence that went beyond their dysfunctional brains. I realized that Miriam spoke to these children as Soul. They talked the only language Soul, a divine spark of God, knows—the language of love. Miriam and the staff used their loving inner connections through Divine Spirit to communicate with the children. Soul to Soul.

"Miriam told me that one boy often appeared in her dreams. He would tell her in the dream what he wanted to learn next. In a day or two, he'd learn the new task.

"I asked if there was a baby Miriam wanted me to hold and give a little special attention to before I left. She said that a child named Mickey had an enlarged brain and was likely to die soon. I sat in a rocking chair while Miriam placed Mickey in my arms. I sensed that Mickey wanted me to hold his head against my heart. I felt him soaking up the love.

"Silently I began to sing HU, a sacred love song to God that connects all life. After singing to Mickey, I told my sister that I had the impression Mickey lived on love.

"Miriam confirmed my observation. She said that the doctors had predicted Mickey's death long ago. But his parents loved him so much that, beyond the ability of medical science, their love was keeping Mickey alive.

"The next day Miriam called to tell about what happened after my visit.

"Miriam held Mickey's hands. She looked into his eyes and said, 'I love you, Mickey.' For the first time in his life—Mickey smiled!

"It was a smile Miriam would never forget.

"She was so excited that she called the rest of the staff to see it. Mickey held his first smile in place while the entire staff clapped and cheered for this break-through that unconditional love had made possible."

Singing HU brings your attention and awareness into alignment with the love of God.

HOW TO OPEN YOUR HEART TO LOVE

One of the best ways to open your heart to the love that is all around you is to do as the ECKist did in the story above. Singing HU brings your attention and awareness into alignment with the love of God.

Here's a spiritual exercise an ECKist designed to experience more divine love.

Since God loves me, I can love me too.

> ### Try This Spiritual Exercise Today!
>
> In the morning sing HU for five minutes. Then repeat two or three times, "Since God loves me, I can love me too."
>
> Be still, and feel God's love.
>
> Remember this feeling throughout the day. When you meet someone, silently say, "God loves you," and allow your heart to fill with love for the person.
>
> Next, if you get angry with someone or a situation, say to yourself, "There must be something in this situation I can be grateful for. What is it?"
>
> You'll find with practice that you can indeed find something to be grateful for.
>
> At the end of the day, as you lie in bed, review the events of the day and sing HU again. Go to sleep resting in the loving arms of Divine Spirit.
>
> Repeat this exercise for two or three days. You're likely to feel good about yourself in a way you haven't experienced before.

QUESTIONS AND ANSWERS

Here are a couple of questions you may have as you think about how to reach the goal of divine love.

1. How can you love people you don't like?

In the musical *Les Misérables,* there's a line "To love another person is to see the face of God."

Having divine love means viewing the highest and best part of the person and leaving the rest to God. Try remembering a time when you sensed a sliver of something to love in the person. Keep looking for the face of God.

2. *How can a relationship grow into unconditional love?*

When love enters, there's no room left for fear, anger, jealousy, blame, and criticism.

You must practice giving without expecting a return. If you have a mental counter that keeps track of who picked up the most dirty socks around the house, you'll stay at the level of human consciousness in your relationship. Instead, look for ways to give silently and lovingly, to make it easier for the other person. Divine love brings about the miracle of a changed consciousness. When love enters, there's no room left for fear, anger, jealousy, blame, and criticism.

DIVINE LOVE OPENS THE DOOR TO SELF-DISCOVERY

With the next spiritual goal you'll look into the mirror of Soul to see who you truly are.

Here, you'll discover the secret to spiritual mastery.

MASTERY

The way to God is difficult to those who struggle against the little self and look to the obstacles in the path. The difference between heaven and earth is not hardly a hairbreadth's in difference.

I will illustrate it by telling you of a great Saint who struggled for God, intensely in silence, holding to the robe of the divine Soul with grasping fingers and begging to maintain his grasp. When awakened, he discovered that his hands were grasping his own robes. You see?

—Rebazar Tarzs to the seeker,
Stranger by the River[1]

27. It's Your Birthright to Know Who You Are

Any man who desires to give the truth or do the work of God must first be faithful and true to that divine self within him.

— Rebazar Tarzs to the seeker,
Stranger by the River[2]

> **The Spiritual Goal of Self-Realization:**
> *Gain Self-Realization and spiritual freedom. Know who you are, and discover your purpose in life.*

Throughout history human beings have asked, Who am I?

Here's Golden Key Number 27.
It's your birthright to know who you are.

If you define yourself as someone's spouse, friend, or parent, then you've only found a partial answer to who you truly are. When you achieve Self-Realization, you'll have a sense of self and purpose unknown to most people on earth.

Sri Harold Klemp, an inner and outer spiritual guide who leads Souls back to God, defines Self-Realization this way:

> *Spirit wants to uplift us so that we develop what we call the spiritual consciousness, or Self-Realization. This is the self-recognition of truth: to know who and what we are and what our mission in this life may be.*[3]

The Self-Realized person is not a victim of life.

HOW WOULD YOU LIKE TO CREATE YOUR OWN DESTINY?

In an interview for this book, Sri Harold gave some pointers about how men and women today can recognize and achieve Self-Realization.

1. *The Self-Realized person takes full responsibility for his thoughts, words, actions, and feelings.* He sets goals. He charts his own course. He knows what to do without a lot of doubts or fears. He doesn't tremble on the threshold.

    The Self-Realized person is not a victim of life. He creates his own universe, his own life, without destroying others. He has self-responsibility and self-discipline. He modifies the passions of the mind so he doesn't harm himself or others.

2. *The Self-Realized person has a divine and true understanding of who and what he is in relation to God.* Self-Realization is like God-Realization but to a lesser degree. (More about God-Realization in chapter 29.)

    The person who is Self-Realized is a master of his

own universe. This is the microcosm. The God-Realized person is master of the universes of God. This is the macrocosm.

Self-Realization is truly realizing yourself as Soul. Beginning to learn what it means to be Soul. Little by little, learning through experience.

3. *Self-Realization is expressed by having sure inner direction.* The Self-Realized person has an openness and ability to surrender his fears and concerns to the direction of the Mahanta. The Self-Realized person knows how to trust his own heart and inner perception. This can apply to the simplest things such as finding a job or buying a car. It's a knowingness that you are in tune with life.

4. *The Self-Realized person is no longer controlled by the mind.* He works with the mind as a tool, a good servant, but doesn't allow it to constantly create doubt.

The Self-Realized person has learned to follow inner nudges. To listen. A person who isn't Self-Realized wavers back and forth. He argues with his inner guidance. He doesn't have the clarity of knowing clear inner direction.

5. *Self-Realization may come gradually or as a dramatic experience.* Self-Realization occurs in an area known as the Soul Plane. It may happen the first time you allow Divine Spirit to direct your life. But, for most, Self-Realization comes quietly in a natural way so the person doesn't lose balance.

Self-Realization doesn't come as a marker in neon letters that says, "Now you're Self-Realized." It's not usually a peak experience, but a process.

The Self-Realized person has learned to follow inner nudges. To listen.

The Self-Realized person sees, hears, feels, and moves within the heartbeat of God.

People who are living in a mental area of consciousness may claim to lead Spirit-directed lives, but claiming to be Self-Realized doesn't make it so. Watch the behavior. The proof is in how the person treats others.

The Self-Realized person sees, hears, feels, and moves within the heartbeat of God. He is living life as the HU, the holy Sound of God which brings God's love and grace into all life.

A Self-Realized person can look back at the way he used to be and see improvement. He's becoming more loving.

6. *Self-Realization isn't cosmic consciousness.* The person who has achieved cosmic consciousness moves from the mass sea of the victim consciousness to a point where he feels he's risen above it. But the cosmic-consciousness person is still run by ego. He has only been fine-tuned.

Walt Whitman is an example of a person who achieved cosmic consciousness. He had astute insights but was an ego-directed man. The cosmic-consciousness person likes fanfare. He can't get beyond it. He thinks cosmic consciousness is more than it is. The cosmic-consciousness person doesn't integrate seamlessly with life.

7. *The Self-Realized person has a real, sincere love for life that he expresses in his behavior.* His way of approaching life is like the image of a Native American Indian who brushes out his tracks as he moves through the forest. He lives in this world without harming the environment, not due to social values, but because he respects himself and all life.

A Self-Realized person would make his bed in the hotel room even though he doesn't have to do that. The Self-Realized person leaves things better than he found them. His only tracks are those that would serve to help others. The Self-Realized person brushes out the tracks of his own explorations through the inner heavenly worlds. He moves through the planes of heaven to learn lessons.

Self-Realization gives peace, freedom, assuredness, and grace.

The goal of Self-Realization is one well worth working toward. Self-Realization gives peace, freedom, assuredness, and grace.

SOME WORDS OF WISDOM FROM ANOTHER SPIRITUAL TRAVELER

Paul Twitchell, the modern-day founder of Eckankar, taught about Self-Realization also.

Here's how he described the process:

When we have the ability to Soul Travel and enter into the worlds where all knowledge is ours through the expansion of the consciousness, all the questions which we are rushing about to have answered will no longer plague us. They will be answered to our utmost satisfaction.

When this occurs, we . . . have become purified as Soul. We are in the state of Self-Realization, and nothing is able to stop us from reaching the highest realm, which is God-Realization. We are now in the region where Soul is a free agent with a sense of independence and divine wisdom. Here Soul recognizes that It, too, will soon become a spiritual traveler and operate as a Co-worker with God.[4]

HOW TO GAIN SELF-REALIZATION

The Self-Realized person is in training to become a Co-worker with God. His first step is to become a Co-worker with the Mahanta. He is sent on spiritual assignments in dreams and in waking life. Inwardly guided to be in exactly the right place at the right time, he gives humble service and love to those who've earned the blessings of Spirit.

The Self-Realized person is sent on spiritual assignments in dreams and in waking life.

But there are two major aspects of Self-Realization. The first is learning who you truly are. The second aspect of Self-Realization will bring you even closer to being a Co-worker with God.

It's knowing why you're here.

28. It's Your Legacy to Know Why You're Here

*The heart must be willing and aspire to serve
God through love. By this joyful performance,
the heart fulfills God's great principle of love,
and becomes known through the worlds of
God; for none can withhold himself from love.*

—Rebazar Tarzs to the seeker,
Stranger by the River[1]

As you work toward Self-Realization, you'll be learning more about who you truly are. You'll grow to recognize yourself as a divine spark of God. As Soul, an atom of God with godlike qualities.

But why are you here?

Here's Golden Key Number 28.
It's your legacy to know why you are here.

You have a spiritual mission. It's your legacy as a beloved child of God to learn what your purpose is in life. And to fulfill it.

When you know who you are and why you're here, you'll have spiritual freedom. This is the ability to move beyond life's problems and see the spiritual gift in each experience.

A KEY TO SPIRITUAL FREEDOM

One key to spiritual freedom and to knowing your purpose in life is an often overlooked virtue.

Gratitude.

Your heart will open wider and wider as you learn to find the gifts of God buried inside even the most challenging aspects of life.

Below is my own story of how recognizing three important gifts from Divine Spirit led me to a deeper understanding and appreciation for life. As you read, think about stumbling blocks in your own life. See how love and gratitude could transform your challenges into stepping-stones.

ACT II: RECOGNIZING THE GIFTS OF SPIRIT

As a child I always thought I wouldn't live past the age of forty. By the time I neared my early demise, I'd packed a lifetime of experiences into those forty years. I lived recklessly. Not valuing my health or happiness.

One day while driving home from a business trip, suddenly I could see future possibilities.

One day while driving home from a business trip, suddenly I could see future possibilities. This is known in Eckankar as the ECK-Vidya, the ancient science of prophecy. From the viewpoint of Soul, an eternal spark of God, I saw the proverbial fork in the road. Two paths, either of which could have been my future, appeared. In one direction, I saw myself dying before my fortieth year, just as I always knew my life would end.

The other road showed me starting a new life with a man I'd met recently. Together we would raise my two children from a previous marriage.

After seeing the two possibilities, I asked my inner spiritual guide, the Mahanta, to renegotiate the original contract for my life span. There was so much more for me to do, I felt. Such love and spiritual potential unfulfilled.

The Mahanta had the power to lift this death sentence. I didn't need to be a victim of fate.

RECOGNIZING THE FIRST GIFT

I had begun to recognize the first gift from Spirit. One I'd shamelessly taken for granted. *The gift of life on this earth.*

With all my heart I visualized myself walking on the road that led far past my fortieth year. It was with great gratitude that I realized I didn't have to accept the future as unchangeable. The Mahanta had the power to lift this death sentence that had haunted me all my life. I didn't need to be a victim of fate.

From the moment I saw the ECK-Vidya, it was as if Act I of my life had ended. What I didn't know about was Intermission. The transition from my first life plan to the new life contract was to last nine years. During Intermission I married the man I loved. Together we raised our children. My husband and I became ordained members of the clergy in Eckankar. And in the fifth year of Intermission, our family moved to Minnesota.

INTERMISSION INVOLVED MORE THAN BUYING POPCORN

Also during Intermission something I'd read in the teachings of Eckankar but didn't fully understand came into focus. I discovered for myself that the Mahanta takes over the management of his chelas' (students') karma (effects of past actions).

As a good trustee or guardian, the Mahanta manages, with wisdom and compassion, the spiritual accounts of those in his care. He allows their debits and credits with life to return to them in amounts and ways they can handle.

I had a lot of karmic debt from this life and from past lives. Part of my debt with life was incurred by not taking care of my body in those years when I hadn't respected the gift of life.

The Mahanta led me in the dream state to meet teams of inner-world health specialists.

During Intermission the Mahanta helped me work out many effects through dream experiences. I had dreams which paralleled my waking life. The Mahanta led me in the dream state to meet teams of inner-world health specialists. These "dream teams" used advanced technology, knowledge, and equipment to reconstruct the spiritual bodies that had been programmed to last only to my fortieth year.

In the waking state I went to doctors who diagnosed potentially serious problems. Conditions that would have ended my life were detected early and healed.

But in the eighth year of Intermission, it looked as if the curtain for Act II wouldn't rise after all. I came perilously close to death.

WOULD ACT II EVER BEGIN?

My job had become too physically and emotionally taxing for me. It required world travel and a lot of stress. In addition, I'd grown lax in my physical exercise and nutrition. My health withered. I again forgot to love my body, the sacred temple of Soul, which the Holy Spirit had been healing all these years.

I went to doctors who couldn't discover what was causing my severe fatigue and weakness.

One day I awoke from a dream and had a clear direction from the Mahanta. I must resign from my job and regain my health.

The following year, I stayed home and began to heal in every way possible. I put my life back in order. Made new plans. As my strength returned, I resurrected my previous career as a professional writer. After a while, I realized that mostly I wanted to write about God. The spiritual life was all that really intrigued me.

I began to read and study Eckankar books and discourses written by Sri Harold. I'd barely had time to skim through them when my work schedule had been so full.

I contemplated earnestly about why I was here. What did Eckankar and the Mahanta really mean to me? And what was my spiritual mission in life?

Then I began to talk to others about God. I interviewed about twenty-five people for a book I wanted to write. I asked ministers, rabbis, spiritual counselors, therapists, and psychics about God.

RECOGNIZING THE SECOND GIFT

I discovered something pretty startling to me. I'd been studying Eckankar for almost twenty years. During this time I'd lost some of my initial appreciation for the incredible insights gained through the Spiritual Exercises of ECK and the guidance of the Mahanta. I'd started to take the miracles for granted.

I'd started to take the miracles for granted.

As I listened to other people talk about God, I found that they didn't have one-tenth of what I'd found in the ECK teachings. Some of them even admitted that greater wisdom of God was out there, but they had no idea where to look or how to find it. This discovery led me to start interviewing ECKists. I asked them: "How did you get into Eckankar? What has being in Eckankar meant to you?"

Wonderful life-changing stories poured out. We laughed and cried together as they relived memories of what their lives had been like before finding Eckankar—and since. Pretty barren for many of them B.E. (Before ECK)!

The holy fire of God relit the flame of love in my heart.

I began to appreciate anew the second gift from Spirit: *Having the teachings of Eckankar and the Mahanta in my life.* The holy fire of God relit the flame of love in my heart.

While writing my book about God, I'd sit in coffeeshops and quiet restaurants. It became commonplace for strangers to talk to me about their dreams, their spiritual searches. With renewed love and joy I shared with them spiritual principles from Eckankar that had helped me. Mostly, though, I listened and learned from each new person I met.

Then I began to have dreams that I was working at the Temple of ECK. Soon I was asked to work in a position where I would help to share the teachings of ECK with others.

THE INNER AND OUTER MASTER

About six months into my new job, even though I kept promises to take care of my body better, my health began to ebb. I was very disappointed. Finally I was doing something I loved to do—bringing the joy of these teachings into the lives of people who wanted them. But now it looked as if I wouldn't be able to continue.

One day, exhausted, I took time off from work and went to a health food store hoping to find some magic potion.

As I swung my cart around the aisle, I saw Sri Harold. He stood alone carefully examining the shelves of vitamins.

As most ECKists do, I usually met Sri Harold as the Mahanta, the Inner Master, in dreams and while doing the Spiritual Exercises of ECK. The chances of physically meeting the Living ECK Master were slight.

But this is one of the advantages of having a living Master. It's like being able to bump into Jesus or Krishna or Buddha at the grocery store. And you can ask, "What's the matter with me? And will you help?"

Later that day I sang HU, the holy name for God which has the power to lift us to a higher state of consciousness. I then sat in quiet contemplation and had an inner vision of Sri Harold.

I asked, "Why did we meet today near the vitamins?"

His face had a grave expression as he answered, "I'm trying to decide what to do about your health."

RECOGNIZING THE THIRD GIFT

A few weeks later, early on a Sunday morning, I lay in bed thinking about the talk I was to give for a worship service at the Temple of ECK later that day. Although resting, I wasn't asleep or dreaming.

Suddenly I found myself floating out of my body to a house in the inner worlds of heaven. Hundreds of people were gathering in a room there. They wore clothes from different eras in history. I felt a rush of joy as I recognized them instantly even though my mind couldn't recall their names. I intuitively knew that they were Souls with whom I'd spent past lives.

I walked over to a woman who is one of my dearest

Suddenly I found myself floating out of my body to a house in the inner worlds of heaven.

friends in this lifetime. She was there in her spiritual body. She greeted me lovingly, but there was sadness in her eyes.

At once I realized why all these Souls were there. I asked my friend, "Am I dying?"

With tears in her eyes she answered, "Yes."

We held each other and cried. I said, "I'm not afraid to die. I know it's only the physical body that will go. But my husband will grieve over losing me. We love each other so very much. And my spiritual work isn't finished on earth."

Inwardly he communicated that I was now faced with a choice between life on earth or life in heaven.

At this moment, a young man came to get me. I instinctively recognized this beautiful angel as an ECK Master. I'd studied the teachings of the Light and Sound of God with him during an ancient lifetime. Tenderly, the young man took my hand. He showed me to an open door leading to a dark tunnel. Next to the tunnel a bank of blue doors formed a wall.

Inwardly he communicated that I was now faced with a choice between life on earth or life in heaven. He told me that something was moving through my entire body. It could result in my death.

If I walked through the open door, I would enter the tunnel. This led to heaven where I, as Soul, could continue helping the Mahanta in the inner worlds by sharing the teachings of the Holy Spirit.

Visions of my husband, children, friends, and pets came to mind. These were all important aspects of my life. But something else moved me to choose as I did. A surge of love swelled inside and poured through me like a mighty river. With all my heart, I proclaimed, "I want to serve God!"

The young man folded the blue doors over the

entrance to the tunnel. Immediately I was aware of being back in my physical body.

I sat up. Tears streamed down my face. After a few minutes, I realized that I had to pull myself back together emotionally. I must get out of bed and prepare to give my talk at the ECK Worship Service. But, I thought, everyone will think I'm nervous because this is my first time speaking at the Temple. Nobody will know that I'm rattled because I've just been to my own inner-world funeral!

I realized that this experience had caused me to recognize the third important gift from Spirit: *The gift of service to God and all life.* My burning desire to be a Co-worker with the Mahanta and with God had brought me back to life. And life back to me.

My burning desire to be a Co-worker with the Mahanta and with God had brought me back to life.

THE HEALINGS

A month later a friend introduced me to a new doctor. He diagnosed a blood infection that was invading my whole body, just as the ECK Master in my experience had told me. Untreated, the infection would have become life-threatening.

Within a month after treatment all my symptoms disappeared. And, after months of fatigue, my energy returned.

To make sure that I'd appreciate this renewed opportunity I'd been granted, the Mahanta gave me one more experience. I met a woman who said that she was a palm reader. Before I could stop her, the woman grabbed my palm and turned it upward. Looking shocked, she asked, "How old are you?"

I answered, "Forty-seven." The palm reader

exclaimed, "You're supposed to be dead by now!"

Then she showed me a center line which ran from the end to the middle of my palm. She explained that this lifeline meant that I would only live till midlife. Talk about a midlife crisis! She examined my palm again and pointed out a second lifeline. It ran parallel to the central one and across my palm to the end of my hand.

My turning point was the commitment I'd made to be a conscious vehicle for God's love in this world.

She explained, "This line predicts a long life ahead."

"I know," I said. "Act II."

By recognizing the three gifts—the gift of life on this earth, the gift of the Mahanta and the teachings of Eckankar, and the gift of service—I was able, with the Mahanta's help, to change the course of my life. My turning point was the commitment I'd made to be a conscious vehicle for God's love in this world.

FINDING THE TURNING POINTS IN YOUR LIFE

Author Mary Carroll Moore in her book from Eckankar, *How to Master Change in Your Life: Sixty-seven Ways to Handle Life's Toughest Moments,* teaches how to recognize the gifts of Divine Spirit that come wrapped in a pretty little package called change.

The following exercise is one she offers to help you discover your own turning points. She says these are times when life is trying to show you that change is coming and how to grow from it. A turning point is "a window of spiritual opportunity."

Finding your own patterns and cycles then learning to handle change gracefully are giant steps toward living in the Self-Realized state of consciousness.

Try This Spiritual Exercise Today!

1. Write down all the negative feelings you may have about yourself and your abilities, in all the areas you can think of. Imagine you are just letting all the negativity in your life flow out on the paper. Try not to censor yourself— no one but you will see this page. When you run out of things to write, take a clean sheet of paper.

2. Now write down all the gifts you have received from life. You can start small at first; include even things you may take for granted like your ability to breathe, run, eat, or even to smile at someone else. Move on to bigger items that enhance your life.

3. Take a third page. Write down what you hope to learn from life. You can divide the page into different areas, such as work or career, family, spirituality, finances, creativity, etc.

4. To carry this exercise one step further, get a colored highlighting marker. Highlight any parallels you see between the three sections you wrote—the negatives, the things you are grateful for, and the things you wish to learn.[2]

Write down all the gifts you have received from life.

FREEDOM TO KNOW GOD

The spiritual freedom you gain through Self-Realization leads you to the next spiritual goal. It's one you've secretly desired for lifetimes.

The full awareness of God and God's love for you.

29. It's Your Destiny to Know God

When man has dwelled in God through inner silence for any length of time, he must return to the earth again. He finds that it is God who has now become the earth and its living beings.

—Rebazar Tarzs to the seeker,
Stranger by the River[1]

The Spiritual Goal to Be a Co-worker with God:
Become one with the Holy Spirit and a Co-worker with God. Have the full capacity to love as God loves.

Here's Golden Key Number 29.
It's your destiny to know God.

Y ou, as Soul, a divine spark of God, also have the spiritual destiny to be a Co-worker with God.

The God-Realized person is a blend of the human and the divine.

It's not easy.

But you can do it.

Others have.

The ancient teachings of ECK offer the opportunity to achieve this level of spiritual mastership in this lifetime. When a person reaches God-Realization, he or she becomes a living, breathing, walking, talking, thinking, acting vehicle for the Holy Spirit. The God-Realized person is a blend of the human and the divine.

The ECK Masters are God-Realized Souls. They serve, under the direction of the Mahanta, the Living ECK Master of the times as vehicles for God's love. There are ECK Masters, male and female, from all corners of the globe and eras in history. The common denominator among them is the immense love they show toward all life. Many people have experienced these ECK Masters and considered them to be guardian angels. Some are known in the ECK literature. They work directly with the students of the spiritual leader of Eckankar today, Sri Harold Klemp. (See chapter 15 for more about ECK Masters.)

WHAT IS GOD-REALIZATION?

If it were possible, I would make a list of the points that characterize a God-Realized person. But for people who do not have the eyes to see, it would be like trying to discern words written with invisible ink. Most people could not read or understand them.

—Harold Klemp, *The Eternal Dreamer*[2]

God-Realization is an awesome goal. Consequently, there are a lot of misconceptions about what a God-Realized person is and is not. Let's take a look at some of the myths surrounding the God-Realized. (Note: the terms God-Realization and God Consciousness are used interchangeably.)

SOME TRUTHS ABOUT GOD-REALIZED INDIVIDUALS

1. *The God-Realized don't interfere in the natural rhythms and cycles of life.* While an ECK Master may perform miracles, these are to restore spiritual balance. They don't bend natural or man-made law to suit their purposes.

   A person can't just proclaim himself to be God-Realized. Or gather followers and make it so. The God-Realized person serves quietly and humbly.

2. *The God-Realized aren't immune from problems and difficulties.* In fact because they're one with the pure positive ECK (Holy Spirit), the negative power by its nature will oppose them. Often even the simplest tasks are made more difficult for ECK Masters. They must exercise the infinite patience that helped to bring them to this high consciousness of God.

   God-Realization doesn't take away life's problems. But the God-Realized are constantly turning negatives into positives; they are skilled at hearing God's answers all around them.

3. *The God-Realized aren't perfect.* The God-Conscious person is not God. He is one with the Holy Spirit, not one with God. The God-Conscious person long ago passed beyond the Universal Mind Power.

   God Consciousness isn't ultimate perfection or a state of constant euphoria. In many ways, it's only the beginning. Now the God-knower has to learn to operate in the physical world with this great spiritual awareness.

Sri Harold says, "Once an individual has God-Realization, he finds it difficult to ever again accept mediocrity or the ambitions of the average person."[3]

Yet a Zen saying sums up the necessities of daily life for the enlightened one: "After ecstasy, the laundry."[4]

"After ecstasy, the laundry."

HOW DOES A GOD-CONSCIOUS PERSON LIVE IN THIS WORLD?

Think about how it must be for a God-aware person to live in a spiritually dark world.

Sri Harold writes:

The experience of God will certainly transform the thoughts, feelings, and behavior of anyone, but weeks or months may pass before he reestablishes himself in society. The individual with true God-Realization is suddenly out of key with social conventions, yet he eventually discovers that to serve the SUGMAD [God] may mean enduring life among the spiritually dead — Souls with darkened lamps. God-Realization may span from a profoundly beautiful experience to the ruthless tearing away of one's final illusions.[5]

He also shares this insight:

The hard part came after God-Realization. Now I had to return to the problems of life and confront them. The specter of God's haunting love was always with me, but I found it was a highly personal state of being. No one else could

*share it. The Secret of the Ages had been given
to me, but there was no way to tell anyone of it.
It carried me beyond the pleasant cooing of belief
and faith, thrusting me into a brilliant world of
light shorn of all illusion.*[6]

Sri Harold shares the experiences above and other
wisdom about what God Consciousness *really* is in two
of his books. *Soul Travelers of the Far Country* and *Child
in the Wilderness* chronicle his experiences reaching
this exalted state. And then learning to live with it.

He writes, "The proof of a real God-Realized experience is: Does the person come down off the mountain
and reenter life?"[7]

BENEFITS OF GOD-REALIZATION

*All the strength that the individual has ever
gathered over the centuries to bring him to
this high plateau is without meaning, for the
majesty of the SUGMAD is beyond anything
in ITS creation.*

—Harold Klemp,
Soul Travelers of the Far Country[8]

In an interview for this book, Sri Harold talked
about some of the advantages to being God-Conscious.
As hard as it may be to come down from the Holy
Mountain of God, the good news, Sri Harold says, is
that the benefits of God Consciousness far outweigh
the disadvantages.

Here are some of the exciting aspects of God-
Realization.

*Some of the
advantages to
being God-
Conscious.*

1. *The God-Conscious person has the opportunity to
    serve.* For example, the ECK Masters live with a
    sense of contentment and fulfillment. That feeling

of doing something for someone just because it makes you happy is one that ECK Masters have all the time.

Sri Harold writes, "You have to give of yourself. There is no other way you can unfold spiritually and rise into the high heavens of God."[9] He defines God Consciousness in terms of service with these words: "God-Realization is not a state where one becomes self-serving. It's a state where one serves others."[10]

2. *The God-Conscious person has the opportunity to learn.* Sri Harold writes, "God Consciousness did not assure me of a comfortable life, but only of the chance to go on forever as an eternal student of the Sound and Light of God."[11] As you can see, even the ECK Masters continue their studies of God and explore ever higher realms beyond God Consciousness.

The God-aware Soul now has the omniscience of God—spiritually. But physically and mentally one is still human and works within the normal capacity of the human mind and body.

Interestingly enough, an ECK Master doesn't have to clutter his mind with a lot of facts and figures of worldly knowledge. Because his relationship with God is now fully realized, whatever information he needs comes to him when he needs it. Living in the full consciousness of God, the ECK Master speaks and acts with confidence that his thoughts, words, and actions pulse with the pure love of God. For he is an agent for God's love.

3. *The God-Conscious person has the opportunity to explore.* To enjoy the adventure of spiritual travel. Everywhere. Beyond your wildest imagination.

The ECK Masters continue their studies of God and explore ever higher realms beyond God Consciousness.

Sri Harold writes that to advance in your spiritual life you develop the "confidence, through experience, to go anywhere in this world and in the other worlds. This is the point I am trying to bring you to. When this state is achieved, you have reached God-Realization."[12]

4. *The God-Realized person has been enjoying the process all along.* As you grow toward achieving God-Realization, you're constantly expanding your ability to give and to accept more and more of God's love. You're becoming a stronger spiritual being. And you're benefiting from the guidance and protection of the Mahanta and other ECK Masters who are working with you every step of the way.

Sri Harold writes about learning to become an ECK Master:

> *The Adepts in ECK have a single purpose in mind when a seeker comes to them for relief: to give that Soul the opportunity for achieving wisdom, power, and freedom, three attributes of God-Realization. This means simply that an individual learns to be like the Adepts, enjoying a 360-degree viewpoint, the center of which is love for all living things.*[13]

5. *The God-Conscious person is fully aware of his own worlds at all hours of the day and night.* He never has an unconscious moment but lives in total awareness. He can survive anywhere.

While the God-Conscious person's physical body sleeps, he's fully aware and explores the dream worlds freely.

While the God-Conscious person's physical body sleeps, he's fully aware and explores the dream worlds freely. He doesn't really dream anymore in the traditional sense. He takes Soul journeys. He vividly remembers these real experiences in the heavenly worlds and applies them to what is happening in his daily life.

6. *The God-Conscious person works on global, universal, and interplanetary levels.* The ECK Masters are known to appear to people to bring healing, comfort, and protection. They can perform miracles. In heaven and on earth. Even on other planets.

They're vehicles for healing, protection, and guidance of the Holy Spirit. Let's put it in practical terms.

The physical body of Sri Harold may be working in his home in Minnesota. But as the Mahanta, the Living ECK Master he may appear to people thousands of miles away. The stories in Eckankar books contain examples of this. People in Africa, Australia, New Zealand, Singapore, Europe, the Netherlands, Mexico, Canada, and the United States report incidents of being helped by Sri Harold, even seeing him as a vision, while he's physically far away.

Because an ECK Master is one with the Holy Spirit, he or she can materialize away from the physical body anywhere, anytime, to any number of people at the same time.

ECK Masters are Co-workers with God.

WHAT DOES IT MEAN
TO BE A CO-WORKER WITH GOD?

One of the definitions of Co-workers with God is "partners with life."

Harold Klemp, *Be the HU*[14]

Co-worker has that uncomfortable little word *work* in it, doesn't it? How could that be much fun?

Well, think about it.

Most people believe that when you die, you go to heaven or hell for all eternity. And then what?

Wouldn't eternal bliss be boring with nothing more to learn or experience?

Is an eternity in heaven nothing more than living on the spiritual dole? Wouldn't eternal bliss be boring with nothing more to learn or experience?

Co-workers with God go to heaven. But they don't have to stay there. They live in heavenly consciousness daily. And they work to bring gifts of heavenly blessings to all Souls. Their lives are constantly filled with spiritual adventures.

You've seen programs on television or in movies where angels appear and help people or animals. How would you like to be one of those angels?

That's one of the things a Co-worker with God can do.

A Co-worker with God is one with the love of God. He or she is God's divine love in motion.

Yet a Co-worker with God maintains his or her individual identity. Co-workers with God have special talents and interests. They serve by using their unique perspectives and skills to help God's children in need.

Here's how Sri Harold describes being a Co-worker with God:

> *Being a Co-worker doesn't mean you hear the Voice of God talking to you as you're serving on the inner planes [levels of heaven]. It's more a matter of realizing that something at that moment needs doing; you are the one most qualified to do it, so you do it. The people around you, on the inner planes even as here, are often unaware*

of what you are doing or of the service you are giving. The joy comes from loving God; and because you love God, you don't have to take credit for the little things that you do. [15]

LEARNING TO BE A CO-WORKER WITH GOD

Unless we learn to work together, we cannot become Co-workers with God. We must somehow find a way to work with those we find it hardest to work with.

—Harold Klemp, *Be the HU* [16]

You learn how to be a Co-worker with God by practicing every day of your life. Good coworkers are team players with individual skills that they contribute for the good of the whole.

In the training for ECK Mastership, people in Eckankar begin to be sent by the Mahanta on spiritual assignments.

When people become spiritual students of the Mahanta, they can begin serving as Co-workers with the Mahanta. This is a part of the training to become a Co-worker with God, and is a great privilege. In the training for ECK Mastership, people in Eckankar begin to be sent by the Mahanta on spiritual assignments. They are placed into situations where they can give love and service to those in need.

A chela (student of Eckankar) who has achieved advanced initiation into the Light and Sound of God can learn to work consciously with the Mahanta. (More about initiations in chapter 20.) Co-workers with the Mahanta are becoming conscious sparks of God. The Co-worker with the Mahanta is there to be a conscious vehicle for God's love. They are divine atoms of God in expression.

The following story from Sri Harold offers an example of how a Co-worker with the Mahanta saved a family's life.

An ECKist was driving home late one night when she had a strong nudge from the Inner Master to take an alternate route. As she drove along the unfamiliar streets, she smelled smoke. She looked to the left side of the road and saw a garage on fire. The garage was attached to a house.

Since it was late at night, the family was asleep. The ECKist stopped the car and went up to the house, banging on the front door to wake the family. They called the fire department. Right next to the garage was a garden hose, so the ECKist began spraying water on the flames.

Later, as the initiate drove away, she began thinking about how she had been able to serve as a Co-worker to save the family's lives. "It was the Master urging me to turn down this road," she said.

Because she listened, she was able to help prevent these people from going through unnecessary grief and karma.[17]

WHY WASN'T GOD THERE TO HELP ME?

When a person has earned a blessing, a Co-worker with the Mahanta is often sent to deliver it. They serve as vehicles to assist in averting karma (effects of actions) when people have earned this help.

When a person has earned a blessing, a Co-worker with the Mahanta is often sent to deliver it.

People who are in training for Mastership are learning to serve not for recognition but out of their love for God. Think of what life could be with more open vehicles who aren't blocked by ego and the need to take credit for miracles.

Co-workers with the Mahanta learn to give with total, unconditional love. They can help people keep

God uses us as vehicles to bring divine love to Its creation.

from "going through unnecessary grief and karma," as in the story above.

So often we complain. Where was God? Why didn't God stop this tragedy from happening? As strange as it may seem, God uses us as vehicles to bring divine love to Its creation. God could be working through you as a channel for love.

This, after all, is why you're here.

And one of the best parts of this divine plan is that all your needs are taken care of in the process of serving God and all life.

CO-WORKERS WITH THE MAHANTA HAVE ALL THE HELP THEY NEED

Co-workers with the Mahanta have discovered a wonderful secret: It's impossible to give more to life than life gives to you. The return to the giver is so astounding it takes your breath away.

Here is a dream I had which helped me understand the reciprocal nature of being a Co-worker with the Mahanta.

In this dream, I had a yard full of leaves. My next-door neighbor turned out to be Sri Harold.

He came over to borrow my rake. I wondered how I would rake the leaves in my own yard, if I gave my only rake away. But I decided to give the rake to Sri Harold even if it meant a sacrifice to me.

To my surprise, he took the rake. And he raked the leaves from both our yards.

This was an important dream for me. It showed that it's impossible to outgive the ECK.

In Training to Give Love and Serve All Life

Here's a spiritual exercise Sri Harold gives to help begin our journey toward God-Realization.

Try This Spiritual Exercise Today!

Pick one day a week where you will do more than just get by. On that day put your whole heart into taking care of your family, your work, and yourself.

So many people spend their lives just trying to get by. That's all they really want to do. A person like that isn't material for God Consciousness; his cloth is different from one who is striving for the highest spiritual states.

People of the Golden Heart care about things. They are filled with love, they finish what they start, and they like to see it done well.[18]

People of the Golden Heart care about things.

Questions and Answers

You've been given a lot of new information about a goal that most people don't even know exists. Here are some questions you might have by now.

1. *Why are Co-workers needed? Why doesn't God do everything?*

I asked Sri Harold these questions. Here's how he explains why the Mahanta uses us as vehicles to bring God's love and blessings into the world.

My elementary education was in a two-room schoolhouse. Fifth graders helped third graders with math or phonics while the teacher worked with the other students.

Being a Co-worker with the Mahanta is similar to this situation.

The student tutor is closer to the age and development of the younger child. He's able to explain ideas with examples and language the teacher wouldn't use. Because the older child isn't an authority figure, the younger student often learns faster and more comfortably from someone nearer his age.

The older student benefits by preparing material for someone else to learn. The tutor grows in confidence and self-esteem as he teaches his less-experienced classmate.

2. *What's it like to be a Co-worker with the Mahanta?*

Co-workers with the Mahanta receive inner instructions in the form of nudges or a sense of knowing exactly what to say or do. Usually the Co-worker with the Mahanta finds himself in a situation where he can use what he's learned to help others.

The Co-worker with the Mahanta receives daily training—and testing—in how to view life as a spiritual experience. He or she learns that every situation is an opportunity for bringing more of God's love into the world.

ANCIENT WISDOM FOR TODAY

The next chapters will introduce you to the history of Eckankar and the ECK teachings. You may be surprised to discover how ancient they are. Yet how relevant to today's world.

And perhaps, to your life.

Co-workers with the Mahanta receive inner instructions in the form of nudges or a sense of knowing exactly what to say or do.

Spiritual History

This is an important point in the spiritual history of earth, because the chelas [spiritual students] of ECK are now together again.

—Harold Klemp, *The Drumbeat of Time*[1]

30. THERE'S A PLACE YOU CAN GO WHERE HEAVEN AND EARTH MEET

On January 27, 1980, I saw the future site of the Temple in Minnesota. The Vairagi Order felt an urgent need to find a permanent location for the Temple of ECK and the Seat of Power. It is the central vortex from which the Mahanta, the Living ECK Master will give the ECK message to the world.
—Harold Klemp, *The Living Word*, Book 2[2]

Here's Golden Key Number 30.
There are sacred places where heaven and earth meet. They are Temples of Golden Wisdom.

Sri Harold Klemp, the spiritual leader of Eckankar, foresaw a temple from which the ancient teachings of the Light and Sound of God would be brought forth into the world.

This is the Temple of ECK.

Now for the first time in five thousand years the teachings of the Light and Sound of God are being taught openly again.

The Temple of ECK is in Chanhassen, Minnesota, in the metropolitan Minneapolis/St. Paul (Twin Cities) area. It is dedicated to the ways of Divine Spirit.

The Temple of ECK is a sacred, shining, living monument to teachings that never lose their eternal nature or relevance.

Even through years of silence.

Even through religious intolerance and persecution.

Now for the first time in five thousand years the teachings of the Light and Sound of God are being taught openly again.

Sri Harold writes:

> *One of the early schools of ECKANKAR was established in Egypt around 3000 B.C. . . . Then persecutions were set in motion, and the ECK teachings were taken underground by the ECK Masters. From that time until the present, we have worked quietly in the background.*[3]

The modern-day founder of Eckankar, Paul Twitchell, spoke of building a temple of ECK. He foresaw the temple as having a golden dome. But Paul died before establishing a spiritual home for the teachings that he had once again brought out to the public when he established Eckankar in 1965.

For more about the historical and spiritual significance of the Temple of ECK, you may want to read *The Dream Weaver Chronicles* by James Paul Davis. He makes some interesting spiritual links between events in the world and the time when the Temple of ECK was being built.

How the Temple of ECK Came into Existence

In 1986 Sri Harold moved Eckankar's headquarters from Menlo Park, California, to Minnesota. A site for the Temple had been found in Chanhassen. Sri Harold gave directions that a lone spruce tree on a hill overlooking the Temple should serve as a marker. The Temple would be built about one hundred meters north of it.

Sri Harold spoke at the dedication ceremony for the Temple of ECK.

He said:

> *The date, October 22, 1990, is one of the most important dates in spiritual history. . . . Because history is happening and we are in the middle of it, it's easy to overlook the significance of today. But I'm happy you could come to this special ceremony as we now begin, in earnest, our mission of carrying the Light and Sound of ECK to the world.*[4]

What Does the Temple of ECK Look Like?

One of the Temple's most striking features, a golden ziggurat roof, was described in a Twin Cities newspaper. In the January 8, 1991, edition of the *Saint Paul Pioneer Press* staff writer Clark Morphew writes, "From a distance, it looks like a golden pyramid, the steps appearing as symbols of the human path to God."

The ziggurat was a feature of ancient temples in Sumer, Babylonia, Assyria, and Egypt. The Assyrians believed their ziggurats were stairways to heaven, a connecting link between God and man.

The golden ziggurat roof of the Temple of ECK is built with approximately 8,700 square feet of specially designed gold anodized-aluminum panels. The roof

The date, October 22, 1990, is one of the most important dates in spiritual history.

weighs over 15,000 pounds. The Temple building is 50,000 square feet. It has three linked areas: the Temple area itself, a vestibule, and an administration office. All three are modified octagons.

RESPECT FOR THE ENVIRONMENT

The Temple of ECK sits on 174 acres of prairie land adjacent to Lake Ann. It seems to rise out of rolling hills from a gradually curving drive through restored prairie grasses. Twenty-five acres of native Minnesota wildflowers surround the building. "The Temple is integrated through color and design with the preserved landscape of the surrounding countryside," according to Peter Sussman, a Temple of ECK architect.

People sit on trail benches and enjoy the deer, birds, and wildlife that inhabit the Temple grounds.

Before Eckankar purchased the property, the land was known as "High Path Ranch." To share the spiritual enjoyment of this sacred environment, approximately two miles of trails are now open to the public.

In season people walk these contemplation trails for spiritual reflection. The trails are dotted with signs which contain quotes from ECK writings. People sit on trail benches and enjoy the deer, birds, and wildlife that inhabit the Temple grounds.

See the middle of this book for photos of the Temple of ECK. In black and white, the photos only begin to capture its impact. The best way to see it is to come by for a visit and a tour.

YOU'RE WELCOME TO VISIT THE TEMPLE OF ECK

You don't have to leave your religion and become a member of ECK to enjoy the benefits of the ECK Temple; just come.
—Harold Klemp, *How the Inner Master Works*[5]

Thousands of people from around the world tour the Temple of ECK every year. It is also the home of a Cub Scout and a Boy Scout troop. One of the activities that people of many faiths enjoy are the ECK Worship Services at the Temple.

These are held on the first Sunday of each month. What people seem to like about them is how different they are from other worship services. ECK Worship Services feature ECKists telling stories about how the teachings of the Light and Sound of God and the Mahanta have helped them in their lives. The services also include singing HU, an ancient sacred love song to God. In addition, performers share expressions of their love for God through music, dramatic readings, and creative arts performances of all kinds. A male or female member of the ECK clergy serves as an officiator of the service.

It is a special treat when Sri Harold speaks at the ECK Worship Service. He does so when his schedule permits. As the guardian of this Golden Wisdom Temple, his presence at the Temple is a profound spiritual event. People regularly comment on the insights his talks have brought to their lives.

ECK Worship Services feature ECKists telling stories about how the teachings of the Light and Sound of God and the Mahanta have helped them in their lives.

Some Visitors' Impressions of ECK Worship Services

Many people find that ECK Worship Services are alive, relevant, and meaningful. Let's listen to what some visitors from other faiths have had to say about them. The names of the following people were changed to protect their privacy.

Jan, a divorced mother of two children, liked the story format used during the ECK Worship Service.

She could relate to the stories. She said that her life is a story; a journey. She felt this was a church that "would love her for what she is."

Rita is married and attends school. She liked the fact that there wasn't a minister preaching or proselytizing. She enjoyed the loving, peaceful atmosphere.

Brad, an interior designer, was impressed with the detailing in the building. After his visit to the Temple, there were some pretty significant changes and "coincidences" in his life. He feels that everything is becoming interconnected.

Brad liked the welcoming, open, and informative atmosphere for newcomers. He was impressed with the three questions that ECK clergyman Peter Skelskey posed to the congregation: "What is love? What is truth? What is my next spiritual step?"

Meg is a homemaker with two children. She felt that the ECK teachings were familiar, like a déjà vu feeling.

Meg said that the church has a very beautiful building but it's the people who make the church. And she feels the people are wonderful.

She has been impressed with friends who are in Eckankar and likes the way they're raising their child. Meg said that the church has a very beautiful building but it's the people who make the church. And she feels the people are wonderful.

Sally, a financial consultant, said that she'd never heard anything as beautiful as when the people in the worship service sang HU together. She said, "It really moved me. It touched something within me."

Jerry, a ten-year old ECKist, said, "I like the worship service. You get to make things in the children's class. And you get to hear music and a bunch of great stuff."

While the main worship service is going on in the sanctuary, there is a children's program for ages three to thirteen. In another room parents with infants and toddlers can view the worship service on a video monitor while their children play or sleep.

Sri Harold writes about another interesting perspective:

> A Catholic priest has been attending ECK Worship Services in Minneapolis. He finds that it makes him a better Catholic. He said that he has been telling a friend of his, a Protestant minister, that he likes the feeling he gets when he comes to the service. Nobody pressures him to become a member of ECKANKAR, or anything like that. We are there simply to sing HU, the holy name of God, and each person is open to receive whatever he can.[6]

OTHER PLACES TO ATTEND ECK WORSHIP SERVICES

Most major cities in the world have Eckankar centers or places where ECKists get together to hold ECK Worship Services. To find the Eckankar center nearest you, look in the white pages of your phone book under Eckankar or call the Eckankar Spiritual Center in Minneapolis at (612) 544-0066.

For information about worship services, tours, and classes at the Temple of ECK in Chanhassen, call (612) 474-0700. Both of these numbers are open for calls, Monday through Friday, from 8:00 a.m. to 5:00 p.m., U.S. central time.

You don't have to physically get in a car to go to a Golden Wisdom Temple though. To see color photos of

Most major cities in the world have Eckankar centers or places where ECKists get together to hold ECK Worship Services.

the Temple of ECK, visit Eckankar's home page on the Internet's World Wide Web at http://www.eckankar.org. You can also visit these temples in your dreams and contemplations.

You may find yourself in Temples of Golden Wisdom during dreams and while doing Eckankar spiritual exercises and contemplations.

VISITING GOLDEN WISDOM TEMPLES

Would you like to visit Golden Wisdom Temples, including the Temple of ECK? You can ask the Mahanta to take you to otherworld temples for advanced spiritual study. You may find yourself in Temples of Golden Wisdom during dreams and while doing Eckankar spiritual exercises and contemplations.

Within the heavens there are many levels or planes of existence. In II Corinthians 12:2, Paul writes of a man who was lifted up to the third level of heaven. Within these levels of heaven there are Temples of Golden Wisdom similar in many ways to the Temple of ECK in Minnesota.

Each Temple of Golden Wisdom has an ECK Master, a Co-worker with God, as a guardian. These exalted spiritual beings teach from the holy scriptures of Eckankar, the Shariyat-Ki-Sugmad *(SHAH-ree-aht-kee-SOOG-mahd)*. Volumes of the Shariyat are housed at these inner-world Temples.

INNER AND OUTER SCRIPTURES

The Shariyat-Ki-Sugmad is unlike any other scriptures you've ever read because people experience it many different ways. Sri Harold calls the Shariyat "a repository of wisdom that rises from the Sound and Light."[7]

The outer writings of the Shariyat, collected in two volumes by Paul Twitchell, the modern-day founder of

Eckankar, are only a translation of what must be perceived at a higher level than words or language can express. The written Shariyat, as with any book, is composed of imperfect words in an imperfect world.

Sri Harold writes:

> *Paul even explained that the Shariyat-Ki-Sugmad comes out in many different ways. With a certain person as the vehicle or instrument, it comes out as poetry; with someone else, it comes out as parables and stories; and for another person it comes out largely as prose.*[8]

There are reports of an interesting phenomenon in the publishing industry known as parallel writing. Different writers have been known to send similar manuscripts to an editor. The writers live in entirely different parts of the world and have never communicated physically.

Perhaps they were experiencing the same area of the Shariyat or the inner heavenly worlds to inspire their stories.

I even knew a writer this happened to. In a dream, he got an inspiration for a novel that seemed to rapidly write itself. He sent the finished manuscript to his editor. The editor called and told the writer that he'd love to publish his book if he hadn't already just bought it from another writer who lived on the opposite coast.

He said that the two books were identical in many ways — even entire passages. Although the plot and characters were the same, the names of the two main characters were different.

The written Shariyat is designed to help you find the wisdom of the ECK teachings, not in a book, but

The written Shariyat is designed to help you find the wisdom of the ECK teachings, not in a book, but within your own heart.

within your own heart. The words may inspire you, but they won't lead you to God. The Light and Sound and the Mahanta do that.

The writings of the Living ECK Master are the most current expressions of the ECK teachings. He is always updating the ECK teachings for the consciousness of the day.

Although the Shariyat is the bible of Eckankar, it isn't studied in the same way most religions study their sacred scriptures.

THE ECKANKAR SCRIPTURES ARE WRITTEN IN THE HEART

Although the Shariyat is the bible of Eckankar, it isn't studied in the same way most religions study their sacred scriptures. Books in Eckankar are viewed as starting points to lead seekers to their own personal experiences with the Holy Spirit. People who begin studying the ECK teachings with the Mahanta as their guide learn through inner methods such as dreams and contemplations.

Sri Harold explains:

> *The highest truth is not written in any book, it's written in your heart. All the books in the world are useless unless they can help you open your heart.*
> *Open your heart to what? To the love of God.*[9]

A delightful comic book makes the scriptures of Eckankar easy to read and understand. It is *Way of the Eternal,* by Cheng Yew Chung, an illustrated compilation of *The Shariyat-Ki-Sugmad,* Books One and Two.

HOW PEOPLE EXPERIENCE THE SHARIYAT

In the audiocassette of a workshop, *The Temples of Golden Wisdom,* Carol Morimitsu and Phil Morimitsu share many of the ways people have perceived the Shariyat and the inner heavenly temples.

They say that some people experience these sacred scriptures as computer printouts, scrolls, marble tablets, thin glass, on a movie screen or videocassette, or as a column of pure Light and Sound. Phil and Carol's advice is "Don't discount anything. A window that you see may be . . . a window to the Shariyat."[10]

Sri Harold tells a story of a woman from New Zealand who saw the Shariyat long before she'd ever heard of Eckankar.

When Sharon was eleven years old she saw a green light in the corner of her bedroom. In the middle she could see a scroll from which light was flowing. Alphabet letters were written across it.

She had no idea what this meant.

Sri Harold says, "She realized something was leading her on a mystic path with very interesting experiences."

Years later Sharon read a discourse written by Sri Harold. In it he explained that some people experience the Shariyat-Ki-Sugmad in the form of a scroll.

Sri Harold explains:

> *The Shariyat-Ki-Sugmad is the ECK bible. It means* Way of the Eternal. . . . *There are two volumes out here, and there are twelve volumes on the inner planes.*[11]

Sharon had been fortunate to be touched by the eternal wisdom of the Shariyat. Her heart had been opened to discover truth. This prepared her for outwardly finding it later in life.

Some people experience these sacred scriptures as computer printouts, scrolls, marble tablets, thin glass, on a movie screen or videocassette, or as a column of pure Light and Sound.

*Did you know
that as you live
your life and
learn, you're
contributing to
the Shariyat?*

But did you know that as you live your life and learn, you're contributing to the Shariyat?

THE LIVING SHARIYAT

Sri Harold explains a remarkable aspect of the Shariyat. It evolves as we grow in conscious awareness of ourselves and of God. In the quote below he refers to the Nine Silent Ones. These are high spiritual beings who work directly for the SUGMAD (God) moving silently through life on special assignments.

Here's how he says the living Shariyat is written:

> *The Shariyat-Ki-Sugmad is gathered by the Nine Silent Ones. It is drawn from the experiences of the initiates as they go through the lower worlds and meet the hardships of life — as Paul [Twitchell] did and as we do. As we meet these experiences, there is always something to be learned.*
>
> *It reminds me of a story about El Paso, which is in West Texas. One day a young man moved to town during a dry spell. It's nearly always dry, but when it does rain, it's constant. For weeks there wasn't any rain, but when the rain finally started falling, it wouldn't stop. It just flooded everything.*
>
> *The newcomer commented on this to an old man who had lived there for many years. The old man, who usually couldn't put two and two together, came up with an interesting statement which may have reflected the sum total of his observations in life. He said, "I spend 75 percent of my life praying for rain, and the other 25 percent praying for it to stop." This old man's viewpoint displays a certain degree of wisdom.*

The ECK Masters and the Nine Silent Ones gather a statement such as this out of each person's life. Some people have more than one statement; some people have chapters of statements. These are distilled and put together, and they become the teachings in the books of the Shariyat-Ki-Sugmad, which are always being written. They are not yet finished.[12]

The Shariyat Technique

Sri Harold offers a spiritual exercise to receive guidance from the Holy Spirit. You can use this technique with any sacred scripture or uplifting writing such as the Bible or the Koran.

A spiritual exercise to receive guidance from the Holy Spirit.

Try This Spiritual Exercise Today!

The following technique is a down-to-earth exercise that is geared to finding the Light and Sound of God. Many who have had difficulty with the imaginative techniques for Soul Travel will find this method successful.

1. Form a question about a problem that has been bothering you in your life. The question can be about health, prosperity, love, or any other subject that has been troubling you.

2. Open *The Shariyat-Ki-Sugmad,* Book One or Two, at random. Read one paragraph and then close your eyes. Sing, or chant, HU eight times (eight corresponds to the eight outer initiations) and then contemplate the passage you have just read. Continue this quiet contemplation for about five minutes, then chant HU eight more times. Again, return to quiet contemplation on

the paragraph from *The Shariyat.* Follow this procedure a third time. The entire contemplation will take from fifteen to twenty minutes.

3. Open *The Shariyat* at random again and read another paragraph. See how this paragraph relates to the first paragraph, how both offer a new insight and approach to your problem.

The usual reason a problem exists for us is that we are afraid to take the next step. Often we can think of four or five solutions to a problem, but we argue with ourselves, trying to decide what the next step should be.

The Shariyat may tell you what the next step is. You may wish to go through the technique again on the following day to carry the solution one step further or to explore some new question of a spiritual nature.[13]

The usual reason a problem exists for us is that we are afraid to take the next step.

A SPIRITUAL COMMUNITY HELPS YOU ADVANCE

Many of us appreciate the emotional and spiritual support of people who view life as we do. It helps us share insights, get questions answered, and enjoy life more.

The next chapter shows some ways to satisfy your growing need for spiritual advancement.

31. You're Invited to Get on the Spiritual Fast Track

So many of you—in one way or another, once or twice in your lifetime at least—have had some kind of experience that the average person hasn't had. These may be near-death experiences, out-of-the-body experiences, Soul Travel, astral projection, or seeing visions. . . .

Then one day you're watching a television program, and you see that others have experienced this too. "All these experiences that these other people have been reporting are true," you say. And you wonder, Where can I meet other people like this? Often you can't. They're scattered all over the country, and the television program seldom gives out names and addresses.

But Eckankar is here again in the twentieth century. It's out in the open again. And one of the advantages of Eckankar and ECK seminars is that you can meet others who, in one way or

another, have had experiences beyond what
most people experience in life today.
—Harold Klemp, *The Slow Burning Love of God*[1]

illions of people are just like you. They've
been touched by the Holy Spirit. They've
had some kind of profound spiritual awakening, such as an out-of-body, near-death, or otherwise
miraculous experience. They've experienced déjà vu,
moments of incredible insight, or the presence of God.

Here's Golden Key Number 31.
You can join others on the spiritual fast track to God.

You can meet these kinds of people in Eckankar. You
can meet people who want more love, deeper meaning,
a stronger relationship with God. Just as you do.

You can meet
people who
want more love,
deeper mean-
ing, a stronger
relationship
with God. Just
as you do.

GETTING ON THE SPIRITUAL FAST TRACK

Eckankar offers a spiritual fast track which leads
directly home to God. It is an inner and outer teaching
led by a living spiritual guide, Sri Harold Klemp, the
Mahanta, the Living ECK Master.

Meeting and getting support from spiritual adven-
turers helps you move along the spiritual fast track
with greater ease and a lot more fun. Eckankar is a
path on which human beings learn to fly like eagles in
their spiritual lives. But in the meantime, we walk this
earth together.

THE JOY OF SHARED VALUES

Perhaps you have already discovered the joy of
associating with people who love God as much as you
do. It's a pleasure to spend time with those who consider spirituality to be a priority.

Most ECKists don't wear their religion like a badge. They try to live it, quietly and with dignity and grace.

Mari, an entertainer and actress, explains how she feels about sharing spiritual interests.

"I met this man from New York. He's a brother. Eckankar actually got him off the streets. He turned his life around. He has an amazing story to tell.

"I believe it could make a difference in race relations if all people were knowingly connected by ECK. To be in worship services together. In Eckankar classes. Goodness. Think of the sharing.

"Each race has a different background and experiences. Everybody has so much energy to bring to the party."

I believe it could make a difference in race relations if all people were knowingly connected by ECK.

You're Invited to the Party

Enjoy yourself at the spiritual new year's party tonight, because Soul is a happy being. When you are with others, realize that they too are Lights of God who are also trying to find their way home to a better, happier, more graceful life.

—Harold Klemp, *How the Inner Master Works* [2]

Speaking of the party, you can also enjoy Eckankar's celebrations of Spirit. Officially they're called seminars. These international gatherings bring a happy mix of spiritual upliftment, reunion with old friends, and meeting new ones. And at many of them there *are* parties with dancing after the workshops and programs are done for the day.

There are three major Eckankar seminars held in North America each year. The first is the ECK Springtime Seminar, usually on Easter weekend. The second is the ECK Summer Festival, sometime in June. Then on or around October 22 is the ECK Worldwide seminar to which thousands of ECKists from all over the world come to celebrate the beginning of Eckankar's spiritual new year.

In addition to being the beginning of the spiritual new year, October 22 commemorates the birth of Paul Twitchell, the modern-day founder of Eckankar. It's also historically the date when the each Living ECK Master of the times receives the Rod of ECK Power and takes on the spiritual leadership of Eckankar.

Other large ECK seminars are held in Europe, Africa, Asia, and the South Pacific. States, provinces, and countries around the world hold ECK regional seminars.

Sri Harold speaks at many of the major Eckankar seminars.

SRI HAROLD'S TALKS AND STORIES

Sri Harold speaks at many of the major Eckankar seminars. His talks and presence are highlights of the event. He often surprises newcomers with his practical nature and warm wit.

He uses storytelling to bring out the spiritual principles of the ECK teachings. Because, he says:

> *The stories that happen in Eckankar today are very similar to the stories that happened way back at the beginning of Christianity. The same sorts of stories and miracles are still going on today.*[3]

Sri Harold's stories contain the inner and outer elements that are fundamental to the teachings of Eckankar. He shares an experience that shows how his stories convey greater truth and awareness than may appear on the surface.

He says:

> One time an ECKist gave me a story that had happened to his father. When I told the story I added a detail that he hadn't told me. I said, "And Rebazar Tarzs was the person." Rebazar Tarzs is an ECK Master who helps people. Rebazar Tarzs was one of the people who came and helped [this man's] father. Later this ECKist described Rebazar to his father. His father said, "Yes, as a matter of fact, there was this man here, and he did look like that. But I don't think I told you about him." I see the rest of the story, and I report it as I see it. I try to be accurate.[4]

The Experience of Hearing Sri Harold Speak at a Seminar

Here's one young college student's impressions of her first time hearing Sri Harold speak at a seminar.

"My father told me there was going to be an Eckankar seminar near where I lived. I decided to go just to appease him, but I'd go Sunday, the very last day.

"My dad had said he'd send me the money to make the trip. But I said, 'No, if I'm going to do this, I'll pay for it too. This will be my thing.' That way I'd owe nothing. I could just check it out for myself.

"On the way to the seminar traffic was horrible. My mother kept saying, 'Let's just turn back.' But I knew I had to get there. By this time, it had become a personal mission.

"When I finally got there, I sat down and waited to be bombarded with 'spirituality.' I expected to be

I knew I had to get there. By this time, it had become a personal mission.

lectured to. Instead, I was washed over with love and light humor and teachings spoken in a way I could understand.

"Everything Sri Harold said related exactly to my life. Whatever he talked about spoke directly to me.

"I came out completely energized.

"Then I got a seminar program and saw all the things I'd missed. All the youth activities. The topics. The workshops. I was so excited I talked all the way home."

INSTRUCTION FOR CHILDREN AND YOUTH

It's not always easy to be a spiritually minded young person in today's world.

As the ECKist above mentioned, you'll find special programs designed for the spiritual needs of youth and young adults at ECK seminars. Families are encouraged to go to the seminars with their children.

It's not always easy to be a spiritually minded young person in today's world. These seminars give youngsters the opportunity to share ideas and form friendships with others who view life as they do.

To help youth apply the ECK teachings to their lives and to be sure Eckankar is doing everything to help them, Sri Harold formed the ECK Youth Council. These are young people from around the world who offer encouragement, advice, and support to Eckankar's spiritual programs for youth and young adults.

The youth also have a publication, *Letter of Light,* to which they contribute stories and share ideas for applying the spiritual principles of ECK in school and with friends and family members. "Questions for the Master . . ." is a special section in this newsletter where Sri Harold answers questions young people ask about Eckankar and life in general.

Here's a sample:

Q: *How did Wah Z [Sri Harold's spiritual name] become the Mahanta?*
                                        —A nine-year-old girl

A. *It was like going to a spiritual school for a long time. There were tests every day. I had to learn to get along better with my problems and with people. Once I passed those tests, the SUGMAD [God] thought it was time to let me have a bigger challenge. It was to help others find their way back to God too.*
                                        —Harold[5]

You'll enjoy meeting people of all ages at ECK seminars.

The Party Isn't Really Over

When you look around the audience at an Eckankar seminar, you'll see people from all walks of life, corners of the world, and nationalities. They're laughing and crying together. They share a wonderful zest for life that is so common among ECKists. You're likely to feel such love that you'll come away glowing.

Sri Harold spoke about the lasting effects of Eckankar seminars. He said, "We'll try to give you something that you can carry with you for more than a few weeks—perhaps your whole lifetime."[6]

Finding Out How Much Love Is All Around You

The heart of the seminar experience is feeling the divine love that comes through on an occasion such as this. The ECK flow is stronger than usual when we all get together.

When you look around the audience at an Eckankar seminar, you'll see people from all walks of life, corners of the world, and nationalities.

You can then carry some of this love home with you after the weekend is over.

—Harold Klemp, *The Drumbeat of Time*[7]

One of the most fascinating aspects of Eckankar gatherings is the validation people receive for their inner spiritual experiences.

One of the most fascinating aspects of Eckankar gatherings is the validation people receive for their inner spiritual experiences. Because Eckankar is unique in being both an inner and outer teaching, people often have dreams or visions of spiritual events. Then later they're inwardly guided to verification that what they experienced was real. This is the prove-it-to-yourself beauty of the ECK teachings.

An ECKist named Joan went to her first Eckankar seminar and had a profound experience that proved to her the abiding depth of the Mahanta's love.

THIS IS THE PLACE!

"About three years before I ever heard about Eckankar I had the strangest dream. I was brought to a place where there was an open pavilion. A man with long blond hair and blue eyes was there. I realized I was out of my body.

"But who was this guy?

"He was saying things that I had waited all my life to hear. When I woke up, I didn't know how I had gotten there. And I didn't know how to get back.

"For about three years the man with the blond hair and blue eyes showed up maybe five or six times. Each time I had a pretty extraordinary experience with him in a dream. Sometimes in meditation. I tried to hear his name. I only found out that it had two A's in it.

"Then I heard about the teachings of Eckankar from a friend. At first I didn't want to have anything to do with it because I thought it was really strange stuff. Then about a year later I went to an introductory program at an Eckankar seminar in Hartford.

"In the seminar art gallery I found out who the man with the blond hair and blue eyes was—the ECK Master Gopal Das.

"There was a wall mural that showed the place I had gone to in my dream. I stood there crying. That was how I learned about the ECK Master who had been coming to me.

"Then my knees just went out from under me. I bumped into the opposite wall and into a life-size portrait of the man with blue eyes and golden hair!

"I went to find my friend. I was sobbing, 'I found the place. I found the place.' "

Gopal Das is depicted as having shoulder-length blond hair, light blue eyes, and a round face with fair features. Because of his long hair and clothing, he's sometimes mistaken for Jesus by those who don't know him by name but see him in dreams, visions, or spiritual experiences.

The painting that so profoundly affected this new ECKist was done by an ECK artist. Eckankar encourages and supports creativity and spiritual growth among its members.

Eckankar encourages and supports creativity and spiritual growth among its members.

ECK SPECIAL INTEREST GROUPS

A highlight of Eckankar seminars for many people is meeting with ECKists who share common interests. In addition to the main program and workshops, there are also meetings of ECK special interest groups. These groups help ECKists learn how to use their skills and talents in service to God and life.

The special interest groups currently in Eckankar are in the areas of writing, music, theater, art, film and television, computer bulletin boards, and the licensed health-care professions. Each special interest group holds meetings and some have newsletters so their members can share ideas and get to know each other better. The groups meet at major Eckankar seminars. Many local ECK centers also have circles that meet regularly to discuss how the ECK teachings apply to members' special skills and interests.

The ECK writers have a conference prior to the ECK Summer Festival each year. It's a quality writing conference that is focused on spirituality and writing. Here's a sample from the ECK Writers Group newsletter, *The ECK Writers Update.*

An ECKist named Alice writes:

> *The activities in the ECK writers circle have helped me sharpen my sense of creativity and expand my imagination. I've been able to develop personal spiritual exercises that have brought me through crises, healings, and personal growth.*[8]

Another way ECKists get to know each other and advance spiritually is to attend classes called Satsangs.

ECK CLASSES

Another way ECKists get to know each other and advance spiritually is to attend classes called Satsangs. Each month Sri Harold sends a discourse which is like a letter to the members of Eckankar. Currently there are seventeen years of monthly ECK discourse lessons for ECKists. These discourses come in series of twelve and are studied one per month.

An ECKist shared what attending Satsang meant to him when he first started to study the teachings.

"My wife took me to an Eckankar introductory talk in Berlin. I didn't feel I really understood much. But I had this inner feeling that this was my path.

"When I went to my first class, it helped me to understand what Eckankar is really about.

"I found that the individuals and, of course, the Living ECK Master are really authentic people. Their outer actions are congruent with what they say.

"In other paths I've met people who talked a lot about good things, but I never had the impression that they were really that good themselves. It was different in Eckankar."

"All the folks I meet, and especially the ECK Masters, provide people with truth. That's amazing today. It's something that assures me that this is the right path."

You Can Also Study Eckankar Privately

You can study Eckankar discourses privately in your own home. Receiving a discourse is like having your own personal meeting with the Mahanta. You don't have to meet with other ECKists, if you don't want to.

But what a treat you're missing!

Satsang classes provide fellowship, validation, and support on your spiritual journey, which can be a lonely one at times. You're welcome to visit a Satsang class to see what it's like.

Another ECKist told how he and others benefit from being around a community of spiritually minded people.

"People are absolutely delighted to know that they can meet in fellowship with others like themselves.

Receiving a discourse is like having your own personal meeting with the Mahanta.

Sri Harold also writes special articles to communicate with members quarterly in a publication called the Mystic World.

They can talk about real issues in their lives, spiritual or otherwise. They can read holy books and writings together."

SRI HAROLD COMMUNICATES WITH THE ECK CHELAS REGULARLY

Sri Harold also writes special articles to communicate with members quarterly in a publication called the *Mystic World*. Through the written word, the Living ECK Master is able to keep his students current with the important spiritual issues of the moment.

Sri Harold's discourses and articles are always inspiring, timely, and uplifting.

In a *Mystic World* article to ECK members he writes:

> *If your troubles seem too much to bear sometimes, please remember that they are also giving you a greater capacity for love and compassion.*[9]

When life is beating you down, it can help to read inspiring words like these.

VISITING TEMPLES OF GOLDEN WISDOM

Each seminar, Eckankar event, or class becomes a virtual Temple of Golden Wisdom as the love of the Mahanta infuses those who are gathered together to learn more about the Light and Sound of God. Here's a spiritual exercise you can use to have an inner experience with these advanced spiritual teachings called Eckankar.

Try This Spiritual Exercise Today!

Before you go to sleep, say to the Mahanta, "If it's for my spiritual well-being, please take me to . . ." (choose one of the following):

- ಜ a Temple of Golden Wisdom
- ಜ an Eckankar seminar
- ಜ an ECK Worship Service
- ಜ a class to study the ECK teachings
- ಜ a fellowship gathering of ECKists or like-minded spiritual friends

Be sure to record in your journal any dream experiences you have. Try not to censor yourself or judge what you write. You may have some ideas about what your experiences should be, but be open to whatever you experience.

QUESTIONS AND ANSWERS

You're probably pretty curious now about the Eckankar advanced spiritual teachings. Here are some questions you may be asking.

1. *What kinds of activities would I see if I came to an Eckankar seminar in my area?*

You'd be able to hear people talk onstage about their personal experiences with the ECK teachings. You could also attend workshops, roundtable discussions, and worship services where people share their insights and learn new ways of exploring the ECK teachings.

One of the most enjoyable features of ECK seminars is the creative arts. ECKists express their love for

You're probably pretty curious now about the Eckankar advanced spiritual teachings.

Divine Spirit through original music compositions and performances. Some seminars also display original art by ECKists.

At most ECK seminars you can buy ECK books and audio- and videocassettes of Sri Harold's talks or ECK music. You can also pick up free literature.

2. *Would I feel welcome at an Eckankar event if I'm not an ECKist?*

By all means. Most areas invite newcomers to Eckankar events and make special arrangements to be sure they feel welcome and comfortable. Not wanting to impose, people may wait until you look as if *you* want to talk.

You might feel as if you've finally come home to people you've known for lifetimes.

Usually there's some kind of social gathering or way for people to chat informally and get to know each other. There's often a part of the seminar program for newcomers. Although a donation is usually requested with seminar registration, none is requested at newcomer workshops. They're open to everyone.

Be forewarned though. You might feel as if you've finally come home to people you've known for lifetimes.

HOW THESE ADVANCED TEACHINGS CAME INTO BEING

In the next chapters you're going to get a brief history of the ECK teachings and the founding of Eckankar as a modern-day religion. You may be surprised at some of what you discover. These teachings have ancient spiritual roots.

Yet not many know the truth about their origins.

32. You Need to Know about the Most Ancient Teachings

The ECK teachings have been here from the earliest times, but they haven't carried the name of ECKANKAR. They have been brought out under different names at different times because they could not be presented openly, but at this point in history they can.

—Harold Klemp, *The Secret Teachings*[1]

The Creator provided a way for creation to learn about its true relationship with God. To find the love that is always pulsing through life itself.

Here's Golden Key Number 32.
The ECK teachings are the most ancient teachings.

This body of teachings originates from the Life Force Itself, the pure, original source of knowledge about God. The ECK teachings are a direct link to this Audible Life Current which is seen as Light and heard as Sound.

And there is always a way for Souls to find the ECK teachings.

THE LIVING ECK MASTER

Throughout history the Living ECK Master of the times has always been the principal teacher of these ancient teachings. He expresses the consciousness of the Mahanta, chief agent for God's love to flow through creation.

During certain eras in history the ECK teachings had to be taught secretly due to religious persecution.

The Living ECK Master leads the ancient order of ECK Masters known as the Vairagi Adepts. He teaches ECK through whatever religion or spiritual path he guides. This becomes the ECK teachings of that day.

Today the ECK teachings are taught in Eckankar, Religion of the Light and Sound of God. They are kept current and pure by Sri Harold Klemp, who is the Mahanta, the Living ECK Master.

THE ECK TEACHINGS HAVEN'T ALWAYS BEEN TAUGHT OPENLY

During certain eras in history the ECK teachings had to be taught secretly due to religious persecution. Until recently the last time the pure teachings of the Light and Sound were taught publicly was five thousand years ago in Egypt. The Mahanta, the Living ECK Master then was Gopal Das. He moved the pure teachings underground when attacks by the orthodox religions in Egypt became too vicious.

After the ECK teachings were no longer taught openly, they scattered throughout the world.

THE TEACHINGS OF ECK WERE SCATTERED

After the ECK teachings were no longer taught openly, they scattered throughout the world. They were taught orally from teacher to students. People learned of them through inner channels of dreams and guidance and the appearances of ECK Masters in various parts of the world.

Native American Indians, Asians, Africans, South Americans all were fortunate to have ECK Masters walk among them. These ECK Masters taught inwardly and outwardly those Souls who were ready for spiritual liberation everywhere on this earth.

The tribal tradition of passing information orally from one generation to the next allowed many of the ECK teachings to remain within the African culture. Truths such as reincarnation, belief in the afterlife, and HU, an ancient name for God taught in Eckankar, have been remembered to this day. Eventually though, without the benefit of having the Living ECK Master as their spiritual leader, most of the religions that had parts of the ECK teachings forgot the origin of their beliefs. Rituals remained to commemorate them, but the essence had been lost.

The tribal tradition of passing information orally from one generation to the next allowed many of the ECK teachings to remain within the African culture.

The ECK Teachings Survived

Every once in a while, proofs emerge in unexpected ways that show how the teachings of ECK survived this five-thousand-year silent period. The following story, for example, shows how a modern-day electrical engineer got quite a shock. And not the electrical kind.

In Africa a retired school principal hired an ECKist to do some electrical work in his home. The homeowner's very old father walked into the room while the two men were chatting. He listened to their conversation.

"What are you doing?" he asked the ECKist. "Telling the secrets of ECK to this child?" He was referring to his son who was anything but a child.

The ECKist replied, "They're not secret anymore.

In 1965, Paul Twitchell brought them out to the public."

The man's father became very quiet. Then he said, "I first heard about Eckankar in 1914."

The old man told about an ECK Master who had introduced him to the teachings. "I see Eckankar has finally made it out to this plane," he said.

This African man had for years been meeting with the ECK Master Gopal Das. During dreams he was taken to study with the ECK Master at a Temple of Golden Wisdom.

When the ECKist showed the old man a picture of Gopal Das, he said, "Yes, that is the man who taught me since I was young, since I first heard of Eckankar in 1914."[2]

As the ECKist in the story mentioned, the pure teachings of the Light and Sound have resurfaced. The world is ready for them again.

And a man who seemed to be a rather unlikely candidate was chosen to bring them back out to the public.

Paul Twitchell had an unquenchable thirst for spiritual truth.

PAUL TWITCHELL GATHERED THE LOST TEACHINGS

Paul Twitchell had an unquenchable thirst for spiritual truth. The Vairagi Masters gave a monumental assignment to him, a man who had been a seeker all his life.

Paul Twitchell had a twofold mission. He was to gather the ancient teachings of ECK wherever he could find them. He would bring them from ashrams, sweat lodges, rain forests, mountaintops, churches, synagogues, and temples. These were only some of the places where gems of the teachings had been scattered.

The second part of Paul's mission was to create a

way for people in the modern world to learn of the ECK teachings. People needed to have the Light and Sound of God in their lives every day. In our modern society, we work, raise our children, and live in our communities. Most people aren't able or willing to become monks or practice religious austerities to find a deeper relationship with God.

Sri Harold writes about how the pure ECK teachings had been obscured:

> *The different masters each had parts and pieces of it [the ECK teachings], but they attached little requirements, or strings, to it: You must be a vegetarian, or you have to meditate so many hours a day if you want to really be a true follower on the path to God. And this was wrong for our day and age. It was geared for another culture.*[3]

The Vairagi Masters knew this. They commissioned Paul to separate truth from the cultural trappings, rituals, and practices that surrounded the scattered ECK teachings over the years. To bring the teachings of the Light and Sound within the grasp of ordinary people.

It was an awesome job.

Paul's Search for Truth

The past is fine; certain people need a historical foundation. But the historical aspect is not essential to any Soul on the path to God. All that is really needed is a linkup, or connection, with the Light and Sound of God.

—Harold Klemp, *The Golden Heart* [4]

The Vairagi Masters commissioned Paul to separate truth from the cultural trappings, rituals, and practices that surrounded the scattered ECK teachings over the years.

As with most of us, Paul's spiritual mission wasn't always clear to him. He knew that he loved God. He knew that he wasn't finding the whole truth about God in the orthodox religions of his time.

He was aware that there was something more. And he spent most of his life sifting through every religion and spiritual teaching he could find, looking for the truth. Paul searched everywhere. You name the teaching, and he studied it. He fell in and out of love with his spiritual teachers as he began to grow beyond them into the God-Realized state of consciousness. But each religion or spiritual path taught him more than he'd known before.

Paul fell in and out of love with his spiritual teachers as he began to grow beyond them into the God-Realized state of consciousness.

Paul was drawn to Eastern teachings such as Hinduism, Buddhism, and the Sant Mat traditions. They seemed to be close to presenting truth as he understood it at the time. Many terms Paul found to describe spiritual experiences and beliefs are Eastern. These were the only words that came close to conveying what is beyond comprehension.

The word *Eckankar* itself derives from a Pali word meaning *one*. Paul coined the word Eckankar to describe the religion that would house the ECK teachings and lead Souls to become one with the Holy Spirit. *Eckankar* is now defined as "Co-worker with God."

PAUL'S FIRST ECK TEACHERS

In the book *The Drums of ECK* Paul Twitchell tells about his past-life serving under General Zachary Taylor in the American-Mexican War during 1846–48. In that lifetime, as Peddar Zaskq, he studied under the Mahanta, the Living ECK Master Rebazar Tarzs.

Paul Twitchell was born on October 22 or 23 between 1908 and 1910. Different people who saw his family Bible have reported conflicting birth dates.

None of his relatives, except for his father and sister Kay-Dee, recognized Paul's spiritual abilities. At the age of eight, he met a being of light who told him, "You are under my charge until you grow up, and at that time your development will be turned over to other Masters."

As Paul progressed toward Mastership, he tried to identify the spiritual guides who came to him during his inner experiences. He sometimes simply identified them as the teacher he was following in his outer studies. Later, as he grew in consciousness, he recognized them as the ECK Masters who were guiding him toward his spiritual destiny.

As Paul progressed toward Mastership, he tried to identify the spiritual guides who came to him during his inner experiences.

During Paul's personal search for truth he first met the ECK Master Sudar Singh in 1935 who introduced him to the ECK teachings. Later he began to receive instruction from Rebazar Tarzs who was the Mahanta, the Living ECK Master at that time.

ECK Masters helped Paul to sift the wheat from the chaff of what he had learned in his spiritual search. In addition to *The Tiger's Fang*, several other classic books present Paul's early experiences with the ECK Masters and his discovery of the ECK teachings.

Paul's writings reveal much about Paul, the seeker. But others remember Paul, the man.

PAUL TWITCHELL, THE MAN

Paul was quite athletic. He was short, of course—five-and-a-half-feet tall—with a very powerful upper physique. He was also rather bowlegged. Some people who didn't think so kindly of him joked that when he was walking down the street, you could almost run a billy goat between his legs.

—Harold Klemp, *The Secret Teachings* [5]

Paul has been described by those who knew him as an enigma, a man of mystery and surprise, a man of puzzling contrasts with a fine sense of humor. His friends knew him as a teacher who used unconventional means to get his students' attention. As a thoughtful man who had a great love for all life.

Paul has been described by those who knew him as an enigma, a man of mystery and surprise, a man of puzzling contrasts with a fine sense of humor.

He was an eccentric with a wry sense of humor. For example, Paul developed a personal seal of approval with his own sticker, "Recommended by Paul Twitchell."

It was a cartoon drawing of him wearing a sports cap. Underneath he had a hand with thumb and forefinger formed into a circle. He sent these seals of approval to Eleanor Roosevelt; Milton Caniff, the creator of the *Steve Canyon* comic strip; and a manager of a Shakey's Pizza Parlor, among others.

Paul also had a sticker for his Sour Grapes award. He'd place these inside books he didn't like. And sometimes he sent his Sour Grapes to people and corporations.

Sri Harold describes Paul as a rascal, feisty, a character, a master compiler, and his own best drumbeater. He also says that Paul led a checkered life.

Paul called himself the *Cliff Hanger.* A bold spiritual adventurer who wanted to touch the sky. He was creative, diplomatic, mercurial. Most of all Paul was compassionate and kind to sincere seekers.

Paul went through many trials and hardships. Sometimes he was vain and cocky. There were times when he despaired. Then he would have peak experiences with God that helped him realize his efforts were worthwhile.

He had a roller coaster of a life filled with joy and heartache.

A good resource for firsthand accounts from people who knew Paul is the Eckankar audiocassette *The Many Faces of Paul Twitchell.*

Paul's Monumental Task

Paul was instructed in the secret teachings that underlie all the spirituality known on this planet. Yet he still had to somehow fit in with the consciousness of his day.

Most of the time, he didn't.

Paul had about as many jobs as he had former religions. Through much of his life he supported himself as a writer. Under a pen name, he even wrote pulp fiction!

He wrote Westerns and philosophy under pen names. One of his stories sold to *Colliers* magazine. While in the Navy during World War II he wrote public-relations copy.

Paul was instructed in the secret teachings that underlie all the spirituality known on this planet. Yet he still had to somehow fit in with the consciousness of his day.

So we have this man with a thick Southern accent from Paducah, Kentucky. Who would believe the results of his years of research?

There was a period when Paul's writing hit good times. He sold two books to a major Hollywood movie studio. This allowed him to quit his job and travel. To continue his search for truth and love.

WHO WAS EVER GOING TO BELIEVE HIM?

So we have this man with a thick Southern accent from Paducah, Kentucky. Who would believe the results of his years of research? Who would accept the fact that he could travel to the heart of God and return with the keys to spiritual freedom?

First Paul would have to promote himself as a person with credentials. He did this type of self-promotion shamelessly. All his life. He managed to get himself listed in *Who's Who in Kentucky* by the age of twenty-seven. And he nominated himself to be highlighted in *Ripley's Believe It or Not.*

Whatever he did to get himself known, it worked!

During his stint in the Navy in World War II, Paul had photos of himself with the actor Pat O'Brien, President Franklin Delano Roosevelt, and General Eisenhower.

As a result of the savvy he gained through all his years of research, travel, and racking up writing credentials, Paul was able to begin speaking with some credibility.

THE TIMES

Put yourself back in time. It's the late 1960s. The Vietnam War has thrown people into a spiritual frenzy. They're questioning authority. Seeking answers that they can't find through traditional sources.

This unknown man named Paul Twitchell—a Westerner, not dressed in a long flowing robe, but an amazingly profound man—comes on the scene.

He has answers.

He can show people how to have their own direct experiences with the Holy Spirit.

He's dramatic.

He's fascinating.

He's right. What he's teaching works.

The Beatles are traveling to visit the Maharishi. But people who attend Paul's lectures are traveling out of their bodies.

It's a time of adventure. Of wonder.

And Paul Twitchell is at the center of it all.

But how will he bring these ancient teachings into a world that isn't nearly as interested in truth as it is in lava lamps and protest marches?

He can show people how to have their own direct experiences with the Holy Spirit.

33. You Have the Opportunity to Discover Truth for Yourself

Truth isn't something "out there" or words written down on paper. We ourselves are the living, walking, expanding truth.
— Harold Klemp, *The Eternal Dreamer*[1]

*B*eauty, it is said, is in the eye of the beholder. The same could be said of truth.

Paul Twitchell was a truth seeker. He searched all his life for the purest source of truth, wisdom, and love. He found it in the ancient ECK teachings.

Here's Golden Key Number 33.
You can discover truth for yourself.

In 1965 Paul Twitchell made spiritual history. He founded the modern-day religion of Eckankar.

And did he ever have a tiger by the tail!

PAUL BROUGHT ECK TO THE PUBLIC

In 1965 Paul started to present the ECK teachings to anyone who would listen.

He did weekly lectures at the California Parapsychology Foundation on the Ancient Science of Soul Travel. With Soul Travel, Soul could walk freely in the heavens while still maintaining a human body. He first referred to Soul Travel as bilocation but later stopped using that term.

All the time, he was learning too.

Paul had to write for the consciousness of his times which was essentially looking for dramatic phenomena rather than deeper spiritual truth.

PAUL HAD A ROUGH TIME OF IT

Paul made mistakes. He changed his mind about whom he admired and didn't. He had to write for the consciousness of his times which was essentially looking for dramatic phenomena rather than deeper spiritual truth.

As Paul's writings and workshops became more successful, he was taken advantage of and misquoted by people he trusted. He wrote discourses to his students on a manual typewriter with a carbon copy. These weren't proofread or edited carefully.

In his letters to Gail Atkinson who was to become his wife and helpmate, Paul listed incredibly long lists of some of the books he had read during his spiritual search. He compiled vital truths and ideas forgotten by many. Paul had a mind filled with years of facts, figures, myths, legends, and interpretations of the deeper meaning he understood from what he was reading.

Paul was basically a one-man show.

He only had his wife and a few dedicated volunteers to help him. He didn't have the time or resources to meticulously research and acknowledge the origins of every thought or idea he had ever read or heard.

Sri Harold writes about Paul's writing and research methods:

> As a book gets older, publishing houses are sold, management changes, and records are lost or thrown out. This is only one of many problems encountered in doing research. . . . It should have taken more than a lifetime for Paul to gather the ECK teachings, and yet he put it all together. This is what Paul did.[2]

PAUL'S ORIGINAL SOURCES FOR THE ECK TEACHINGS

Sri Harold explains that because Paul became such an adept spiritual traveler he could do research in the inner heavenly worlds. He visited libraries that held information accessible to only a few, such as Julian Johnson and Paul Brunton who went to some of the same primary inner sources as Paul did.

Like a master architect using both new and old materials, Paul pieced together the truths that he found. But he took everything a step further. He recast the seed ideas so they fit into a grander, more compelling spiritual framework. One which would allow the Sound and Light to shine through.

An ECKist who was a spiritual seeker for many years tells about his first impressions of Paul's writings.

"At first I would read things, especially in Paul's works, and I'd think, *Well, I already read that.* I was comparing mentally how it stacked up with other things.

"But generally there were two things. First, the overall approach and the principles were, even from a

Paul took everything a step further. He recast the seed ideas so they fit into a grander, more compelling spiritual framework. One which would allow the Sound and Light to shine through.

mental point of view, the best I'd found. Paul's writings covered everything from A to Z. They didn't leave any questions unanswered, at least for me. I thought his writings were the best around.

"But also I started noticing the subtler parts. The books themselves were like Light. They had that quality. So they made you feel good to read them. Some of the things I'd read by other writers didn't."

OTHER SEEKERS RESPONDED

Interest in the ECK teachings grew beyond Paul's wildest dreams. People began to ask for the ECK teachings in writing. Paul started to write and send out ECK discourses. These were in the form of monthly letters to his new spiritual students. Sri Harold writes, "Paul wrote discourses when he was too busy, too tired, or too sick to write them. Why? Because the monthly mailings were scheduled to go out on a certain date, and Paul did what he had to.[3]

By 1967 Paul's name was becoming better known. He wrote a series of articles for the *New Cosmic Star,* a new-age magazine. He grew into one of the publication's most popular writers.

PAUL'S WRITINGS

After the first rush of interest in his work, Paul became the quintessential man with a mission. He worked as fast as he could.

After the first rush of interest in his work, Paul became the quintessential man with a mission. He worked as fast as he could. Those who knew him said he would have three typewriters, with three manuscripts going at once.

He'd make corrections on originals and hoped he remembered to make them on the carbons or vice versa. He researched constantly. Something inside of him knew that he had so little time. Fine points of grammar and punctuation were often left to the printer's copy editor. Sometimes his writings appeared contradictory. He didn't have the time to go back and see how he'd expressed something earlier. He tried to put into words what was beyond language to express or the mind to comprehend.

Paul wrote for the consciousness of the day. Sri Harold explains:

> *In the late 1960s, when Paul was introducing the ECK works to the public, its consciousness was quite low. He found that people were bored with pure truth. The Living ECK Master's mission is to find a doorway to Soul. Partly as protection for his family, Paul created the town of China Point, which does not exist. Paul dressed up some outer writings, like a myth form, to acquaint seekers with underlying truth. He had to reach them at their state of consciousness, which was very low when compared to people's understanding today.*[4]

Paul Twitchell wrote books, novels, poetry, discourses. Whatever might best communicate to the seekers of his day.

Paul Twitchell was an amazingly prolific writer and teacher. He wrote books, novels, poetry, discourses. Whatever might best communicate to the seekers of his day.

In six short years he published incredible spiritual-history-making books such as *ECKANKAR: The Key to Secret Worlds.* That book, first released in 1969, continues to sell in bookstores around the world.

ECKANKAR TEACHINGS BECAME MORE ESTABLISHED

In 1970 on the advice of attorneys Paul established Eckankar as a nonprofit organization. This would give

Out of his immense love for God and his desire to satisfy truth seekers everywhere, Paul continued an incredible output of writing and teaching even though he was dying.

the teachings stability and insure that they could continue in this world.

By 1970 Paul was traveling all over the world lecturing and giving workshops. During a trip to Spain, a young man poisoned him. Paul knew that the beverage the man offered to him would harm him, but he drank it anyway. He had come to see the man out of love.

The poison severely damaged his body. Sometimes his body looked black. Other days he would appear to glow with health. Out of his immense love for God and his desire to satisfy truth seekers everywhere, Paul continued an incredible output of writing and teaching even though he was dying.

In *ECKANKAR: Illuminated Way Letters*, January 1971, Paul wrote that he was serving as the Mahanta until the time came to appoint an interim ECK Master. This person would serve as the Living ECK Master until the next Mahanta, who was still in training, was named.

At a 1971 ECK seminar in Cincinnati, Paul translated (died) of a heart attack. Some ECKists said Paul appeared to them afterward.

People today continue to report meeting the ECK Master Peddar Zaskq, which is Paul Twitchell's spiritual name, in dreams and visions. Even in person.

PAUL TWITCHELL TODAY

Sri Harold writes about an inner-world encounter he had with Paul:

> *Since he left the physical body, Peddar Zaskq, or Paul Twitchell, continues to work on the inner planes to bring together the common language of ECK in books.*

I saw Paul. . . . standing in an alcove in the library on the mezzanine level of a Temple of Golden Wisdom. The room was rather dark except for a shining golden light that was glowing over Paul and the book on the desk in front of him.

Paul just stood there, reflecting and thinking. As I watched him, I recognized that the gifts he gave through his writings and teachings of ECK were understood and appreciated by only a very few. He didn't expect praise, and he didn't wait for applause. He just kept doing what had to be done and bringing out truth, without thanks or reward.

He continues to do a number of things, but he especially enjoys research. He loves to find the hidden truths among us so that they can be shared with the people on all the planes.[5]

> He didn't expect praise, and he didn't wait for applause. He just kept doing what had to be done and bringing out truth, without thanks or reward.

THE INTERIM LIVING ECK MASTER

After Paul translated (died), Gail, his widow, said that he had let her know that the next Living ECK Master should be a man named Darwin Gross. Gross was an initiate of Eckankar who had, at times, worked closely with Paul.

Gross served as the Living ECK Master from 1971 until 1981. Sri Harold Klemp was chosen by the Sugmad [God], and appointed by Gross, to receive the Rod of ECK Power, the spiritual leadership of Eckankar, on October 22, 1981. History shows Gross tried to hold on to the Rod of ECK Power even though he had passed it on to Sri Harold. Gross's fall from grace is written about in Sri Harold's autobiographical book *Soul Travelers of the Far Country*. Today Darwin Gross is no longer associated with Eckankar.

ECKANKAR TODAY

At the time of this writing, Sri Harold has been the Mahanta, the Living ECK Master and Eckankar's spiritual leader for sixteen years. As the Living Word, at the helm of what has always been and always will be an evolving spiritual teaching, he *is* Eckankar today.

In chapters 1 through 3 there is a description and history of Sri Harold Klemp and his role as spiritual leader of Eckankar. For more information you can read the trilogy of his autobiographical books: *The Wind of Change, Soul Travelers of the Far Country,* and *Child in the Wilderness.* They give an honest and sometimes startling account of what it takes to attain, live with, and operate from the highest consciousness of God.

Sri Harold has a threefold mission that he's shared with members of Eckankar.

Sri Harold has said that there are three parts to his mission as the spiritual leader of Eckankar.

SRI HAROLD'S MISSION

Sri Harold has said that there are three parts to his mission as the spiritual leader of Eckankar. His global mission is to tell people everywhere about the Light and Sound of God.

The first phase of the Mahanta's mission was to establish a core of leaders known as Regional ECK Spiritual Aides (RESAs). These men and women are somewhat analogous to cardinals in the Catholic Church. They are volunteer clerics who help bring Eckankar to entire states, provinces, and countries. The RESAs are appointed by the Living ECK Master.

RESAs also lead efforts to bring the ECK teachings to those who want to know about them. This is called the Vahana (*vah-HAH-nah*) aspect of Eckankar, its missionary element. RESAs, with the help of volunteers, oversee the Eckankar centers. Eckankar is supported through donations and revenues from its spiritual literature, tapes, and other materials. Most large cities have ECK centers. There are about two hundred ECK centers around the world. These are often in office buildings or storefronts. Some areas plan to have Eckankar temples in the future.

The ECK center is the heart of a local area. It is here that seekers and members gather to attend Eckankar classes and ECK Worship Services, and get to know each other in spiritual fellowship.

Phase Two of the Mahanta's Mission

Phase two of the Mahanta's mission was to build a home for Eckankar. As mentioned earlier, the ECK teachings had been taught secretly for thousands of years.

After Paul Twitchell established the religion of Eckankar, he knew that it still needed a Seat of Power, such as the Vatican is for Catholics. This could be a place from which the teachings of the Light and Sound of God would be given to the world.

For more about the Temple of ECK which was completed in 1990 in Minnesota, see Chapter 30. This truly special building is a Golden Wisdom Temple that serves as the spiritual center for Eckankar. It is also a local community church.

The Temple of ECK is open to all who love God.

Phase Three of the Mahanta's Mission

Eckankar is a missionary teaching. But a missionary in Eckankar is not interested in converting people. He or she has the opportunity to grow and learn

Eckankar is a missionary teaching. But a missionary in Eckankar is not interested in converting people.

spiritually by bringing the love of God into every aspect of life. Sri Harold says, "An ECK missionary will learn at least as much as he or she has to teach." [6]

The third phase of the Mahanta's mission is to tell all people about the Light and Sound of God. The ECK teachings, the teachings of divine love, are much needed in our spiritually hungry world.

The ECK teachings, the teachings of divine love, are much needed in our spiritually hungry world.

ECKANKAR AROUND THE WORLD

Today Eckankar is established in over one hundred countries. Because the Eckankar books are available in ECK centers and bookstores around the world and many people study the teachings privately, it's impossible to say how many people consider themselves to be ECKists.

It's clear that interest in Eckankar is growing. Thousands of seekers each year request information about Eckankar to help them take the next step on their spiritual journey.

WHEN HAVE WE MET BEFORE?

Would you like to know about your own history with the ECK teachings before this lifetime? Even more important: What did you learn?

Most people who encounter Eckankar today have studied the teachings of the Light and Sound in previous lifetimes with one or more of the ECK Masters. You can ask for an understanding of what these teachings have meant to you in the past. And what they offer to you now.

Try This Spiritual Exercise Today!

Sit quietly before going to sleep or when you first wake up in the morning. Allow a period of fifteen to twenty minutes or more depending on whether you're getting results.

Close your eyes, and sing HU (pronounced like the word *hue*) a few times as you exhale long drawn-out breaths. Fill yourself with love, and turn your attention heavenward.

Then read the following passage from *Stranger by the River*. These are the words of ECK Master Rebazar Tarzs to a crowd that had gathered—and to each of us who yearns for God.

> *We have all met before. Centuries ago under a banyan tree ye all sat listening to my words. In many lands, here in this earth world and in the beyond we have been together, and shall always be together in thy long journey to reach God's eternal goal.*[7]

Now ask the Mahanta to show you when you encountered the ECK teachings in another place, another time.

Ask the Mahanta to show you when you encountered the ECK teachings in another place, another time.

FREEDOM OF RELIGION

The ECK teachings offer spiritual liberation. Most of us aren't as free as we'd like to believe we are. Often we're bound by social and family pressures to at least pretend to accept what others think we should believe. Not what we really suspect or know to be true in our hearts.

The next chapter offers you some options. Let's go on a spiritual shopping spree. And behave as if we had all the freedom in the world to create the ideal religion.

TRUE RELIGION

Come share the dreams you have inside
Come hear the story—come alive.
Come to a place where dreams can be
A part of you—a part of me.

We are a part of something more
Something we've never seen before.
We're part of a dream that's coming true
Coming for me—coming for you.

—Bruce Kurnow, Ann Vogle, Fred Vogle,
"Come Share the Dream"[1]

34. You Have the Right to Spiritual Freedom

What benefit do the ECK teachings offer you over those of every other path to God? In the simplest terms, they offer spiritual freedom.
—Harold Klemp, *The Living Word, Book 2*[2]

Here's Golden Key Number 34.
You have the right to spiritual freedom.

Seems obvious, doesn't it? *Of course I'm free,* you might be saying to yourself.

But, are you?

Many people don't follow their hearts because they're afraid of what others will think.

Social and family tradition binds them to the religious beliefs of their childhood, their neighborhood, or their community. Even though people are searching for more satisfying spiritual beliefs in record numbers, they often fear rejection and disapproval if they look outside the orthodox religions.

The following story shows how people can go

417

beyond these limitations as they reach out and exercise their right to spiritual freedom.

THE WORD

"I have a friend who is not a member of Eckankar. One day we were talking about the recent death of a close friend. As I shared my thoughts on death and the continuity of life, I could see she was puzzled. The views I expressed were very different from her Christian ideas, so I explained a little about Eckankar. She was interested and asked a lot of questions.

"My friend went home and told her mother about Eckankar. A strict Christian, her mother told her Christianity was the only true path to God. Still my friend wondered, *Is Eckankar for me?* She came to me with her question. All I could say was, 'I guess that's a question you must answer for yourself.'

"A couple of days later, she called me. She'd had an experience that helped her decide about ECK. She was lying in bed thinking about the differences between Eckankar and Christianity. 'Which is better for me?' she wondered aloud. She closed her eyes to think about it.

She opened her eyes and saw a large Blue Light at the foot of her bed. Within the Blue Light stood a man.

"Suddenly she felt a change in the atmosphere. She opened her eyes and saw a large Blue Light at the foot of her bed. Within the Blue Light stood a man. She had never seen the man before, yet it seemed that she knew him. As soon as she blinked her eyes, he and the light were gone. Then softly, musically, almost inaudibly, a word came to her.

"Later, she came to ask what the word meant. When I told her, she knew that Eckankar was right for her. The word? It was *Wah Z*, the spiritual name of the Mahanta, the Living ECK Master, Sri Harold Klemp."[3]

Free to Find the Mahanta

The Mahanta calls your name when Soul is ready for a direct link to the Holy Spirit, the Light and Sound of God. This awakens a longing in Soul to return to Its true spiritual heritage. To discover Its true identity.

The mind and ego, fearing change and the unknown, erect barriers for Soul's search beyond the status quo. The mind's job is to keep Soul in ignorance of Its spiritual destiny. If the mind is successful, it may be lifetimes until an individual is ready to answer the call of the Mahanta to find who he is and why he's here. To exercise Soul's birthright to spiritual freedom.

Many people have sought and found spiritual freedom in Eckankar. What has spiritual freedom meant to them? It may surprise you how much a person's life can improve when he takes this direct path to spiritual liberation in one lifetime.

Many people have sought and found spiritual freedom in Eckankar.

The Many Sides of Spiritual Freedom

If you look back to how you were before ECK, to a large degree life was just existing. By this I mean wondering what it's all about, what it all means, why are you here.
—Harold Klemp, *The Slow Burning Love of God*[4]

In interviews for this book ECKists were asked: What has Eckankar done for you? What could these teachings offer to others? As you read some of the answers, ask yourself if what they've found in Eckankar is something that would be beneficial in your life.

Free to Go Directly Home

"I think that Eckankar has basically the same thing to offer to every person. And that is the most direct path to God. A way to return home and to understand and experience ourselves as sparks of divinity. And it shows that this is not just a lofty concept but a spiritual, mental, physical, and emotional fact."

FREE TO BE AT PEACE WITH LIFE

"In my company, the secretary joined Eckankar. After three years I asked her, 'Why did you join?'

"She said, 'Well, after working with you for so many years, I looked at you, and there seems to be such a nice feeling or flow that comes from you. You're always happy and looking at life in a more open way.' And that's what attracted her to Eckankar."

FREE TO BREAK ADDICTIONS AND HABITS

Studying Eckankar has helped me to break some of my most harmful habits. The first one that just dropped immediately was my smoking habit.

"Studying Eckankar has helped me to break some of my most harmful habits. The first one that just dropped immediately was my smoking habit. Suddenly after I became a member the desire to smoke disappeared without my having to make any effort. It was a great gift.

"Giving up other mental habits I had has taken longer. Some took years.

"Breaking destructive habits hasn't come from developing this incredible will. More than anything it comes from an inner satisfaction or an inner contentment. It allows me to see and discover, day by day, what my real desires are.

"I'm able to choose what I really desire. To choose what I want in my life. Rather than being driven by the things I fear. The things that at one point made me ashamed of myself."

Free to Accept the Gifts of Divine Spirit

"After becoming a member of Eckankar, I started to feel gratitude for the first time in my life. Soon after I started studying Eckankar, my heart began to open.

"I remember being told in my previous religion, 'You should be grateful because you have faith.' But I didn't feel it. It wasn't real for me.

"With Eckankar, I practiced the spiritual exercises and singing HU. My heart began to really open. I began to feel grateful.

"What gifts have I received? It would be hard to talk about all of them. For example, I had been told by doctors that I could never have children. Yet somehow I was able to have two beautiful children. To me, that is a part of what opening up to the gifts of Divine Spirit can bring. You have things in your life that you never thought you could have.

"That's the outer life. In the inner life there's so much love that I wasn't aware of before. But I am now."

Free to Find Happiness through Simplicity

"Because the lessons of love are never-ending, I find that there's always one more step. A deeper and deeper aspect that one can discover.

"I've found that in my dealings with others, I'm learning to give and receive love. Instead of trying to be right about something. Instead of demanding that everything in my life turn out the way I expected. I'm having a lot more joy, tolerance, and compassion. Which I find extremely helpful.

"When I look back I can hardly recognize my life twenty years ago. It's not that there are grand things

I've found that in my dealings with others, I'm learning to give and receive love.

happening in my life, although they are, every day. But it's the smaller things that are very beautiful and happy.

"Just the simple things of life like enjoying a meal and being with my family. To really enjoy an afternoon with my son or daughter playing in the garden.

"Being here and being happy."

FREE TO LOVE AND BE LOVED

"Eckankar has shown me how important love is in my life. I didn't know that before. When I received my Second Initiation, one of the things I discovered was that, for the first time in my life, I felt loved.

"It wasn't that I had had such a hard life before. I was loved by my family and friends. But I never felt loved.

"I'd never felt divine love in my life. I never felt God could love me. That I could really be loved.

"Suddenly with the Second Initiation, I had an incredible feeling that someone—the Mahanta, the Living ECK Master—loved me. He really loved me as Soul. With divine love.

"That shook my foundation. It was a new starting point. From then on I began to look for that love. Not only from him but in life around me. Within myself.

"I looked for ways to reach this love within myself so I could bring it out. To see it in my life."

FREE TO GET IN THE FLOW

"Let's say I rush off in the morning without doing my spiritual exercise. Often the day doesn't go as well.

"When I begin the day with a spiritual exercise, I notice my writing improves both in quality and sometimes quantity. Everything flows better."

When I begin the day with a spiritual exercise, I notice my writing improves both in quality and sometimes quantity.

Free to Start the Day with Serenity

"I like living the path of ECK every day. I like to start the day with Divine Spirit, tuning in by singing HU. I also put my attention on the Inner Master and on the dreams I've had. I know that the ECK is taking me places and teaching me things.

"I like to recognize the presence of Divine Spirit in my life. I find that it has a huge effect on the quality of my day by setting the tone early in the morning. It really changes my day in a way that's very noticeable.

For me Eckankar is a way of living my life.

"For one thing, I can handle stress better when I'm in tune. I can remember to sing HU to myself for a second or two before I respond to an irate individual who's in anguish over something. To be a little more patient with my explanation. To dig deep, and try to find another way to say it rather than being impatient.

"For me, Eckankar is a way of living my life."

Free to Find God in All Life

"I talk with a lot of people who are hearing about Eckankar for the first time. Sometimes I ask them, 'When have you felt the presence of God?'

"Many say that they never have.

"For most, though, their first response is usually something like they feel spiritual when they're in nature. Or at the death of a loved one. Or the birth of a child. They only really feel the presence of God when they're completely absorbed in their lives.

"No one I've talked to has ever immediately answered that question by saying that they felt the presence of God while sitting in a church.

"This is why I treasure Eckankar. It's taught me

I think the primary benefit comes from understanding what life and death are about. How to put all the pieces together.

how to recognize and appreciate the presence of God in every aspect of my life."

FREE TO MAKE SENSE OUT OF LIFE

"I see the relationship of Soul with the Mahanta, the Inner Master, as teaching lessons of love. I've been looking at the fundamentals of ECK. The ability to truly contemplate the ECK works, the ability to integrate something into your being. To me this is a tremendous opportunity.

"There are so many tools in Eckankar. Dreams. Soul Travel. I think the primary benefit comes from understanding what life and death are about. How to put all the pieces together."

THE BASICS OF ECKANKAR IN REVIEW

The ECKist above referred to the fundamentals of ECK. Below are some key principles of Eckankar taken from *ECKANKAR—Ancient Wisdom for Today,* a quick, easy-to-read pocket-size book that many people have found valuable in helping them to understand what Eckankar teaches about many subjects. See the offer at the back of this book to learn how to request a free copy.

The Basic Beliefs of Eckankar

- Soul is eternal and is the individual's true identity
- Soul exists because God loves It
- Soul is on a journey of Self- and God-Realization
- Spiritual unfoldment can be accelerated by conscious contact with the ECK, Divine Spirit
- This contact can be made by the use of the Spiritual Exercises of ECK and by the guidance of the Living ECK Master

- ⁀ The Mahanta, the Living ECK Master is the spiritual leader of Eckankar
- ⁀ Spiritual experience and liberation in this lifetime is available to all[5]

Eckankar is a religion for the individual who wants to explore his or her unique way of having more love in this life.

Create Your Ideal Religion

Do you like some of the aspects of spiritual freedom that people have mentioned so far? Maybe you want to be free now. Here's a spiritual exercise to use your freedom of choice.

Ask: What is the next step for me on my spiritual journey?

Try This Spiritual Exercise Today!

Write down everything you'd like a religion to be or to have. If you don't like religion, write anything that you think would help you have a better relationship with God. It's your life. You can create your ideal religion.

Now, put the list away.

Close your eyes. Fill your heart with love. Open yourself completely to the guidance and direction of the Holy Spirit.

Ask these three important questions: What is the next step for me on my spiritual journey? What would most help me find my ideal religion? How can I become spiritually free?

For a few minutes, sing HU, God, or the name of your spiritual master. Then sit quietly. Let the love of God seep gently into your heart.

In the next twenty-four hours, be a skillful observer. Watch for signs and signals the Holy Spirit sends to answer your questions. Guidance may come in the form of comments people make that seem to light up for you. You may read something. Or have a dream or insight. These are all ways the Holy Spirit can communicate with you.

Continue with this spiritual exercise once or twice a week. Reread and revise your list of qualities for an ideal religion as new ideas come to you. Do this exercise gently. Don't push one way or the other.

When you finish the exercise each time, end it by saying the ancient blessing of the ECK Masters. It means, "Thy will be done."

Say, "May the blessings be."

FREE TO CHOOSE

In the next chapter you'll meet some more ECKists. They'll share the stories of their uniquely individual spiritual journeys. Perhaps you'll recognize in their stories your own search for love, purpose, and true religion.

35. You're Free to Choose the Next Step on Your Spiritual Journey

You'll find that many of the people in ECK have come from just about every religion on earth.

We have people from all over, from every religion, every philosophy. Some people have been in three, four, five, or six different ones because they desire truth, God, and divine love so sincerely.

When they found the answer was missing in one of the paths, they kept moving. They wanted to move from darkness into light.

—Harold Klemp, *The Slow Burning Love of God*[1]

Moving from darkness into light.

Does this interest you?

Some people want what Eckankar has to offer, but they aren't interested in leaving their religion now, or ever.

There are some initiates in Eckankar who continue with their life's work of serving Souls in other religions.

Here's Golden Key Number 35.

You can choose the next step on your spiritual journey.

You don't have to leave your religion to study Eckankar. You can study the teachings and begin working with the Mahanta as your spiritual guide right now. Right this very moment.

There are some initiates in Eckankar who continue with their life's work of serving Souls in other religions. The Mahanta's love and the ECK teachings are universal. The important thing is that you find what's uniquely best for you spiritually.

An ECKist told this enlightening story about an experience she had when she lived in a Muslim country. This ECKist is a member of the ECK clergy and has also been appointed to facilitate the outer ceremony of initiation into the Light and Sound of God. The inner initiation is given by the Mahanta.

A RELIGION THAT SUPPORTS ALL OTHERS

"I received a phone call from a student of Eckankar who asked if I could give the ECK initiations. When I replied yes, the gentleman asked, 'You are a woman, and yet you can give initiations?'

"I was living in a Muslim country at that time. Women there are often looked upon as not equal to men. I realized why he was asking.

"After we got over this hurdle, he explained that he had received notification from the Eckankar Spiritual Center that he was invited by the Mahanta, the Living ECK Master to take the Second Initiation in Eckankar. We scheduled a time and place to meet.

"I greeted him at the door. We settled in and began

to talk. Since I was the only ECKist he'd met since joining Eckankar, he asked many questions. After a while, we went on with the initiation ceremony. Once the initiation was completed, we talked more. He said that he had been raised as a Muslim on his grandfather's knee. His religion would always be Muslim.

"This startled me. I quietly asked the Mahanta, 'What now? What should I ask?'

"Our conversation went something like this.

" 'Why did you join Eckankar?' I asked.

"He said that he was given a book on an airplane. He loved the HU.

" 'Why did you take the initiation of Eckankar?'

" 'To find out more about the spiritual exercises.'

" 'When do you do the spiritual exercises?'

" 'When I go to the mosque five times a day and roll out my prayer rug.' "

It then occurred to the woman how HU, the ancient love song to God taught in Eckankar, is truly universal. Singing HU is a basic element of the Spiritual Exercises of ECK.

The man said, "Once a week, after the noon prayer, the men have a discussion on the Muslim holy works. Lately the men are asking me, 'Where are you coming up with your viewpoint and understanding of these works?' "

In this moment, it was as if time stood still. The woman was being shown how this man served as a vehicle for the ECK in his own religion. By singing HU and having a yearning to explore more of the inner worlds, he was enhancing the understanding and truths of his Muslim religion.

By singing HU and having a yearning to explore more of the inner worlds, he was enhancing the understanding and truths of his Muslim religion.

"I am so thankful and grateful for this enlightening

experience," the woman said. "I invite all to explore Eckankar regardless of their current religion."

HOW SOME PEOPLE DECIDE ECKANKAR IS RIGHT FOR THEM

The teachings of ECK are to fit you and your life. It's not the other way around, where you try to bend yourself into a pretzel trying to fit ECKANKAR.

—Harold Klemp, *Ask the Master,* Book 2[2]

In writing this book, I interviewed ECKists from around the world and asked, "How did you find Eckankar?" The following are some answers to that question.

One comment that many made is how familiar the teachings were. Not that they'd ever heard of Eckankar before—most hadn't. But the ECK teachings struck a chord deep within and answered a longing.

These ECKists are on the road to spiritual freedom. Perhaps their experiences will help you decide if you'd like to exercise your freedom to study the ancient teachings of the Light and Sound of God.

I had some amazing experiences during my first spiritual exercise. Paul's face appeared to me in beautiful clarity. Three dimensional.

THE PROOF OF PERSONAL EXPERIENCE

"I was in Eugene, Oregon, in the summer of 1971; and I saw a poster on the wall saying that Paul Twitchell [the modern-day founder of Eckankar] was going to be in Portland. So I decided to go.

"I went to the seminar and met Paul at his last seminar in Portland. He translated [died] a month later. By that time I'd started taking his discourses.

"I had some amazing experiences during my first

spiritual exercise. Paul's face appeared to me in beautiful clarity. Three dimensional. It was so real, I felt I could touch it. And I'd never had anything like that happen to me before.

"I felt that there was something real here, and I wanted to pursue it."

I had an experience when my father died. I sat by his bedside. I saw a little sparkling of light come from his heart region.

A Profound Experience to Recognize Truth

"I was an atheist. I didn't believe in God or in anything. I didn't think there was life after death.

"But I had an experience when my father died. I sat by his bedside. I saw a little sparkling of light come from his heart region. Then a little white bird sat in the window and flew away.

"I was shocked. I thought this must be Soul. I had never worked with those things.

"So then I started searching for something.

"Paul Twitchell came to Oslo, Norway, in 1970 and gave a talk. A friend of mine and I went. By then I understood that there was something after death.

"I just listened to Paul and asked him, 'Can I do this? Can I study Eckankar?'

"He said, 'Give me two years, and you will know.'

"I thought, *Two years. Must I study two years before I know?* But I had done so many other things. Why not try? And here I am, twenty-two years later.

"Earlier I was never in doubt about anything, but I was empty. When I saw Soul leave my father's body, I became so confused. It took everything out of me that was old. So in a way it was easy for me to understand these new ideas. I could be open to them."

A LIFELONG SEEKER

I found a book by Paul Twitchell in a bookstore when I was eighteen years old. I think the book clicked for me because of my having been a Tibetan lama. The teachings felt familiar.

"I've been a seeker since the age of five. I had questions about life and death. At age twelve I left Christianity. I wondered if there were realities beyond life and death. I went searching through religion and psychic experiences.

"I found a book by Paul Twitchell in a bookstore when I was eighteen years old. It was about his studies with the Tibetan ECK Master Rebazar Tarzs. I couldn't take my eyes off Paul Twitchell's photo. I kept staring at his eyes. These weren't a dead man's eyes.

"I knew I had been a lama, a Tibetan monk, in a past life. I think the book clicked for me because of my having been a Tibetan lama. The teachings felt familiar."

HE SPOKE MY LANGUAGE

"When I was eighteen, I was listening to a radio program in English. French was my native language, and I understood about 10 percent of the English words. The words that caught my attention then were *Soul Travel.*

"At that time, I was into astral travel. After the person spoke about the book *The Tiger's Fang*, I went into a bookstore close by. On the top shelf were about three or four copies of *The Tiger's Fang.*

"I bought one. I marked in red all the words I did not understand so I could reread the book afterward. By the time I finished the book, it was almost all red.

"I spoke with a friend of mine and passed him the book. I never saw it again.

"Three weeks later I went to the same bookstore to buy another copy of the book. I spoke to the clerk, and he said that they'd never had that book there. He said that he was the one who bought books for the store, and they never had that kind of book.

"I guess that's when I became an ECKist."

A Step Further

"I started seeking when I was twelve or thirteen years of age. I read things by Rudolf Steiner and about Ram Dass and astral travel. Then the Rosicrucians and Transcendental Meditation. I tried many things.

"When I started in ECK, it was another search. And it still continues. Because in ECK there's always another step.

"I learned about Eckankar through my brother. I was about eighteen and studying metaphysics.

"The first thing that attracted me to Eckankar was that there were higher planes. Even my teacher at the time knew there was something higher, but he told me he couldn't go there. But he knew.

"He just said, 'I can't take you there.'"

Even my teacher at the time knew there was something higher, but he told me he couldn't go there. But he knew.

It Had to Be My Decision

"I was seventeen when my father introduced me to the teachings of Eckankar. It had been about fifteen years since I'd last seen him.

"At first my father just told me, 'You need to know this word *Mahanta*.'

"And I would say, 'Uh huh. OK, fine.'

"Then I decided to get to know my father better. So I went up to Canada to spend some time with him. I was introduced into an ECK household there. My brother and sister, stepmother, and father were all in Eckankar.

"I would see the others doing their contemplations.

And I would ask, 'What are they doing?' Then my father would explain.

"He gave me a couple of Eckankar books to read when I went home. Then he called me every weekend and asked, 'What page are you on?'

"For several weeks, I'd answer, 'I'm on page three.' And the next week, 'I'm on page three and a half.'

"Then something just clicked. I guess I found an answer to a question which I'd even forgotten I had. All of a sudden I started going through the book quickly. I felt a great spiritual hunger. I was just ripping through the book and getting answers. There was a feeling of coming home, of remembering, of understanding something I knew.

"I always knew that Eckankar would have to be my choice. It wasn't something I could do just because my father was in it. It had to be something that was really for me."

LOOKING FOR A CHANGE

"I first heard about Eckankar from a friend who was an ECKist. She gave me a book which I read and couldn't really grasp.

"But I felt something in my heart starting to open. I felt that there was something here for me.

"Even so, it took about eighteen months for me to decide to become a member. I decided because my friend said, 'Look, if you join Eckankar, your life is going to change.'

"Those were the words I wanted to hear. At that point my life at work, my emotional life, everything seemed to be stuck, not moving anywhere. I felt I needed a change. I needed to start moving.

I always knew that Eckankar would have to be my choice. It wasn't something I could do just because my father was in it.

"I was no longer active in the religion I had grown up in. But I had always, since I was very young, had a very deep spiritual longing.

"So I felt that this might be just what I was looking for to change things for me.

"To bring more life into my life.

"I joined a couple days after that. And my life started to change—quite a lot!"

Looking for an Inner Guide

"It all started about fourteen years ago. I had gone through a very, very dark period of my life—the dark night of the Soul. And what helped me out of that was that I learned to meditate.

"Then about six months before I heard about Eckankar, I started to feel this incredible longing. It would come to me when I was meditating. At first I didn't know what was making me weep.

"I became aware that this was a longing to find the Inner Master. I didn't know that such a thing existed, I just felt a longing to meet this Master.

"I had had no esoteric or mystical inclinations before. But when I came across the teachings of Eckankar some months later, I was invited to an introductory talk. At this introductory talk I didn't understand much of what was going on. But I could perceive that there was something very special. More like an inner freedom that suddenly opened for me that night.

"It wasn't the outer knowledge because I could hardly remember anything of the talk. But beginning right there that night, my life began to change immediately.

"I found myself having to take full charge of my life.

But beginning right there that night, my life began to change immediately. I found myself having to take full charge of my life.

I knew this was for me; I knew I was going to have to grow.

"It took about one and a half months for me to decide to become a member. Two months after I joined Eckankar, I attended my first major seminar in the United States. That was 1981 when Sri Harold received the Rod of ECK Power and became the Mahanta, the Living ECK Master.

"The moment I saw Sri Harold, I knew he was the Master. I knew it because I could perceive this incredible Blue Light coming out of him. It was very gentle. I still remember how sweetly it shone for me that night. It was very special.

"I knew that was what I'd been longing for. I wept with gratitude.

That evening I received the Darshan, the meeting with the Master and the enlightenment that comes with it.

"That evening I received the Darshan, the meeting with the Master and the enlightenment that comes with it.

"It was such a great gift.

"And suddenly all that longing stopped. What remained was this incredible joy and gratitude for having found my inner guide."

Which Religion Is Best for You?

It is important to remember and understand that no human being's vision of God is a perfect vision. This is why there are so many different religions on earth.
—Harold Klemp, *The Drumbeat of Time*[3]

The ECK, Divine Spirit, is the love of God pouring from the Creator to all creation.

The ECK infuses and inspires all religions. At the

heart of every true religion is the ECK. The leaders of each spiritual teaching catch a wave of love from the Creator and develop their teachings according to their own states of consciousness. This explains the differences among religions.

There comes a time in many people's lives when they ask the question: Is my religion satisfying my spiritual needs?

How can you know which religion or spiritual teaching is the next best step for you? There comes a time in many people's lives when they ask the question: Is my religion satisfying my spiritual needs?

If the answer is yes for you, then continue with that religion and infuse it with all the love, commitment, and service you can. Study its teachings and apply them to the best of your ability.

If you find a need for more than what your religion is offering, consider the teachings of Eckankar or another religion that may offer more to your present state of consciousness.

Above all, exercise your right to pursue spiritual freedom in this lifetime.

THE SECRET TEACHINGS

When people come into Eckankar, I say, "Welcome. It's good to have you back."
—Harold Klemp, *The Slow Burning Love of God*[4]

It's been a pleasure introducing you to thirty-five golden keys for discovering more love, peace, and purpose in your life. This book can present only a fraction of the wonder, wisdom, and love contained in the ancient teachings of Eckankar, Religion of the Light and Sound of God. And, of course, the true teachings of ECK are the secret teachings, found within your own heart.

Can you hear the ECK, the Voice of God, in the breath of the wind? Or in the happy laughter of children? Or in the wailing of deep sorrow?

Life knows who you are and why you're here.

God's love is bringing you home.

Listen. The Mahanta is calling your name.

NOTES

Chapter 1. The Mahanta Is Calling Your Name

1. Harold Klemp, *The Living Word* (Minneapolis: ECKANKAR, 1989), 207.
2. Harold Klemp, *Soul Travelers of the Far Country* (Minneapolis: ECKANKAR, 1987), 107.

Chapter 2. The Mahanta Is Guiding You Home

1. Harold Klemp, *Ask the Master,* Book 1 (Minneapolis: ECKANKAR, 1993), 187.
2. Catherine Ball (Talk given at 1990 ECK Springtime Seminar, San Francisco, Calif., April 1990).
3. Barbara Kantrowitz with Patricia King, Debra Rosenberg, Karen Springen, Pat Wingert, Tessa Namuth, and T. Trent Gegax, "In Search of the Sacred," *Newsweek,* 28 November 1994, 52–55.
4. Harold Klemp, *The Slow Burning Love of God,* Mahanta Transcripts, Book 13 (Minneapolis: ECKANKAR, 1996), 168.
5. Harold Klemp, *The Secret of Love,* Mahanta Transcripts, Book 14 (Minneapolis: ECKANKAR, 1996), 164.
6. Harold Klemp, *Unlocking the Puzzle Box,* Mahanta Transcripts, Book 6 (Minneapolis: ECKANKAR, 1992), 102.

Chapter 3. You Can Meet the Mahanta

1. Klemp, *Slow Burning Love,* 71.
2. Harold Klemp, "Questions for the Master . . .," *Letter of Light,* October 1993, 3.
3. Jelaluddin Rumi, "A Subtle Theological Point," trans. Coleman Barks, *Delicious Laughter: Rambunctious Teaching Stories from the Mathnawi of Jelaluddin Rumi* (196 Westview Drive, Athens, Georgia 30606: MAYPOP BOOKS, 1-800-682-8637, 1990), 102–4.
4. Harold Klemp, *The Cloak of Consciousness:* Mahanta Transcripts, Book 5 (Minneapolis: ECKANKAR, 1991), 256.

439

5. Victor Girolomoni, (Talk given at 1991 ECK Summer Festival, Anaheim, Calif., June 1991).
6. Klemp, *The Secret of Love,* 165.
7. Klemp, *Unlocking the Puzzle Box,* 69.

Chapter 4. Some People Know Who They Are

1. Harold Klemp, *What Is Spiritual Freedom?* Mahanta Transcripts, Book 11 (Minneapolis: ECKANKAR, 1995), 80.
2. Klemp, *The Secret of Love,* 166.
3. Hausa (West African saying) quoted in *A World Treasury of Folk Wisdom,* comp. Reynold Feldman and Cynthia Voelke (New York: HarperCollins Publishers, 1992), 119.

Chapter 5. Some People Know Why They're Here

1. Klemp, *The Secret of Love,* 168.
2. Klemp, *Slow Burning Love,* 223.
3. Harold Klemp, *Ask the Master,* Book 2 (Minneapolis: ECKANKAR, 1994), 125.

Chapter 6: The Holy Spirit Is with You Now

1. Harold Klemp, *The Drumbeat of Time,* Mahanta Transcripts, Book 10 (Minneapolis: ECKANKAR, 1995), 139.
2. Klemp, *The Secret of Love,* 87.
3. Klemp, *Slow Burning Love,* 219–20.
4. Catherine Kirk Chase (Talk given at 1992 ECK Worldwide Seminar, Minneapolis, Minn., October 1992).
5. Harold Klemp, *We Come as Eagles,* Mahanta Transcripts, Book 9 (Minneapolis: ECKANKAR, 1994), 74–75.
6. Harold Klemp, *HU: A Love Song to God* (Minneapolis, ECKANKAR, 1990), audiocassette.
7. Katherine de Guia (Talk given at 1990 ECK Worldwide Seminar, Orlando, Fla., October 1990).
8. Michael Kachig, *A Special Gift* (Minneapolis: ECKANKAR, 1992), videocassette.
9. Paul Twitchell, *ECKANKAR—The Key to Secret Worlds,* 2d ed. (Minneapolis: ECKANKAR, 1969, 1987), 99.

Chapter 7: You Can See the Light without Nearly Dying

1. Klemp, *The Drumbeat of Time,* 142.
2. Harold Klemp, *Stories to Help You See God in Your Life,* ECK Parables, Book 4 (Minneapolis: ECKANKAR, 1994), 287–88.
3. "Psychiatry Finds Religion Sane," *Minneapolis Star Tribune,* 11 February 1994, 4A.
4. Klemp, *Slow Burning Love,* 226–27.
5. Harold Klemp, *How the Inner Master Works,* Mahanta Transcripts, Book 12 (Minneapolis: ECKANKAR, 1995), 62.
6. Ibid., 63.

7. Klemp, *Stories to Help You,* 291–92.

Chapter 8: You Can Hear the Sound of God's Voice

1. Klemp, *The Drumbeat of Time,* 217.
2. Raymond Reyes (Talk given at 1991 ECK Worldwide Seminar, Minneapolis, Minn., October 1991).
3. Twitchell, *Key to Secret Worlds,* 100.
4. Hans Jenny, *Cymatics: Wave Phenomena Vibrational Effects Harmonic Oscillations with Their Structure, Kinetics and Dynamics, vol. 2* (Basel, Switzerland: Basilius Presse, Basler Druck- und Verlagsanstalt, 1974), 100.
5. Ronald L. Fields and Julia S. Fields, *A Special Gift.*
6. Harold Klemp, *The Spiritual Exercises of ECK* (Minneapolis: ECKANKAR, 1993), 87.
7. B. K., letter, *The Mystic World,* Summer 1986, 5.

Chapter 9: You Don't Have to Fear God

1. Paul Twitchell, *Stranger by the River,* 3d ed. (Minneapolis: ECKANKAR, 1970, 1987), 192.
2. Harold Klemp, *Wisdom of the Heart* (Minneapolis: ECKANKAR, 1992), 196.
3. Gaelic proverb quoted in *World Treasury of Folk Wisdom,* 66.
4. Klemp, *Slow Burning Love,* 202.
5. Joyce Helens (Talk given at 1991 ECK Worldwide Seminar, Minneapolis, Minn., October 1991).
6. Francis Thompson, *The Hound of Heaven* (Dallas: Amrita Foundation, 1989), 17.
7. Lam. 3:37–38 Authorized (King James) Version.
8. Isabel Wilkerson, " 'It Is the Death of Things the Way You Knew It,' " *Minneapolis Star Tribune,* 6 September 1992, 25A.
9. Klemp, *Spiritual Exercises,* 119.

Chapter 10: God Loves You

1. Klemp, *We Come as Eagles,* 139–40.
2. Harold Klemp, *The Book of ECK Parables,* Vol. 3 (Minneapolis: ECKANKAR, 1991), 141–42.
3. Fredrick Buechner, quoted in *Simpson's Contemporary Quotations,* comp. James B. Simpson (Boston: Houghton Mifflin, 1988), 186.
4. Harold Klemp, "What We So Far Know of God," *ECKANKAR Journal* (1992): 2–3.
5. Kabir, quoted in *Zen to Go,* comp. and ed. Jon Winokur (New York: New American Library, 1989), 148.
6. Harold Klemp, *The Eternal Dreamer,* Mahanta Transcripts, Book 7 (Minneapolis: ECKANKAR, 1992), 114.
7. Harold Klemp, "The God Seeker," *ECK World News* (January 1978): 6.

Chapter 11: You Don't *Have* a Soul

1. Rumi, "The Ocean Duck," *Delicious Laughter,* 116.
2. Klemp, *The Secret of Love,* 44.
3. Klemp, *Inner Master,* 127.
4. Sharon Begley, "Science of the Sacred," *Newsweek,* 28 November 1994, 56, 59.
5. "Auguries of Innocence," 1–4, *The Complete Poetry and Prose of William Blake,* rev. ed., ed. David V. Erdman (Berkeley and Los Angeles: University of California Press, 1982), 400.
6. Klemp, *Slow Burning Love,* 242–44.
7. Joseph Campbell, *The Hero with a Thousand Faces,* 2d ed. (Princeton, N.J.: Princeton University Press, 1968), 58.
8. Klemp, *Ask the Master,* Book 2, 278.
9. Twitchell, *Stranger by the River,* 114–15.
10. Klemp, *Spiritual Exercises,* 281.

Chapter 12: You've Lived Before

1. Klemp, *Slow Burning Love,* 207.
2. François-Marie Arouet Voltaire, "La princesse de Babylone," quoted in Ian Stevenson, *Children Who Remember Previous Lives: A Question of Reincarnation* (Charlottesville, Va.: The University Press of Virginia), 25.
3. Klemp, *Ask the Master:* Book 1, 112.
4. Paul Twitchell, *The Shariyat-Ki-Sugmad,* Book One, 2d ed. (Minneapolis: ECKANKAR, 1970, 1987), 152.
5. Stevenson, *Children Who Remember,* 103.
6. Klemp, *Inner Master,* 10.
7. Ibid., 147.
8. Doug Culliford, "Checkers," *Earth to God, Come In Please . . .* (Minneapolis: ECKANKAR, 1991), 15–16.
9. Klemp, *Inner Master,* 11.
10. Ibid., 16.
11. Klemp, *The Secret of Love,* 172–75.
12. Klemp, *What Is Spiritual Freedom?* 186–87.
13. Ibid., 186–88.

Chapter 13: You'll Live Again

1. Harold Klemp, *The Dream Master,* Mahanta Transcripts, Book 8 (Minneapolis: ECKANKAR, 1993), 91.
2. Klemp, *Ask the Master,* Book 1, 62.

Chapter 14: You're in Training to Become More Than an Angel

1. Twitchell, *Stranger by the River,* 39.
2. Klemp, *Stories to Help You,* 279.
3. Klemp, *Ask the Master,* Book 2, 102.

4. Walt Wrzesniewski, "My Spiritual Tour of Duty," *ECKANKAR Journal* (1993): 30.

Chapter 15: Ancient Spiritual Masters Are with You Today

1. Klemp, *The Secret of Love,* 173.
2. Harold Klemp, *The Golden Heart,* Mahanta Transcripts, Book 4 (Minneapolis: ECKANKAR, 1990), 97.
3. Klemp, *Inner Master,* 170.
4. Paul Twitchell, *The Shariyat-Ki-Sugmad,* Book Two, 2d ed. (Minneapolis: ECKANKAR, 1971, 1988), 173.
5. Mi Ja Coyle, "An Encounter with an ECK Master," *ECKANKAR Journal,* (1995): 52–54.
6. Lobsang P. Lhalungpa, trans., *The Life of Milarepa,* rev. ed. (Boston: Shambhala Publications, 1977), xxix, 3, 5.

Chapter 16: You Live in Parallel Dimensions

1. Klemp, *The Dream Master,* 15.
2. Ibid., 130.
3. Klemp, *The Secret of Love,* 42–43.
4. Klemp, *Slow Burning Love,* 105.
5. Klemp, *We Come as Eagles,* 70.
6. Stevenson, *Children Who Remember,* 108–10.

Chapter 17: You Can See and Change Your Future

1. Klemp, *The Eternal Dreamer,* 115–16.
2. Paul Twitchell, *The ECK-Vidya, Ancient Science of Prophecy* (Minneapolis: ECKANKAR, 1972), 25.
3. Klemp, *The Dream Master,* 128.
4. Twitchell, *ECK-Vidya,* 84.
5. Klemp, *What Is Spiritual Freedom?* 183.
6. George Gallup, Jr. and Jim Castelli, *The People's Religion: American Faith in the 90's* (New York: Macmillan Publishing Company, 1989), 72.
7. Klemp, *The Dream Master,* 212.
8. Klemp, *Spiritual Exercises,* 229.
9. Klemp, *Ask the Master,* Book 1, 55.
10. Ibid., 65.
11. Harold Klemp, *The Book of ECK Parables,* vol. 1 (Minneapolis: ECKANKAR, 1986), 25–26.

Chapter 18: *Spiritual* Laws Bring Harmony to Your World

1. Klemp, *The Dream Master,* 37.
2. Rosa Worth (Talk given at 1991 ECK Summer Festival, Anaheim, Calif., June 1991).
3. Richard J. Maybury, *Whatever Happened to Justice?* (Placerville, Calif.: Bluestocking Press, 1993), 31.

4. Paul Twitchell, *The Key to ECKANKAR*, 2d ed. (Minneapolis: ECKANKAR, 1968, 1985), 29.
5. Klemp, *Inner Master*, 244.
6. Henry David Thoreau, quoted in *2500 Anecdotes for All Occasions*, ed. Edmund Fuller (New York: Avenel Books, 1980), 283.
7. Albert Camus, *The Fall*, quoted in *Simpson's Contemporary Quotations*, comp. James B. Simpson (Boston: Houghton Mifflin Company, 1988), 223.
8. Klemp, *Spiritual Exercises*, 147.

Chapter 19: You Need to Know the Most Powerful Prayer

1. Klemp, *The Drumbeat of Time*, 254.
2. Ibid., 162.
3. Klemp, *We Come as Eagles*, 10.
4. Klemp, *Inner Master*, 194.
5. Klemp, *We Come as Eagles*, 140.
6. Mike DeLuca, "HU, A Love Song to God," *ECKANKAR Journal* (1994): 9–10.
7. Klemp, *Spiritual Exercises*, 129.

Chapter 20: You Can *Soul Travel*

1. Klemp, *The Golden Heart*, 82.
2. *Soul Travel Workshop with Millie Moore* (Minneapolis: ECKANKAR, 1979), audiocassette.
3. Klemp, *The Dream Master*, 16.
4. Klemp, *The Golden Heart*, 262.
5. Klemp, *Spiritual Exercises*, 235.
6. Harold Klemp, *The Wind of Change* (Minneapolis: ECKANKAR, 1980), 47.
7. Klemp, *Inner Master*, 33.

Chapter 21: Expanding Your Consciousness Is the New Frontier

1. Klemp, *Stories to Help You*, 63.
2. Twitchell, *The Key to ECKANKAR*, 29.
3. Klemp, *Spiritual Exercises*, v.
4. Ibid., 231.

Chapter 22: Your Dreams Are Real

1. Harold Klemp, *The Living Word*, Book 2 (Minneapolis: ECKANKAR, 1996), 64.
2. Naomi Epel, *Writers Dreaming* (New York: Carol Southern Books, 1993), 6.
3. Klemp, *The Secret of Love*, 97.
4. Benjamin Kilborne, "Ancient and Native Peoples' Dreams," *Dreamtime and Dreamwork: Decoding the Language of the Night*, ed. Stanley Krippner (Los Angeles: Jeremy P. Tarcher, 1990), 197.

5. Wilse B. Webb, "Historical Perspectives: From Aristotle to Calvin Hall," *Dreamtime and Dreamwork,* ed. Krippner, 179.
6. Edward Dolnick, "What Dreams Are (Really) Made Of," *The Atlantic Monthly,* July 1990, 41–45, 48–53, 56–61.
7. Klemp, *Inner Master,* 217.
8. Klemp, *Slow Burning Love,* 174.
9. Dolnick, "What Dreams Are," 48.
10. Peter Occhiogrosso, *Through the Labyrinth: Stories of the Search for Spiritual Transformation in Everyday Life* (New York: Penguin Group, 1991), 373–74.
11. Klemp, *Spiritual Exercises,* 35.

Chapter 23: The Key to Your Success Is Setting *Spiritual* Goals

1. Twitchell, *Stranger by the River,* 132.
2. Ibid., 20.
3. Kantrowitz et al., "In Search of the Sacred": 55.
4. Klemp, *The Golden Heart,* 126.
5. Gloria Lionz, "Releasing Hidden Fears," *ECKANKAR Journal* (1991): 25–26.
6. Klemp, *Spiritual Exercises,* 225.

Chapter 24: You Can Master Spiritual Survival Skills

1. Twitchell, *Stranger by the River,* 89–90.
2. Harold Klemp, *How to Find God,* Mahanta Transcripts, Book 2 (Minneapolis: ECKANKAR, 1988), 307.
3. Klemp, *What Is Spiritual Freedom?* 156.
4. Klemp, *The Eternal Dreamer,* 66–67.
5. Harold Klemp, *Child in the Wilderness* (Minneapolis: ECKANKAR, 1989), 172.
6. Guy Stevens (Talk given at 1991 ECK Springtime Seminar, Washington, D.C., March 1991).
7. Klemp, *Spiritual Exercises,* 213.
8. Klemp, *The Secret of Love,* 166–67.
9. Klemp, *How to Find God,* 152.

Chapter 25: It's Your Right to Discover Truth and Wisdom

1. Twitchell, *Stranger by the River,* 175.
2. Harold Klemp, *Be the HU* (Minneapolis: ECKANKAR, 1992), 277.
3. Nancy Landon, "The Spiritual Art of Relationships," *ECKANKAR Journal* (1990): 27.
4. Twitchell, *Stranger by the River,* 80.
5. Klemp, *Spiritual Exercises,* 13.
6. Klemp, *How to Find God,* 157.

Chapter 26: You Can Have the Greatest Love of All

1. Twitchell, *Stranger by the River,* 46.

2. Allan Luks with Peggy Payne, *The Healing Power of Doing Good: The Health and Spiritual Benefits of Helping Others* (New York: Ballantine Books, 1991), 10–11, 68.
3. Giovanni Riva, "Dissolving Karma with Others the Easy Way," *ECKANKAR Journal* (1996): 30–31.

Chapter 27: It's Your Birthright to Know Who You Are

1. Twitchell, *Stranger by the River,* 156–57.
2. Ibid., 108.
3. Klemp, *How to Find God,* 151.
4. Twitchell, *Key to Secret Worlds,* 72.

Chapter 28: It's Your Legacy to Know Why You're Here

1. Twitchell, *Stranger by the River,* 51.
2. Mary Carroll Moore, *How to Master Change in Your Life: Sixty-seven Ways to Handle Life's Toughest Moments* (Minneapolis: ECKANKAR, 1997), 87.

Chapter 29: It's Your Destiny to Know God

1. Twitchell, *Stranger by the River,* 187–88.
2. Klemp, *The Eternal Dreamer,* 6.
3. Klemp, *Soul Travelers,* 238.
4. Anonymous Zen statement, quoted in *Simpson's Contemporary Quotations,* 218.
5. Klemp, *Child in the Wilderness,* 125–26.
6. Ibid., xi–xii.
7. Klemp, *Be the HU,* 182.
8. Klemp, *Soul Travelers,* 141.
9. Klemp, *How to Find God,* 310.
10. Klemp, *Be the HU,* 210.
11. Klemp, *Child in the Wilderness,* 239.
12. Klemp, *The Eternal Dreamer,* 15.
13. Klemp, *Ask the Master,* Book 1, 57.
14. Klemp, *Be the HU,* 211.
15. Klemp, *Unlocking the Puzzle Box,* 63.
16. Klemp, *Be the HU,* 214.
17. Klemp, *ECK Parables,* vol. 3, 273.
18. Klemp, *Spiritual Exercises,* 197.

Chapter 30: There's a Place You Can Go Where Heaven and Earth Meet

1. Klemp, *The Drumbeat of Time,* 4.
2. Klemp, *The Living Word,* Book 2, 159.
3. Klemp, *How to Find God,* 38.
4. Klemp, *The Drumbeat of Time,* 6.
5. Klemp, *Inner Master,* 43.
6. Klemp, *We Come as Eagles,* 28.
7. Klemp, *Ask the Master,* Book 2, 277.

8. Harold Klemp, *The Secret Teachings,* Mahanta Transcripts, Book 3 (Minneapolis: ECKANKAR, 1989), 147.
9. Klemp, *Inner Master,* 5–6.
10. Carol Morimitsu and Phil Morimitsu, "The Temples of Golden Wisdom" (Minneapolis: ECKANKAR, 1986), audiocassette.
11. Klemp, *The Secret of Love,* 163.
12. Klemp, *The Secret Teachings,* 147–48.
13. Klemp, *Spiritual Exercises,* 125–26.

Chapter 31: You're Invited to Get on the Spiritual Fast Track

1. Klemp, *Slow Burning Love,* 26.
2. Klemp, *Inner Master,* 17.
3. Klemp, *The Secret of Love,* 170.
4. Ibid., 162.
5. Harold Klemp, "Questions for the Master . . . ," *Letter of Light* (January 1993), 3.
6. Klemp, *The Secret of Love,* 161.
7. Klemp, *The Drumbeat of Time,* 109.
8. Alice De Filippo, "An Arahata's Notes: Creating Your Own Connection with Divine Spirit,"*ECK Writers Update* (May 1995), 6.
9. Harold Klemp, "Notes on Health and Healing," *The Mystic World* (June 1995), 1–2.

Chapter 32: You Need to Know about the Most Ancient Teachings

1. Klemp, *The Secret Teachings,* 144.
2. Klemp, *Stories to Help You,* 331–32.
3. Klemp, *The Secret Teachings,* 159.
4. Klemp, *The Golden Heart,* 122.
5. Klemp, *The Secret Teachings,* 142.

Chapter 33: You Have the Opportunity to Discover Truth for Yourself

1. Klemp, *The Eternal Dreamer,* 35.
2. Klemp, *The Secret Teachings,* 160.
3. Klemp, *The Golden Heart,* 9.
4. Klemp, *Ask the Master,* Book 2, 195.
5. Klemp, *The Golden Heart,* 155–56.
6. Klemp, *The Dream Master,* 43.
7. Twitchell, *Stranger by the River,* 67–68.

Chapter 34: You Have the Right to Spiritual Freedom

1. Bruce Kurnow, Ann Vogle, Fred Vogle, "Come Share the Dream," *Come Share the Dream* (Minneapolis: ECKANKAR, 1992), audiocassette.
2. Klemp, *The Living Word,* Book 2, 45.
3. Cybil Fisher, "The Word," *Earth to God,* 275–76.

4. Klemp, *Slow Burning Love,* 86.
5. *ECKANKAR—Ancient Wisdom for Today,* compiled by Todd Cramer and Doug Munson (Minneapolis: ECKANKAR, 1993), 11–12.

Chapter 35: You're Free to Choose the Next Step on Your Spiritual Journey

1. Klemp, *Slow Burning Love,* 84.
2. Klemp, *Ask the Master,* Book 2, 18.
3. Klemp, *The Drumbeat of Time,* 87.
4. Klemp, *Slow Burning Love,* 107.

GLOSSARY

Words set in SMALL CAPS are defined elsewhere in this glossary.

ARAHATA. An experienced and qualified teacher for ECKANKAR classes.

CHELA. A spiritual student.

ECK. The Life Force, the Holy Spirit, or Audible Life Current which sustains all life.

ECKANKAR. Religion of the Light and Sound of God. Also known as the Ancient Science of SOUL TRAVEL. A truly spiritual religion for the individual in modern times, known as the secret path to God via dreams and SOUL TRAVEL. The teachings provide a framework for anyone to explore their own spiritual experiences. Established by Paul Twitchell, the modern-day founder, in 1965.

ECK MASTERS. Spiritual Masters who can assist and protect people in their spiritual studies and travels. The ECK Masters are from a long line of God-Realized SOULS who know the responsibility that goes with spiritual freedom.

HU. The most ancient, secret name for God. The singing of the word HU, pronounced like the word *hue,* is considered a love song to God. It is sung in the ECK Worship Service.

INITIATION. Earned by the ECK member through spiritual unfoldment and service to God. The initiation is a private ceremony in which the individual is linked to the Sound and Light of God.

LIVING ECK MASTER. The title of the spiritual leader of ECKANKAR. His duty is to lead SOULS back to God. The Living ECK Master can assist spiritual students physically as the Outer Master, in the dream state as the Dream Master, and in the spiritual worlds as

449

the Inner Master. Sri Harold Klemp became the MAHANTA, the Living ECK Master in 1981.

MAHANTA. A title to describe the highest state of God Consciousness on earth, often embodied in the LIVING ECK MASTER. He is the Living Word.

PLANES. The levels of heaven, such as the Astral, Causal, Mental, Etheric, and Soul planes.

SATSANG. A class in which students of ECK study a monthly lesson from ECKANKAR.

THE SHARIYAT-KI-SUGMAD. The sacred scriptures of ECKANKAR. The scriptures are comprised of twelve volumes in the spiritual worlds. The first two were transcribed from the inner PLANES by Paul Twitchell, modern-day founder of ECKANKAR.

SOUL. The True Self. The inner, most sacred part of each person. Soul exists before birth and lives on after the death of the physical body. As a spark of God, Soul can see, know, and perceive all things. It is the creative center of Its own world.

SOUL TRAVEL. The expansion of consciousness. The ability of SOUL to transcend the physical body and travel into the spiritual worlds of God. Soul Travel is taught only by the LIVING ECK MASTER. It helps people unfold spiritually and can provide proof of the existence of God and life after death.

SOUND AND LIGHT OF ECK. The Holy Spirit. The two aspects through which God appears in the lower worlds. People can experience them by looking and listening within themselves and through SOUL TRAVEL.

SPIRITUAL EXERCISES OF ECK. The daily practice of certain techniques to get us in touch with the Light and Sound of God.

SUGMAD. A sacred name for God. Sugmad is neither masculine nor feminine; It is the source of all life.

WAH Z. The spiritual name of Sri Harold Klemp. It means the Secret Doctrine. It is his name in the spiritual worlds.

451

FOR FURTHER READING AND STUDY*

Journey of Soul
Mahanta Transcripts, Book 1
Harold Klemp

This collection of talks by Eckankar's spiritual leader shows how to apply the unique Spiritual Exercises of ECK—dream exercises, visualizations, and Soul Travel methods—to unlock your natural abilities as Soul. Learn how to hear the little-known Sounds of God and follow Its Light for practical daily guidance and upliftment.

The Dream Master
Mahanta Transcripts, Book 8
Harold Klemp

If you don't believe dreams are important, you're missing out on more than half your life. Harold Klemp, the Dream Master, can show you how to become more aware of your dreams so you can enjoy a better life. But *The Dream Master* is not just about dreams. It gives you the keys to spiritual survival, and is about living life to the fullest on your way home to God.

The Spiritual Exercises of ECK
Harold Klemp

This book is a staircase with 131 steps. It's a special staircase, because you don't have to climb all the steps to get to the top. Each step is a spiritual exercise, a way to help you explore your inner worlds. And what awaits you at the top? The doorway to spiritual freedom, self-mastery, wisdom, and love.

How to Master Change in Your Life:
Sixty-seven Ways to Handle Life's Toughest Moments
Mary Carroll Moore

In your life, you always have a choice. You can flee from change, a victim of fate. Or, as the hero, you can embrace each challenge you face with courage and grace. Included are sixty-seven powerful techniques to help you understand change, plan the future, conquer fear and worry, and resolve problems of the past.

*Available at your local bookstore. If unavailable, call (612) 544-0066. Or write: ECKANKAR Books, P.O. Box 27300, Minneapolis, MN 55427 U.S.A.

There May Be an Eckankar Study Group near You

Eckankar offers a variety of local and international activities for the spiritual seeker. With hundreds of study groups worldwide, Eckankar is near you! Many areas have Eckankar centers where you can browse through the books in a quiet, unpressured environment, talk with others who share an interest in this ancient teaching, and attend beginning discussion classes on how to gain the attributes of Soul: wisdom, power, love, and freedom.

Around the world, Eckankar study groups offer special one-day or weekend seminars on the basic teachings of Eckankar. Check your phone book under **ECKANKAR**, or call **(612) 544-0066** for membership information and the location of the Eckankar center or study group nearest you. Or write **ECKANKAR, Att: Information, P.O. Box 27300, Minneapolis, MN 55427 U.S.A.**

☐ Please send me information on the nearest Eckankar center or study group in my area.

☐ Please send me more information about membership in Eckankar, which includes a twelve-month spiritual study.

Please type or print clearly   940

Name _____
　　　　first (given)　　　　　　　　　last (family)

Street_____ Apt. # _____

City _____ State/Prov. _____

ZIP/Postal Code _____ Country _____

About the Author

Linda C. Anderson is an ordained minister of Eckankar with over twenty years' experience as a professional writer. Former literary manager for a regional repertory theater and winner of national awards for playwriting, her plays have been performed in the United States and Europe. Her articles and short stories have been published in newspapers, magazines, and literary journals. Currently Linda works in the Public Information department at the Eckankar Spiritual Center in Minneapolis. Hundreds of radio and television stations and newspapers have interviewed her about spiritual subjects and the teachings of Eckankar. She is an international speaker who leads workshops on spirituality that participants have called life-changing.

Raised as a Roman Catholic, Linda studied to be a nun while she was in high school and college. She left the convent before taking final vows and began teaching in a Catholic school. But one day while preparing second graders for their first confession, she was confronted with the fact that she didn't believe these little children were sinful. Although she felt her childhood religion had given her a strong spiritual foundation, one doubt led to another. For the next twelve years Linda searched through a variety of religious and metaphysical paths for answers to her questions. Even though her career was doing well, Linda felt she was unsuccessful in her personal life, and she yearned for deeper spiritual meaning. For something more.

In 1976 Linda was awakened from sleep by a vision of blue

light and a voice telling her that she was going to be loved as she had never been loved before. This profound religious experience changed the course of her life and culminated in her finding and embracing the teachings of Eckankar. The blue light, she discovered, was the Mahanta, Keeper of the Secret Wisdom, inviting her to begin the journey home to God.

Linda now lives in a Twin Cities suburb. She is married, with two grown children and a menagerie of pets to enrich her life. She travels around the world, offering to seekers the golden keys that have brought her so much love, peace, and joy.

For information about workshops on Eckankar or to share stories about your own spiritual journey, write to:

ECKANKAR
Att: Public Information
P.O. Box 27300
Minneapolis, MN 55427 U.S.A.